A SURVEY OF
CATHOLIC THEOLOGY
1800–1970

A SURVEY OF CATHOLIC THEOLOGY
1800-1970

MARK SCHOOF, O.P.
With an introduction by
E. Schillebeeckx, O.P.

Translated by N. D. Smith

WIPF & STOCK · Eugene, Oregon

Wipf and Stock Publishers
199 W 8th Ave, Suite 3
Eugene, OR 97401

A Survey of Catholic Theology, 1800-1970
By Schoof, Ted Mark, OP
Copyright©1970 by Schoof, Ted Mark, OP
ISBN 13: 978-1-55635-817-3
Publication date: 2/26/2008
Previously published by Newman Press, 1970

Original language edition, Aggiornamento, published by Het Wereldvenster, 1/1/1968

ACKNOWLEDGEMENT

I would like to take the opportunity to thank my friends at Blackfriars, Oxford, for their generous help in preparing the English version of the book, in particular Cornelius Ernst, Osmund Lewry and Andrew Lascaris. More than gratitude is due to the translator. For anyone who has struggled with the complexities and obscurities of theological language the painstaking and sensitive translations of David Smith, who in his own field has re-established the age-old connections between his home-town, Norwich, and the Low Countries, are an ever growing source of wonder.

CONTENTS

INTRODUCTION	1
THE ENIGMA OF THEOLOGY WITHIN THE CATHOLIC CHURCH	6
IN SEARCH OF AN EXPLANATION IN HISTORY	14
By Way of Guidance	14
Nineteenth-century Changes in Catholic Theology	21
The Hope of the 'Modernists'	45
Germany in Movement	72
The Challenge of the 'World' in France	93
After the War in Germany and the Netherlands	121
Results of a Hundred Years of Neo-Scholasticism	146
FREEDOM FOR A NEW UNDERSTANDING OF THE GOSPEL	157
Only via a Side-Road	157
The Unchanging Truth	160
The Tübingen School	165
Newman's Way	170
Neo-Scholasticism and the First Vatican Council	175
History and Dogma in Modernism	180
Re-orientation within Neo-Scholasticism	188
The Development of Dogma in Le Saulchoir	194
The Heart of the Problem in the 'New' Theology	201
Progress between 1950 and 1958	210
The Result	222
THE APPEAL TO THE WORLD'S BISHOPS	228
Freedom for a Realistic Dialogue	228
The Fate of the 'Two Sources' Schema	235
The Council's Final Judgement on Dogma and History	247
GETTING USED TO THE NEW FREEDOM	265
EPILOGUE IN 2007	276
ERRATA	284

INTRODUCTION

THIS book's point of departure is clearly stated in the title of the first section—'The *Enigma* of Theology within the Catholic Church'. This suggests from the very outset that Catholic theologians occupy a very special position within their Church, a position which is not entirely the same as that occupied by theologians in other Churches. In the theology of the Reformed Churches, our attention is again and again drawn to a continuing series of peaks of theological authority—Barth, Bultmann, Tillich, Ebeling and Fuchs, Moltmann, Pannenberg and so on. In Catholic theology, however, these 'peaks' are more relative—theology seems more to be borne along by a wider stream which carries all kinds of vessels along with it, but within which a current that is somewhat faster than the stream itself can from time to time be observed. The factors which cause this difference between Catholic and reformed theology are not yet entirely clear to me. The most obvious would seem to be that the hierarchical teaching authority of the Catholic Church exerts an inhibiting and even paralysing influence on the original thought of Catholic theologians, but this is not borne out by the data provided in this book. In my view, the reason is rather to be found in the distinctively Catholic idea of the Church. According to this idea, the radical need for hermeneutic interpretation is recognised as clearly as in Protestant theology, but far greater importance is attached to the *fides Ecclesiae*, the faith of the whole community of believers, than to the finest syntheses of theologians, even though these have a critical function with regard to the empirical form in which the faith of the community appears. This view is not contradicted by the fact that the pastoral teaching authority of the Church has, in the past, repeatedly drawn attention to the 'theologian Thomas Aquinas' as a safe guide. The need for this repeated *admonition* is, after all, a clear indication of the instinctive resistance on the part of Catholic theologians to believing firmly in one theologian. The catholicity of faith seems spontaneously to resist the authority of one personal synthesis, however successful this may be at a given period. The Catholic theologian is always only one small voice within a great movement which began with Christ and the apostolic Church with its Scripture and has continued throughout the ages. Every part of this great historical process is therefore at the same time a criticism of the tendency to make another part of this tradition absolute. In this way, every Catholic theologian knows from the very beginning that he is subject to criticism—not, in the first place, to possible criticism from the teaching authority of the Church, but to the criticism of history. He is, in other words, conscious that he is simply *taking part in* a great social undertaking which is theology and that he can only play a very subordinate part in this undertaking. It is, of course, true that this authentic consciousness sometimes caused him, in the past, to forget that this very ecclesial character of theology also entrusted him, as a theologian, with the task of criticising the Church.

The author of this book was born in Schiedam in 1933. On completing his studies at grammar school, he became a Dominican in 1951. He studied philosophy at the Dominican house of study in Zwolle and then read theology for four years at Oxford. He then studied for his doctor's degree at the Catholic University of Nijmegen, finishing his studies in 1961. Since that time, he has been my assistant at the University, specialising in the history of theology. His present task in the syllabus of the theological faculty at Nijmegen is to direct seminars and guide students in the 'reading of texts'. In addition to this, he is also the editorial secretary of *Tijdschrift voor Theologie*.

I have the greatest admiration for Fr Schoof's book—not only because, in it, he succeeds in putting a very complex history most suggestively into words, but above all because he also shows a clear ability to make analytical distinctions and on this basis provides the reader with a very compelling synthesis. His concise but sensitive analyses have something in common with musical composition, in which not only the impressive whole is important, but every movement, every melody and indeed every note has its own special value. This comparison is not really far-fetched, because the author is in fact an active musician and lover of music. It is probably this that accounts for the meticulous care that he takes in his scientific studies in sensing shades of meaning and in resuming or merging 'themes' that he has already begun, and for his precision in the 'performance' of his text, which he only allowed to be published after many rehearsals.

The publisher asked me to introduce this book above all because it is to be translated into several foreign languages. But, once it has been read, no further recommendation is needed abroad, where the author is still virtually unknown. It deserves to be known internationally because of its contents, not because of any recommendation.

Because the series 'Theological Monographs', in which this book is published, is aimed at a wide circle of readers, the vast critical apparatus that would provide a justification for what is said in this book is omitted. But anyone who is familiar with the development of Catholic theology from the nineteenth century to the Second Vatican Council will know at once how much study lies behind this at first sight so obvious picture of twentieth-century Catholic theology. What is, of course, ultimately at stake is the total picture, which would have remained more or less the same if a few different theologians had, for example, been discussed instead of those selected for review in this book. The writer had to limit himself in one way or another and the best way to do this was not to mention all the theologians who have contributed to the total picture in a row, but to make a responsible choice in which all kinds of chance historical incidents also play a part. The book should therefore in no sense be regarded as a kind of 'theological canonisation' of the theologians mentioned to the exclusion of others. The theological stream has been accurately followed in this book and the author has done this by means of several points of reference. A different system of points of reference might have led to more or less the same result. This confirms once again the distinctive character of theology within the Catholic community of faith.

This book has confronted me with a question that I have not yet been able to answer—what exactly happened in the middle of the nineteenth century? The hopes of the Tübingen school were completely dashed at this time. Like B. Welte, the author of this book suggests that the same problem also occurred in other spheres at the same time—a similar change took place after the death of Hegel and Goethe and, in the world of music, after the death of Beethoven and Schubert, when Franck and Bruckner and Kierkegaard and Newman were not recognised. Many different factors can, of course, be brought forward as influencing this change, but it is still not possible to find a full explanation. What is more, the fact that Rosmini, who had great authority in Italy especially and many sympathisers in the Roman Curia, was ultimately defeated because of a decision of ecclesiastical politics (insisting at any price on 'neo-scholasticism' as the universal theology of the Church) points in the direction of what may be called the beginning of a general 'sclerosis' in all spheres of the life of the Church. Over and against the pluralistic society that was emerging, salvation was, so it seems, only seen in making a uniform stand and deviations which were in themselves legitimate were sacrificed to this.

Fr Schoof's book concludes with a consideration of the Second Vatican Council, but this is regarded not as an end, but as a way of making room for truly Catholic theological speculation in which legitimate pluralism is freely accepted. Another new period of theological thought, then, has commenced since Vatican II and it is, at the moment, not yet possible to predict its future. Some signs of a 'post-ecumenical' phase in theology are already beginning to emerge, because both Protestant and Catholic theologians are conscious that they are confronted with the same problem—the intelligibility of the Christian faith to modern man and the fact that, according to the Christian message, God, Christ and the Church claim to be the salvation of the world, while this world, bowed down beneath great cares and yet full of hope for a self-made and real improvement of the world, increasingly tends to bypass the Church, Christ and God. Theologians have, therefore, begun the task of a general Christian examination of conscience, in which all the various Christian theologies are forced together like sisters in one community and are becoming more conscious of their function to criticise the Church and society.

On the other hand, however, we have also learnt that a dialogue without obligations, in the long run, undermines the dialogue itself. Many Catholic theologians are therefore coming more and more to accept the view that, in an ecumenical attitude, 'putting one's own house in order' is, for the time being at least, a *conditio sine qua non* for any future ecumenical dialogue of any consequence. This shows clearly that post-conciliar Catholic theology, although it is being tossed about on the waves, does not intend to let itself drift and, conscious of the real problem, yet at the same time uncertain of its solutions, still refuses to abandon its critical distance or to revel in the problem for its own sake. Here too, present-day Catholic theologians show that they are aware that the new design of the Church of the future will undoubtedly mean a great change, but that this change will result in a Church that, in faithfulness to the gospel, will be the Church *of Christ*.

E. Schillebeeckx, O.P.
Nijmegen

THE ENIGMA OF THEOLOGY WITHIN THE CATHOLIC CHURCH

In addition to murders, racial disturbances and student demonstrations, the newspapers of today frequently mention and discuss the current unrest within the Catholic Church. What is remarkable about this is that these reports appear not only in newspapers here in the Netherlands, which is still to a very great extent a practising Christian country where everyone, not without some reason, is considered a theologian, but also in the world press. Ever since that massive and unwieldy colossus, the Catholic Church, was set in motion by the Second Vatican Council, there has been a continuous process of current and counter-current within the Church which has fascinated even outsiders and which can therefore be treated as ordinary 'news'. It would probably not be very difficult for a cynic to show that this interest has its origins in distance rather than in close involvement—the style in which some of these reports are written is very reminiscent of that of the sports page, complete with a forecast of the probable winners and, in their letters to the editor, the supporters of both sides are able to air their views.

Even those who are closely involved in the events, however, cannot deny that the real course of affairs is surrounded by a rather mysterious haze and, moreover, it is not clear whether this is the result of genuine awkwardness in dealing with the modern media of publicity or an intentional smoke screen. The leaders of the Catholic Church have never been afraid to use political or generally 'worldly' means, sometimes

The Enigma of Theology within the Catholic Church

of a kind that reminds one unpleasantly of the secrecy of Russia or China. Various people have, not unsympathetically, drawn attention to striking sociological similarities between centralised structures within the Catholic Church, some of which may even be called totalitarian, and certain aspects of life under a rigid Communist administration. There is a remarkable similarity in the way in which a 'liberal' Communist theoretician speaks about Marxism and the way in which a 'progressive' theologian speaks about Catholicism and there is the same parallel between the conservatives in both camps. It would appear as though the same kind of thaw is taking place—the parallels were strikingly evident on both sides, for example, in the conversations between Christians and Marxists at Salzburg—but at the same time there remains an element of doubt which made me use the word 'appear'. Is the 'conversion' of the Catholic Church at Vatican II genuine or not? Has the Church really set off on a new course?

This fascinating uncertainty has recently given even Catholic theologians a place in the news, sometimes quite spectacularly. It would seem as though strange manoeuvres are taking place behind the scenes in the Church of Rome. She no longer seems to be the same powerful fortress, subject to military authority, since the Council as she was before. The central administrative apparatus of the Church is certainly going to be drastically reformed, the Index has disappeared and opinions which are regarded as dangerous are no longer condemned officially without consultation with those directly concerned. The Church is sending friendly delegations to science congresses, cultural gatherings and symposiums on non-Catholic theology—things which she simply rejected in the past. She also appears to be less ready to pronounce her veto in the case of universally human problems. Pope Paul's encyclical on the development of nations sheltered far less than ever before behind wealth and the capitalist countries and even referred to the 'temptation' to use the means of revolution in the face of oppressive injustice. But the newspaper reader also notices that Catholic peace ambassadors are sometimes called to order when their work seems scarcely to have begun or that their negotiations are prematurely broken off. Doubts very soon started to arise concerning the Dutch New Catechism, which had been published under the aegis of a full national episcopate, and reports of mysterious commissions of theologians or cardinals who were reputed to have found errors or even heresies in the book started filtering through in the press. The Council declared that the Church always had need of conversion and purification, but the English theologian McCabe, who used the word 'corrupt' of the Church, was relieved of his function. A monastic community in Mexico, which had given a place to psychoanalysis in its life, was suddenly forbidden, on juridical grounds, to continue with this promising venture that was already bearing fruit. In these and other cases, the names of theologians have been made public and in the less scrupulous journals, these theologians have not only been blamed, but also condemned outright.

These reports inevitably remind us of what is said in the newspapers about Russia or China. Which of the contradictory reports can we believe? Which reporter has managed to escape from the supervision of Intourist? Does the Catholic Church really intend to be 'up to date' now or is she only practising a new form of Catholic duplicity in an attempt to gain a little goodwill?

The position of Catholic theology at the moment can only be understood within this general situation, as an aspect of the Church as a whole, which has suddenly become very agitated. It is not, at first sight, easy to see the reason for publishing a separate volume on the new Catholic theology in a series of books which already includes a general outline of the 'new ways in theology'.[1] Is Catholic thought not at the moment active in the same secular 'countryside' as Protestant theology and is it not guided by its 'reconnoitrers' and its 'beginning of a map'? Is anything more to be expected from such a volume than simply a following of the

The Enigma of Theology within the Catholic Church

same route, an adaptation to the achievement of the theology of the Reformation? Would the only result be a few supplementary details to add to the 'beginning of a map'? Deconfessionalisation is now the order of the day—the Catholic University of Nijmegen is seriously discussing whether or not it should retain its confessional title and, even within the Catholic People's Party of the Netherlands, suggestions to drop the first part of the name are being made. But obviously an adequate description is not provided simply by saying that Catholic theology has reached the level of the leading figures in Protestant theology. Not only will the Catholic theologian who is most critical of the older pattern of theology hardly be able to believe that his own theological tradition has no contribution to make to the theology of today—the interested outsider will also not have any explanation of the enigmatical position occupied by theology within the Roman Catholic Church.

The ground has been breaking up more and more in recent years under the whole of the Christian world. The many experts who use the phrase 'historical crisis' in connection with this continuously spreading phenomenon will probably prove to be right, but it is less easy to predict how—or, as many say, whether—Christianity will emerge from it and no new forecast will be made in this book. It is, however, important to note that the *aggiornamento* set in motion by the Council partly cuts across this process in the Catholic Church. Ten years ago, it seemed impossible for anyone to imagine that the 'rock of Peter' might also break up, but it was precisely during the Council that the wave of radical theology reached the 'ordinary believers' via *Honest to God*, the first of a new kind of paperback book—'theology for the millions'. This was the environment in which Catholics suddenly found themselves when the Council marked the beginning of the gradual ebbing away of strict discipline within the family of their Church. It is hardly surprising, then, that the psychological characteristics of young teenagers who have broken away from a strict family environment and of parents anxiously running around after them in an attempt to entice them to come back home again have, since this time, been noticeable in the Catholic Church. In the Netherlands, there would also seem to be a third catalyst at work—the ultimate completion of Catholic emancipation since the end of the Second World War. This gives a kind of revolutionary flourish to Dutch Catholicism, which was previously so worthily ultramontane. This revolutionary flavour causes confusion among those who believe unconditionally in the plausible reporting of *Time* magazine or in the southern panic of such papers as the *Corriere della Sera*. A pessimist would perhaps apply the fascinating comment made by the English theologian, Alec Vidler,[2] to the situation in the Netherlands, namely that a radical attitude does not usually come from moderate and intelligent conservatism, but from obscurantism.

It is therefore a question of placing Catholic theology in this turbulent movement. How does the 'new theologian' feel within the Catholic Church of today? He may perhaps, from time to time, find himself the victim, unawares, of an inclination to bask in the public interest and to feel satisfied with the result if he looks back at the past—and ten years or so is quite sufficient in this case. Modesty, however, soon returns, since he cannot deceive himself into believing that the recent history of the Catholic Church has really been influenced by these theological agitations. With a few exceptions, such as, for example, the first few years of the pontificate of Pius XII, the Catholic Church tends to present herself as a well organised society which, as far as her practical decisions and, for example, her pastoral reforms are concerned, prefers to rely on the established theological tradition which has so far been found to be sound or on the administrative customs which have grown up in the course of centuries. Among the diplomatic activities, the concordats and the practical encyclicals, the new theological ideas of a few professors have made almost as little impact on the Church as a whole as the petitions of scholars on a ministry of defence. The American bishop who had to admit at the Council that it had never occurred to the hierarchy of his country that a theologian could be useful for any other purpose than that of educating seminarists[3] was not simply describing a personal experience. Even in the present feverish urge for renewal, theology is brushed impatiently aside by those who are rushing so furiously ahead. On the other hand, it is regarded with suspicion by those who are alarmed by the renewal as the source of all doubt and uncertainty. Some of the theologians themselves believe that it is not the function of a science to provide a community with dynamism, whereas others are of the opinion that the real vocation of the theologian is prophecy—to go on pointing out the way towards new interpretations and practical consequences of God's word for us.

What clearly emerges from this medley of feelings and ideas is that Catholic theology certainly has a very distinctive aspect—it seems to be far more closely bound to the Church than the new theology of the Reformed Churches. This is probably the reason why the peaks seem to be less high and also less lonely—in Catholic theology, there is no Barth, no Bultmann and no Tillich. If, then, a separate volume is to be devoted, in this series of books, to Catholic theology, it must automatically concentrate on the enigma of the place which theology occupies within the Catholic Church. It can hardly add anything to the survey of contemporary theological questions already provided by Professor Sperna Weiland in his *New Ways in Theology*. All the same, it may be valuable in that it makes up for the omission to which the author referred in his foreword, by attempting to describe a different pattern of theology and to indicate a distinctive type of theological attitude. In order to do this, it will be necessary to bear in mind what creative theology has in fact meant in the recent past within the Catholic Church—to echo the words of Helmut Thielicke, 'a person is what he has behind him'.[4] This historical account will outline the constantly renewed attempt to bring 'established theology' (and usually the established order in the Church as well) 'up to date', to transform it in such a way that it can translate God's word for the modern world. During this laborious process, attention will be concentrated on the essential problem—how, within the Catholic Church, the lawfulness of such an aspiration, of a new theology, can be made acceptable to a changing world, in other words how, within tradition which is constantly moving forward, continuity with the real message of Christ can be indicated. This process leads, via various impasses, to the surprise of the *aggiornamento* of the Second Vatican Council, at which the great majority of the Fathers acknowledged the lawfulness of the new theological thinking in principle because they recognised it as descriptive of their own pastoral experience.

In this, I have two aims in mind. The first is to clarify to some extent the enigmatical position which theology even today still occupies within the Catholic Church, to provide therefore a kind of glimpse 'behind the theological news', so that it will become clear that the situation, which is still very confused today, has a pre-history, perhaps rather an underground pre-history, a context which is able to throw a great deal of light on the enigma. The second and perhaps more important aim, however, is to give some idea of the position which Catholic theology is beginning to occupy within the whole of Christian thought and at the same time to warn against the one-sided emphases which are to be expected of Catholic theology and also to plead for openness to and understanding of the capital which the Catholic tradition contributes. During the long and laborious process of thawing out on the part of Catholic theology, several remarkable aspects are also coming to the surface of a theological attitude which may be of importance to the whole of Christian theology or rather which are only now beginning to function in a properly balanced way within the whole of theology.

The enigma of the new Catholic theology may perhaps prove to be vital to the whole of Christian thought today.

NOTES

[1] See J. Sperna Weiland, *New Ways in Theology*, Dublin 1968.
[2] See A.R. Vidler, *The Modernist Movement in the Roman Church*, Cambridge 1934, 202.
[3] See R. Caporale, *Vatican II: Last of the Councils*, Baltimore 1964, 92.
[4] '. . . Ein Mensch "ist" doch das, was er hinter sich hat', H. Thielicke, *Ich Glaube*, 2nd ed., Stuttgart 1967, 157.

IN SEARCH OF AN EXPLANATION IN HISTORY

By Way of Guidance

IT seems advisable, before setting out on this historical exploration, to put up a few signposts and to give a general idea of what the traveller may expect to see on the way. In the first place, the theological pioneers within the Catholic Church have followed different routes, but all these routes have ultimately led to the same end and have frequently cut across each other. The direction of the two main routes is connected with the way in which theology functions within the Catholic Church. Travelling along the first of them, Catholic theology attempts to establish contact as directly as possible with the gospel of Christ and to listen to this gospel as purely as possible, through the reaction of the witnesses who heard it. This testimony has come down to us through the centuries both in the speaking and in the whole life of the community of the Church. It has been authentically recorded in Scripture, which the Church has examined again and again, and in certain basic outlines of the life of the community within the Church. By following these tracks, a continuous attempt is made to get as close as possible to the source itself. This, then, is a going back in an attitude of active listening. For some twenty years or so, this process has been known as *ressourcement,* 'going back to the sources'.

The Catholic theologian does not, however, leave his own environment behind like ballast when he sets out on this exploration—he searches as a man of his own period, stimulated by his present experience. He wants to ask new questions of the gospel in order to be able to integrate it, in a more constructive stage, into his own life. For this reason, theology aims to establish contact as closely as possible with all that really occupies the Christian community and the whole world of today, and frequently in precisely that order, since, up to the present time, Catholic theology has, almost without exception, been practised by priests, whose 'contemporary existential experience' has, in the first place, been gained in practical pastoral work. This second main route, then, is not a going back, but an exploration in breadth into the contemporary pastoral reality and present-day secular thought.

In addition to these two main routes, there is also an important subsidiary route, that of non-Catholic Christian thought, which has clearly had a stimulating and fertilising effect on Catholic theology, both in its attitude and in its factual content. The practice of theology in the Catholic Church has, with increasing clarity, become more 'ecumenical' in tone, showing an almost scrupulous concern to integrate the testimony of the whole of Christian theology into Catholic thought. The distant journey to the source of the gospel of Christ and to the reality of our own times has, in fact, often followed the route already sketched out by Protestant, Anglican or Eastern Orthodox theology. This has happened so precisely at so many different points that it is quite possible to speak of an *aggiornamento* brought about by the achievements of non-Catholic theology.

Three themes can therefore be discerned again and again in Catholic theology in its process of renewal—an impulse from the authentic Christian past, an impulse from contemporary existential experience and an impulse from the other Christian Churches. These are the factors which always play a part when a theological revival comes about. They were present at the time of the medieval renaissance—that period of endearing vitality which unintentionally resulted in the building of a theological fortress to which the

Catholic Church still frequently withdraws with rather shameful haste. In the Middle Ages too, the origin of the new theology was an evangelical revival, clearly influenced by the social changes that were taking place at that time. This gave rise to a real hunger for texts which not only brought an exciting, secularising philosophy within reach, but also, and above all, gave access, through the Church Fathers, to the source of the gospel of Christ. What is more, it is even possible to discern an 'ecumenical' aspect of this medieval renewal of theology in its openness to Eastern, Arabic and Jewish theology and philosophy. These three themes in the attempt to renew theology often overlap and consequently cannot be taken as a regulating principle. It can, however, be illuminating to point them out in various theological movements, especially whenever one of them emerges more clearly.

Further, a word must be said about the limits in time of our exploration. The present situation in which theology finds itself in the Catholic Church has clearly discernible roots in the period round about the beginning of this century, the relatively short and rather depressing episode of modernism, a word which has since become so emotionally charged that it is instinctively avoided by the protagonists of renewal, because their attempts are all too readily called (neo-) modernistic. The obvious thing to do, then, would be to follow the course of the theology of renewal from this unfortunate movement onwards. Modernism, however, can only be understood as a reaction against the theological situation at the end of the nineteenth century, which was in turn the result of an interaction between renewal and conservatism which again went back, via certain lines at least, to the beginning of the nineteenth century. An examination, at least in outline, of the history of Catholic theology in the nineteenth century, with particular attention to the change which took place at about the middle of the century and which has since determined the attitude of the Church, is therefore indispensable.

In addition to setting certain limits in time, it is also advisable to provide some kind of geographical outline. It is a remarkable fact that there are only two countries, or rather, linguistic zones, where the Catholic theological revival seems to be able to take root—France and Germany. Of course, the various theological movements extend much farther than this—one has only to think of Newman in the nineteenth century and of Tyrrell and several very active Italian groups during the period of modernism. After the Second World War, Dutch theology also became internationally known on the fringe of the French and German linguistic zones. Nonetheless, the centre of theological renewal does seem to move in waves between France and Germany. It is in these two zones that theologians seem to have both the necessary scientific tradition and sufficient creative energy at their disposal. The same, of course, applies to other spheres of activity—not only theology, but also literature, music and philosophy. This is obviously true of the German-speaking countries from the end of the eighteenth century onwards. It is undeniable that this environment inspired a promising revival in Catholic theology during the first half of the nineteenth century. In post-revolutionary France, Catholics had first of all to find their place in society again and any theology that was able to take root there was to a very great extent determined by this background. What is probably more important is that it was in this climate that modern ultramontanism first came about, an attitude which was to have a decisive influence on the later course of theological renewal within the Catholic Church. Towards the end of the nineteenth century, in the more relaxed atmosphere of the pontificate of Leo XIII, modern historical and biblical criticism gradually became firmly established in France as well, at the Instituts Catholiques, and this, together with the discussions at that time of the new apologetics of the philosopher Blondel, formed the background to the modernist movement. The debate about the questions stirred up by modernism was pushed into the background by the violent experience of the First World War and, round about 1920, it became obvious that another theological revival was beginning in the German-speaking countries, a revival that had its roots in the many 'movements' of that turbulent period. When ascendant Nazism began to suppress German thought, France once more began to show signs of awaking again theologically. This took the form of a creative *ressourcement* within scholastic theology and was centred first in the Dominican house of Le Saulchoir and later in the Jesuit faculty of Lyon-Fourvière. It was the second centre which gave rise to a *nouvelle théologie*, which did not, however, emerge clearly until after the war. When, in 1950, this movement had lost impetus, the initiative went back again to the German-speaking countries and the theology of the Dutch language area also began to take a more and more active part in the debate.

Finally, it is worth while putting up a few practical beacons. The word theology will be used in this book in its narrower, more concentrated sense of deliberate, systematic and methodical reflection about the reality of faith, the scientific integration of the word of God as directed towards us. It is fully recognised in the new theology that the only ultimate aim of this new science is preaching. At the same time, however, it is clear that there is also a phase in our reflection on the faith which is not yet ready to be a proclamation of God's word that is intended for all men. Staff work and research are as necessary within the Church as they are in any other sphere. When Catholic theologians began to open new ways in which modern man could experience faith, the concepts 'contemporary' and 'popular' were at first regarded as synonymous and not all authors and publishers tried to rectify this misunderstanding with equal care. It seems advisable to avoid diluting the term theology to such an extent that it includes every possible idea about the reality of faith, and to require every theologian to dispense with a special theological language, so that everything that he says will always be immediately intelligible to everybody. I should also like to add here, by way of a 'footnote', that this book is no more than a book *about* theologians and that it is written in a style and form that will enable it to be understood by a wide circle of readers.

A little superfluously, perhaps, I would like to point out that in this book only *new* impulses within Catholic theology will be considered. By thus limiting myself I do not intend to pass judgement on other contributions to theology. It just seems a matter of common sense not to try and present a survey of the whole of theology in the Roman Catholic Church. It will be hard enough not to oversimplify the evolution of the theology renewal. The bibliographies which round off each section may to some extent restore the balance. And, finally, there ought to be yet another warning —as a matter of simplification the word 'Catholic' will normally be used in its more popular sense of 'Roman Catholic'.

Bibliography

As in the case of Professor Sperna Weiland's *New Ways in Theology*, to which this book is to some extent a companion volume, the bibliographies which appear after the various sections have been compiled with a practical aim in mind. The books, articles and studies included here will therefore be principally those which are fairly easily obtainable and which themselves refer to further reading. For the same reason, English translations have, as far as possible, been traced of works originally written in other languages.

Studies dealing with the various elements that go to make up Catholic theology can most easily be found in the articles entitled 'Theology' in, for example, *Sacramentum Mundi* VI (Karl Rahner and Cornelius Ernst), London and New York 1968—, in the *New Catholic Encyclopedia* XIV (G. Van Ackeren), New York 1967—, and in the outstanding *Encyclopédie de la foi* (H. Fries), Paris 1965—. The article on theology by E. Schillebeeckx originally published in 1958 and included in his *Revelation and Theology* (London and Melbourne 1967) bears the strong imprint of his own manner of practising theology. A similarly personal exposition can be found in Yves Congar's *A History of Theology* (New York 1968), which is a translation and revision of his monumental, classic contribution 'Théologie' in the *Dictionnaire de Théologie Catholique*, with a brief supplement for the time after 1939—the year in which this article was originally written by Congar. Karl Rahner's view of theology has recently been elaborated by a whole team of specialists in *Mysterium salutis* (Einsiedeln, Zürich and Cologne 1965—), a work in several volumes which sets out to provide a 'street plan' of the dogmatics of the history of salvation. An English edition is in the course of preparation. The first volume includes not only a detailed exposition of the place and function of theology, but also of such basic themes as revelation, faith, tradition and Scripture, which are dealt with later in this book. Finally, the short work by M.D. Chenu, *Is Theology a Science?* (London 1959), the second volume of the useful series 'Faith and Fact', can be recommended.

Congar's work, referred to above, also includes a general survey of the history of Catholic theology. This is in fact the only survey of this subject that is sufficiently wide and deep. In addition P. de Letter's article 'Theology, History of' in the *New Catholic Encyclopedia* XIV, can be used very profitably. Of all the works that set out to describe the more recent situation, the most satisfactory is still *La théologie catholique au milieu du XXe siècle*, by the eminent historian of Louvain University, R. Aubert, even though it was published as early as 1953 in Tournai. His view in this book is, of course, preconciliar and rather 'French'. Later but less strictly theological is his contribution on the Church of Rome in *Twentieth Century Christianity*, edited by Stephen Neill (London 1962). J. Comblin's *Vers une théologie de l'action*, published in 1964 in the series 'Les Études religieuses' in Brussels, is in many ways a remarkable book; it, too, mainly considers the French language area. German Catholic theology is dealt with exclusively in A. Kolping's rather uneven book *Katholische Theologie gestern und heute* (Bremen 1964), which covers the period from the First Vatican Council in 1870 to today. Two American publications deserve to be mentioned, *Current Trends in Theology* (New York 1965), a rather too general survey of theological themes and attitudes in the early sixties, and *Theology in Transition*, a useful 'Bibliographical Evaluation of the "Decisive Decade" 1954-1964' (New York 1965), though perhaps a little impatient with new attempts. In a wider context one will find enlightening comments on Catholic thinkers in J. Macquarrie's *Twentieth-Century Religious Thought* (London 1963).

Finally three books must be mentioned which provide separate 'portraits' of (among others) Catholic theologians. The first two are *Theologians of our Time* and its supplementary *Modern Theologians: Christians and Jews* (Notre Dame, U.S.A. 1964 and 1967 respectively). The third is a fascinating book which so far unfortunately exists only in German, *Tendenzen der Theologie im 20. Jahrhundert* (Stuttgart and Olten 1966), a collection of studies on exactly ninety-nine theologians in chronological order, to which I shall refer again in the bibliographies which follow.

Nineteenth-century Changes in Catholic Theology

If theology could still be called the queen of the sciences after the seventeenth century, the Catholic columnist, Philip Scharper, commented in *The Critic*,[1] then she was at the most a constitutional monarch, who bore the crown but could not impose her will. The real power behind the throne lay with the jurists, the guardians of public order in the Church and those who practised an esoteric art which has recently acquired the special name of 'churchmanship', a sort of clerical politics or business economics. This, in his opinion, applied to Protestant theology until the middle of the nineteenth century or thereabouts, but it was true o Catholic theology until the Second Vatican Council.

A historian would perhaps not wish to be held responsible for this characterisation of the part played by theology, not even if it takes its literary form into account. But it cannot be denied that it does give some idea of the situation in which Catholic theology has been placed for about a century or so. If Catholic thought since, let us say, the Peace of Westphalia, is reviewed in broad outline, the main impression gained is that it has been in the service of polemical apologetics against Protestant theology, the ever increasing supremacy of the secular sciences and rationalistic deism. A violent struggle has also been raging within the Church between Thomism, Scotism and Molinism, of which the debate about Baianism and Jansenism was really no more than an offshoot. It can be no secret that the real cause at stake in these theological polemics has often been very untheological interests, and partly because of this, the conflict sometimes became so violent that Rome had to intervene by declaring the Catholic opponents to be heretics. On the other hand, however, Pope Paul VI made the following comment on the scornful attitude taken by the undoubtedly touchy Synod of Pistoria towards these disputes: 'false, frivolous, harmful to the Catholic schools and undermining fitting obedience to the Apostolic definitions'.[2] But, round about the beginning of the nineteenth century, a new phase began when a creative tendency emerged around the theological faculty of the German university of Tübingen, a movement which, in calm and open dialogue with contemporary philosophy and theology, began to develop a new synthesis.

German theology in the early nineteenth century

In 1803, the *Reichsdeputationshauptschluss* of Ratisbon had handed over large areas of Swabia to the new Elector of Württemberg in exchange for the territory on the left bank of the Rhine ceded to Napoleon. This meant that the

Elector suddenly found himself with a large number of Catholics in his country, which had hitherto been almost exclusively Lutheran. In an attempt to give equal rights to both groups, he established, in 1812, a Catholic theological college in Ellwangen. Five years later, this college was incorporated into the university of Tübingen, alongside the flourishing faculty of Protestant theology there. This provided the climate within which a revival of Catholic theology could take a definite shape.

It did not take very long before this new beginning was made. By the end of the eighteenth century, the traditional late scholastic theology had collapsed as a result of the infiltration of ideas stemming from the Enlightenment and it was virtually forgotten in the Catholic Church—certainly in Northern Europe—in the intoxication of the French Revolution, which had its effect on Catholic intellectual life. Certain Catholics had, for some time already, been criticising the traditional devotions, pilgrimages and indulgences practised in the Church, the unintelligible and individualistic liturgy and the obligatory celibacy of priests. Such Catholics were demanding a biblical devotion and open dialogue, even worship in common, with other Christians. This movement is usually dismissed nonchalantly, but not entirely without reason, as Josephinism and Febronianism in the older Catholic books of Church history. Among these restless Catholics, however, was a genuine theologian, J.M. Sailer, an unusually fascinating figure who had been a member of the Society of Jesus for three years until its dissolution in 1773 and who afterwards continued as a secular priest and theologian. As such, his life was made very difficult because of various manoeuvres of ecclesiastical politics, but nonetheless he died in 1832 as the Bishop of Ratisbon. He was astonishingly well read in Scripture, in the Fathers of the Church and in theology from the early scholastic until the post-tridentine period. He must also have possessed an almost magical power of attraction, which not only made him a great teacher, acknowledged as a pioneer by very many of those who later took part in the Catholic revival, but also gave him access to many of his great contemporaries outside the Church. Catholics discovered in his teaching a close affinity with the spirit of their own times and, of course, in the romantic movement with its interest in the Catholic Middle Ages, which was at that time flourishing, they had the tide in their favour. In his theology, published in the forty-one volumes of his collected works, Sailer looked for links with Kant, Jacobi and Schelling and tried to shift the emphasis from the external structure of the life of the Church to the inner experience of faith and thus to transcend the rationalistic rigidity of religion and faith. In his own elaboration of theology, he concentrated on the subjective experience of faith. In this, his theology was closely related to that of Schleiermacher and had a rather pietistic tendency to throw insufficient light on the objective, historical reality of the Church and revelation. The impulses which he passed on to his many disciples were clearly of greater and more lasting importance. These were gratefully accepted and elaborated into a contemporary theology by the Catholic school of Tübingen, which became the undisputed centre of Catholic thought for many years and has continued its own tradition up to the present.

The theologians of the new Catholic faculty were at first a little uneasy in Tübingen, confronted with the members of the established Protestant faculty, but their reception was encouraging and many years of mutually fruitful contact followed. What was noticeable in the attitude of the Catholics was an unconcealed care to anticipate Protestant criticism, especially in their allusions to the freedom of research within the Catholic Church, and to use terms which their Protestant colleagues could respect. Even in Ellwangen, they had become firmly associated with the continued call to reform Catholic practices. In his first book, written four years after the transfer to Tübingen, the moral theologian J.B. Hirscher demanded the abolition of private Masses, as well as communion under both kinds and the language of the people in the celebration of the Eucharist. As a result of this, the book was, one year after its publication, placed on the Index. The dominating figure of this early period, J.S. von Drey, however, helped to turn his colleagues' interest towards more constructive and more strictly theological fields of activity.

The earliest works of the members of the Tübingen school show beyond all doubt that they were greatly indebted to the romantic movement. The climate of their thought was conditioned by their use of such emotionally charged terms as *Geist*, *Leben* and *mystischer Sinn* and by a preference for dynamism, organic growth and a community inspired by the *Volksgeist*. They were clearly under the spell of Schelling and Schleiermacher. Yet this climate was as fresh and stimulating as that of Schubert's songs or Eichendorff's romantic novel, *Aus dem Leben eines Taugenichts*, and the results achieved by these early theologians of Tübingen still compel us to respect them. They regarded it as their task to integrate, in a spirit of openness, the new attainments in the spheres of history, biblical criticism and philosophy into the Catholic tradition and to express their conviction of faith in the new mode of thinking and speaking. B. Welte has pointed out that the great philosophers of this period directed their attention to Christianity and thus brought philosophy within the reach of theologians.[3] In any case, we have here the spectacle of the Catholic theologians of the Tübingen school trying, in their own way, to come to terms with the tension between the many-sided presentation of the constantly progressing historical event and the enduring, meaningful 'idea' that is expressed in this event—the tension between the unique and non-recurrent word expressed by Christ and the manifold historical way in which this comes to us through the Church. Like Schleiermacher, they also tried to approach the unity of natural and revealed religion from the vantage-point of human experience. It was not entirely without reason that they were accused of following the same course as and imitating Schleiermacher.[4] At the same time, however, they were not afraid to call his 'radical feeling of dependence' an oversimplification which did not do full justice to the unique historical character of revelation and the reality of the living community of the Church. The whole life of the Church, her customs, worship and moral attitudes, were for these theologians as much a basis for theological reflection as the Church's teaching. Detailed and objective historical theology had therefore to precede systematic reflection and this reflection had also to embrace the contemporary life of the community of the Church and to listen to the world in which this community lived, especially the world of contemporary philosophy.

The theologians of the Tübingen school consequently showed a restless activity. On the one hand, they ceaselessly investigated the tradition of the Church and considered the works of those who had gone before them, especially the writings of the Fathers of the Church. On the other hand, however, they were not afraid to incorporate the developing contemporary science of biblical criticism despite the fact that this was, at that time, still strongly influenced by rationalistic assumptions. They also started a fruitful dialogue, not only with Schelling and Schleiermacher, but also with Kant and Hegel and worked in a spirit of ecumenical openness, stimulated especially by their Protestant colleagues at Tübingen.

They thus opened up entirely new ways in such spheres as the knowledge of faith and theological anthropology and approached God's works in the world and in mankind in a highly original way. Above all, however, they stimulated a new understanding of the Church as a historical, dynamically growing reality—a synthesis built up around the biblical concept of the 'kingdom of God'—which, in its living tradition, 'hands down' God's word and salvation to us. The founder of the Tübingen school was von Drey, apparently a rather melancholy man, who none the less exerted such an influence during the thirty years he was a professor at Tübingen that his inspiration was still felt in the second generation of students. He vigorously set out the plan according to which the new faculty was to work in the *Tübinger Theologische Quartalschrift*, which was founded by him and is still a leading theological journal. His colleague, J.A. Möhler, twenty years his junior, has been called the most brilliant representative of all that the Tübingen school stood for. On being appointed to the university in 1823 at the age of twenty-seven, he became, because of his critical spirit and yet at the same time very warm heart and his firm attachment to the Church, the centre of the new faculty, especially after publishing, only two years later, a much praised work on the Church. In 1832, he wrote his major work, *Symbolik*, in which he attempted to synthesise the inner community life of the Church as nourished by God's Spirit, and her visible structure. This book too was widely read and praised, but it involved the author in sharp and public polemics with the equally famous theologian of the Protestant faculty at Tübingen, F.C. Baur. Because of this, he decided, a few years later, to accept a professorship at Munich, where he hoped to find a calmer atmosphere in the circle of the historians Döllinger and Görres. Only a few years after this, however, he died from the consequences of an attack of cholera.

Both von Drey and Möhler came, in later years, to dissociate themselves noticeably from the romantic movement and to clarify their initially rather vague formulations. This change came to an end in the leader of the second generation at Tübingen, J.E. Kuhn, who, after studying at Tübingen and spending a short period teaching at Giessen, returned in 1837, at the age of thirty-one, to Tübingen, where he continued to teach until 1882. Although biblical and patristic theology always continued to fascinate him—his first task as a professor had been exegesis—and he was not only a formidable theological polemicist, but also practised for many years as a politician, he was, in the first place, both naturally disposed and inwardly impelled to speculation and, in the opinion of many, the greatest speculative spirit that the Tübingen school produced. He incorporated the achievements of the school into a comprehensive synthesis that was at the same time finely balanced in all its details. Kuhn completed the process of dissociation from the romantic movement and its ideas that the earlier members of the Tübingen school had begun and turned especially towards Hegel's philosophy of the objective spirit. When he died, however, in 1887, the tide had already turned many years before. The chance that the new synthesis of the school might stimulate renewal in the whole of the Catholic Church had already passed before 1850.

Anyone familiar with the fate of similar theological attempts at renewal within the Catholic Church will probably be surprised that the school of Tübingen was able to continue on its far from traditional course without intervention on the part of the hierarchy. It is, however, a fact that, although a few books were placed on the Index and more accusations and complaints were certainly made, the Tübingers and those whose thinking was directly related to theirs were not condemned or even publicly warned. The situation at that time in Germany was extremely delicate and a false move against the Catholic school at Tübingen, which enjoyed such good will, might have had catastrophic consequences in university circles. The leaders of the Catholic Church were apprehensive of dormant separatist tendencies and of the remarkable sensitivity that the Germans always showed as soon as free scientific research was involved. What is more, Rome condemned remarkably little during the first half of the nineteenth century, in comparison with the period after 1848. Bautain, who tended to underestimate man's knowledge of God, was warned several times and the liberal ideas of Lamennais with their strongly political flavour—something that the authority of the Church is more inclined to take seriously than purely theological modernism —were, of course, censured. Apart from this, there was only the condemnation of the ideas of Georg Hermes after his death in 1835, a pronouncement which was not particularly clear and in which many secondary motives played a part.

Even before the emergence of the Catholic school of Tübingen, this scholarly priest, a most hard-working man of very high standing, two years older than von Drey, had developed a new philosophical system of apologetics which was based on Kant's critique and which aimed to reach religious certainty via self-reflection from the point of departure of absolute doubt. He was never able to find a satisfactory solution to the tension between a philosophical construction of this kind and historical revelation, but there was enough support for his ideas for him to be able to neutralise the growing resistance to them. He himself, anyway, never seems to have suspected that his teaching might be condemned. In contrast to the attempt made by the Catholic school of Tübingen, his work is clearly topheavy, even anachronistic in its one-sided reliance on the philosophy of the Enlightenment.

Hermes' younger contemporary, Anton Günther, who survived him by many years, is often referred to in the same breath as Hermes. Their basic attitudes certainly differ very much—rather like the difference between Kant and Hegel—but it is undoubtedly possible to agree with L. Scheffczyk's comment, that the two men 'are very close to each other in the rear-view mirror of historical reflection'.[5] From a distance, Günther seems to have been the more striking personality. Hardened by a very difficult youth, he took part in all the theological polemics of his time in pithy, rather aggressive language and with feared humour. He seems also to have been as little deterred by growing criticism as Hegel himself. His impressive attempt to construct from and to base in man's creative consciousness of himself the whole of knowledge, including faith, forms the most radical synthesis between faith and knowledge that has ever been evolved by a Catholic theologian. Like Hermes, however, he was unable to find a satisfactory place for the historical fact of revelation, the positive data of Scripture and the tradition and history of the Church. Although he had been able to gain support in high places within the Church, and the investigation of his ideas dragged on for years, his condemnation in 1857 was inevitable. Deeply shocked, Günther, who was by this time seventy-three years old, made his submission, together with a number of his disciples.

The theological climate in Catholic circles had, however, radically changed by then. It was partly the attempts of Hermes and Günther and their ultimate failure which, after the idyll of the Tübingen school in its beginnings, introduced a period of grim skirmishes and alarmed withdrawals into the old fortress of the Church. Round about the middle of the nineteenth century, the life of the Church, and consequently theology too, came under the influence of a deep depression which brought about a structural change in theological attitude.

The change round about the middle of the century

In 1848, the following remarkable sentence occurred in the correspondence between two members of the Oxford Movement, R. Wilberforce and J.B. Mozley: 'A pretty state we are in altogether, with a radical pope teaching all Europe rebellion.'[6] This same pope gave instructions, a few years later, for a list of contemporary errors to be compiled and it was from this list that the notorious Syllabus eventually grew. The Syllabus contained the following sentence, which, as it were, reflects the one just quoted: 'The pope can and must try to achieve a reconciliation and a settlement with progress, liberalism and modern civilisation.' This sentence was—not unexpectedly—condemned.[7]

These two quotations have, as their immediate context, the political and administrative activity of Pius IX, not primarily his teaching function or his attitude towards theology. It is precisely at this administrative level, however, that his significance with regard to Catholic thought during the thirty-two troubled years of his pontificate is really to be found. In this, the fate of the ecclesiastical state occupied a prominent place in Pius' thoughts. This may cause surprise and even irritation now, but at that time it was accepted almost without question. There were very few Catholics in the nineteenth century—not even such an open-minded thinker as Newman—who believed that the pope could fulfil his function without this secular power. And, after the pontificate of the withdrawn and strict Gregory XVI, the cordial and spontaneous Pius had been welcomed with new hope by the 'liberals'—a word that, at that time, above all implied progressiveness. But the year 1848, the year of revolutions, which is said to have made the conservative Dutch king, William II, into a liberal within twenty-four hours, had the opposite effect on Piux IX. He had to flee in haste from Rome and leave power there in the hands of the revolutionaries until French troops were sent to help him. After this experience, he underwent a radical change—whereas he had previously been too optimistic and open, he now became very conservative and cautious. He had ventured too far into hostile territory and had been able to reach the gates of his citadel only at the last moment. From now onwards, everyone would have to remain inside. He was at a loss to explain, now it had happened, what had impelled him to venture outside that safe and familiar fortress. Were the liberals not trying to undermine law and order? Were they not fulminating against Christianity and the clergy?

Ever since the beginning of the century, a growing number of influential Catholics, especially in France, had been appealing to the papacy to protect Christianity from what they regarded as the chaotic aftermath of the French Revolution. The personal good nature and piety of Pio Nono and his dramatic experiences were an ideal target for the insistent mystique of the pope encouraged by these 'ultramontanists'. A French priest had already remarked that no one was expected even to take off his hat when Gregory XVI came past,[8] but Pius IX was called the 'under-God of mankind', the continuation of the incarnate Word.[9] William G. Ward, who, like Veuillot and Cardinal Manning, was one of the most convinced ultramontanists, declared that he would most of all like to find a papal bull on his breakfast table beside *The Times* every morning.[10]

Under pressure from his environment, and especially from his secretary of state, Antonelli, Pius IX felt that it was his sacred vocation to respond to these expectations and, as a result, he began to prepare the Church for a long siege. The ramparts were built higher and higher and warnings and condemnations were followed by further warnings and condemnations. At the same time, it was becoming more and more difficult to raise one's voice in opposition to the prevailing views, because firm unanimity was, within the Catholic fortress, a first requirement. Shortly before the Syllabus was published in 1864, the Pope announced that he intended to convoke a council 'in order to surmount the exceptional needs of the Church with this exceptional means'.[11] This plan gave rise to a short-lived hope among the Catholic 'liberals', but their hopes were not fulfilled. The majority of the bishops who attended the Council ratified the prevailing course and apparently did so because they were convinced that it was right. It was only in connection with the question of papal infallibility that there was any real opposition, but the outcome was not surprising —without this pronouncement, the Church of 1870 would have been convinced that she was in contradiction to the revelation of God.

The theological situation within the Church at this time was strikingly illustrated at the First Vatican Council by the intervention of Bishop Verot of Savannah in Georgia, U.S.A., who said that the view that Negroes had no soul had to be rejected in the Constitution on Faith rather than the obscure errors of the German idealists.[12] The ideas of Hermes and Günther, which were under discussion here, certainly must have seemed to be very far removed from the real needs of the Church, especially in one of the southern States of America, shortly after the end of the civil war. In Germany too, however, the life of the spirit had undergone

In Search of an Explanation in History 33

a radical change under the influence of changing times. It is not easy to find a clear cause for this. Welte, for example, has referred to an extinguishing of the light of genius, to a disappearance of the 'mystical meaning' and to the situation of philosophy after Hegel's death in 1831 and that of literature after Goethe's death at almost the same time.[13] The solid and top-heavy music of Brahms and Reger is also quite different in character from that of Beethoven and Schubert, both of whom died just before 1830, or even that of Berlioz and Chopin. I should not wish to deny the genius of 'mystical meaning' of Franck or Bruckner, but it is a fact that these composers evoked hardly any response in their contemporaries. The situation is similar in the case, for example, of Kierkegaard or Newman.

After this change, thinking was directed towards positive data and verifiable, empirical facts in nature and history. The interest was no longer in synthesis, but in analysis and the isolation of data. The creation of all-embracing structures of thought was no longer regarded as ideal—specialisation became of central importance. A world of technical possibilities was opened up and science was intoxicated by a sense of optimism about the progress that lay in store for mankind. There was at this time such an exclusive concentration on calculable phenomena that everything that could not be grasped by the exact sciences tended to be regarded as illusory. This applied in particular to the reality of God and its manifestation in the world.

Seen against this background and within the context of the increasing isolation of the Church, the relatively sudden structural change of Catholic theology is not surprising. In the first place, the creative theological impulse, which was, in the context of the whole Church, still very weak, went dead to a great extent and its place was soon taken by a new theological attitude. On the one hand, Catholic theologians, together with the whole Church, took up a resolutely defensive position. In opposition to the new thinking that was so concerned with empirical facts, a theology was developed which Welte has strikingly described as a 'theology despite everything' and a 'safeguarding of orthodoxy that was not without a certain nervousness'.[14] On the other hand, scholastic thought, which was dormant in the Church, discovered that it was spiritually remarkably close to the new objective and analytical thought in the world. Scholastic thought is also analytical and deals in an objective and apparently mathematical way with an ever increasing number of more and more precisely defined concepts, thus disintegrating the reality of salvation—so the opponents of scholasticism, who are never absent, say—into separate atoms. In retrospect, it is possible to say that the nineteenth-century theologians who revived scholasticism understood it in accordance with the spirit of their own times—concentrating to such an extent on the separate details of the building that they were too close to be able to see the whole structure of the medieval synthesis.

The direct consequence of these two theological tendencies —the defensive attitude of theology and the interest in scholasticism—was the sudden revival of scholastic thought in a form that was more apologetical and even more polemical than before, namely neo-scholasticism. The Catholic members of the Tübingen school saw their shares fall sharply in value and were conscious of being pushed to the periphery of theological thought—to such an extent that, by the end of the nineteenth century, the school had been almost forgotten, even though some of their ideas continued to survive in the scholastic theology of the period. In Italy, the highly personal and influential thought of A. Rosmini continued to be the target of obstinate attacks, even though he was exonerated initially. These attacks, however, eventually did result in condemnation by the Church in 1887. Rosmini's scholastic critics were of the opinion that his writings contained elements of ontologism, a tendency which was quite widespread round about the middle of the nineteenth century and which claimed to come into contact, in an intuitive knowledge of reality, with the being of God himself. Open dialogue with contemporary thinking and with Protestant theology was viewed in Catholic circles with suspicion and regarded as problematical and dangerous. The language of theology became extremely unimaginative and cautious and Catholic theologians confined themselves to interpreting traditional sources. They were no longer looking for images to give form to creative ideas, but for clearly defined concepts which would, as far as possible, preclude misunderstanding when the traditional ideas were handed on in teaching. In thinking about faith, the sacraments and the Church, it was no longer the subjective, personal and inward dimensions which were emphasised, but the external and objective aspects. No attempt was made to build up a richer and richer synthesis within which the many aspects of the reality of faith would have an organic place—on the contrary, theological thinking tended at this time to move away from the centre. In the end, precisely for this reason, neo-scholasticism could not really evade the criticism of having dealt exclusively with a great number of affirmations in a loose and external context. Man's free personal decision and his individual conscience became deeply overshadowed by an increasingly centralised authority and an objective and easily manipulated law. Never before, perhaps, had the course chosen by the hierarchy of the Church exerted such a rapid and deep influence on theological thinking. It is also perhaps characteristic of the second half of the nineteenth century that it did not produce lay theologians like F. von Baader or J.J. von Görres—the new type of theology remained, almost as a matter of course, in the hands of the clergy.

The most striking aspect of this change that took place round about the middle of the century, however, is the changed theological attitude towards history. The Catholic school of Tübingen tried to understand Christianity as a dynamic, developing element and to integrate the results of positive research into their synthesis. Round about 1850, however, theologians, going back to an attitude towards change and development that had grown up in earlier centuries, began to view historical and biblical criticism as a danger which undermined the besieged fortress and as an element that was foreign to and incapable of being combined with Christian faith. Some of the radical conclusions of biblical criticism above all make it possible for us to understand this attitude, but this reaction of fear inspired a panic-stricken and fundamental rejection of history. The reality of faith was regarded as a timeless, changeless metaphysical 'system' which was therefore able to ignore all new discoveries and to keep the 'spirit of the times' safely outside the walls. In the heated controversy around Loisy towards the end of the century, this attitude was expressed by the none too prudent Abbé Maignen thus: 'Unlike a science that is constantly changing, the Church is fully justified in not attempting to find a useless reconciliation between her dogmas and the provisional results of the sciences. She has only to be concerned with her own teaching, which is dependent on faith alone and to alleviate the distress of souls by protecting them against all that may give rise to doubt and against dangerous and rash views. Science may constantly change, but faith is unchangeable.'[15]

The result of this dissociation from the constantly changing scientific reality was, however, not that positive theological research within the Church was no longer practised. Study of the Bible, the Church Fathers, the medieval theologians, archeology and the history of the Church began, in harmony with the great interest at that time in verifiable facts, to flourish anew, especially after 1880. The historical monographs of this period were in fact the only really original theological works produced during this time. They stood apart, however, from systematic theology and were not integrated into the Church's defensive speculation about the reality of faith. This applies even to the balanced and personal synthesis of the greatest of all the nineteenth-century scholastic theologians, M.J. Scheeben, who, following the Tübingen school, integrated a profound knowledge of the Greek Fathers into his speculative thought, while his theological attitude was, as will appear later in this book, to remain a model for the Catholic renewers. Even his theology, however, did not really integrate the historical and dynamic aspect of their heritage into his otherwise very balanced synthesis. His work consequently also gives the ultimate impression that it is outside time. On the other hand, the positive theologians did not consider dogmatic theology in their research. This mutual aloofness gave rise to a constantly increasing tension of unanswered questions between both groups of theologians, a tension which was all the more explosive because each group was conscious of the fact that it did not have a total view and, uncertain as to which course to follow, tried to put off the inevitable confrontation for as long as possible. The violence of the polemics with opponents inside and outside the Catholic Church and especially the reaction of panic to modernism can only be understood as the result of questions that had been set aside for years.

It is furthermore possible to remark, in the case of a figure like Scheeben, the concept of 'neo-scholasticism' has been used to cover altogether too many theologians. This is one reason why it is such an unsatisfactory label, especially since the First Vatican Council and its establishment in practice as the official theology of the Church. This is why the Catholic renewal itself takes place within the neo-scholastic tradition—from Schell to Rahner and Metz, most of the renewers can thus be called neo-scholastics. The concept 'neo-scholasticism' has therefore become less and less precise and has to be used with great caution. The tendency described above does, however, clearly remain the basis either on which one relies or against which one argues. As such, the concept 'neo-scholasticism' is indispensable.

Two opposite poles

My rather abstract description of the change that took place in Catholic thought round about the middle of the nineteenth century can be given a little more light and shadow if we consider some of the major figures of this period. The first of these is undoubtedly the Jesuit J. Kleutgen. One needs to have no stereotyped prejudices against his Order to observe that Kleutgen, who was the most striking and militant personality in the early neo-scholastic movement, was a splendid commander of the defence of the theological citadel. He showed fight not only against thought outside the Catholic Church, but also against the school of Hermes, ontologism, Günther and the Catholic theologian of the Tübingen school who has gone down in history as 'the noble Hirscher'. Kleutgen had, when he was a young man, been a follower of Günther and his conversion was manifest even in his personal life. After he had been called to Rome in 1851 to work in the Congregation for the Index, which was at that time still a separate organism, he came into closer contact with his fellow Jesuits of the so-called Roman school—Perrone, Passaglia, Franzelin and Schrader—together with whom he had a clear influence on the documents of the First Vatican Council. This Council marked the culmination of neo-scholastic theology, which has since become so closely identified with the teaching of the Catholic Church that every protest within the Church has also automatically been directed against neo-scholasticism and this has in turn quickly been branded as treason against the teaching of the Church itself. More than any other neo-scholastic theologian, Kleutgen made the rather feverish tone which is characteristic of the movement current, a tone which makes one think of someone who says something too loudly and with too much assurance in order to silence his own unease. Although he wanted to extend neo-scholastic thought is a positive and synthetic direction, as Scheeben had done, unrest at the front kept him to the end in active service. It was this that drew these bitter words about his own country from him: 'I want to have nothing more to do with that country or with its confused, yet so inflated minds.'[16]

He undoubtedly regarded the historian Ignaz von Döllinger, the most striking member of the camp of positive theologians, as one of these inflated Germans. Von Döllinger has always remained a rather enigmatical figure. He came from a liberal Catholic environment, went through a phase of sound, even narrow, 'orthodoxy' and finally became an aggressive and feared and certainly expert opponent of the views of the Roman Curia. This was already obvious when the immaculate conception of Mary was declared a dogma in 1854, but was revealed in its most challenging form at the scientific congress convoked by von Döllinger at Munich in 1863. In a great speech at this congress, he proclaimed Germany as the country of the future in the sphere of theology because no other people 'cherished both eyes of theology, philosophy and history, with the same care, love and thoroughness'.[17] In addition to this, he called scholasticism a ruin that could only be replaced by a new building and demanded freedom from the tutelage of the Curia for historical research. It is therefore not surprising that the Archbishop of Munich soon received a strong protest from the Pope and that, a year later, the Syllabus included a condemnation of the affirmation that 'the decrees of the Apostolic See and the Roman Congregations hold back the progress of science'[18] and of the view that scholastic theology was not adapted to the spirit of the times. Von Döllinger was passed over as a theologian for the Council and fulfilled everyone's expectations by resisting violently as soon as a definition of papal infallibility was first discussed. He was excommunicated after the Council, but did not join the Old Catholic Church, which owed much to his impulse. He continued to hesitate for twenty years, on the verge of submission to the Catholic Church, but clung until he was ninety-one to his conviction that 1870 had called 'a new Church' into being.

Looking back, it cannot be doubted that he said many painfully true things. Nor can it be denied that he had a clear vision—perhaps recalling Möhler, whose *Einheit in der*

Kirche had made such a deep impression on him—of the direction which theology should take, namely that of allowing teaching about faith to become permeated with 'purified history and philosophical speculation'.[19] It can, however, hardly be claimed that he himself provided the beginning of any such synthesis. In his case, history remained isolated from thinking about faith—he had effective weapons at his disposal and did not hesitate to use them, but did not seem to realise that this would ultimately have to lead to a conference table and to constructive negotiations. Unfortunately, his opponents were equally unable to see so far ahead. A long series of conflicts was to follow.

John Henry Newman

The tension within the Catholic Church was revealed even in the life of that great and balanced thinker, John Henry Newman, although he remained on the periphery of the arena and yet had already found the key to a synthesis. His life-span was within two years of coinciding with that of von Döllinger, but the distance between the two men was as great as that between Augustine and Jerome. Newman's personality was, in many ways, surprisingly like that of Augustine. Like Augustine, he too concentrated on personal religious life, viewed the world as the sign of God's works, was Platonic in his basic attitude and his way of thinking, was fundamentally original and preferred to write in the form of essays. He had the kind of originality which is able to make even the most worn-out idea sound surprisingly new. According to O. Chadwick, his opponents described his originality as an 'infinite capacity for not reading important books', but it would be better to say that his independent mind naturally forced a distinctive form on everything that he assimilated. In a word, his work never gives the impression of being secondhand.[20]

Even as a young man, Newman was a controversial figure who was never afraid to make a stand in public, but he was never vociferous. On the contrary, he was rather the classic type of learned English gentleman. His English way of thinking, with its attention to the concrete, contrasts refreshingly with the ambitious thought of the Germans, with its passion for abstractions. His language is suggestive and reflects his preference for 'real knowledge', a knowledge based on living experience. The historical dimension of being a Christian had become a personal problem for Newman from the time of the Oxford Movement onwards. The question of the bond between the Church of England and the gospel of Christ made him study history in detail and reflect deeply and personally. This gradually led to his conviction that an 'idea', an original and creative interpretation of the human reality, could retain its identity even through its historical development. I hope to show later how this notion of 'dynamic identity' became the essence of a new concept of tradition, which has shown itself to be more and more fruitful in theology. On the basis of this concept, historical studies and contemporary thought can be admitted to the very heart of theology, not in opposition to the gospel of Christ and the dogmas of the Church, but as indispensable guides to the authentic meaning and the present-day implications of the gospel and the Church's dogmas.

It was not in fact Newman's plan to provide a theological synthesis of this kind. What he did was to put forward, at various points, ideas that were surprisingly new for the period in which he was living. One example was his idea that it was necessary to consult the laity in matters of faith. The Anglican theologian, A. Vidler, has rightly pointed out, however, that Newman himself had no need of any change in or re-interpretation of the Church's teaching. It was not the content of the teaching of the Church that he found unsatisfactory, but the reasons on which faith was based in current theology.[21] He regarded himself neither as a theologian nor as a philosopher in the sense in which these were understood in the Church of his time. He refused an invitation to attend the Council as a theologian and he was never able to feel at home in scholastic thought. He did not even go in for the new historical criticism of von Döllinger which had been acclaimed with such enthusiasm by the turbulent group gathered round Lord Acton. It was Newman's fate, as England's most prominent Catholic, to bear the burden of occupying, by conviction, a middle position. He was too conservative for the young liberals and too unmanageably radical for the ultramontanists and especially for Cardinal Manning. A great man, he always remained on the outside. When he was made a cardinal in the second year of the papacy of Leo XIII, he was rehabilitated for a short while, but he was regarded with suspicion until deep into the twentieth century as having been a forerunner of modernism. This is mainly because Loisy and Tyrrell, uncritically but understandably, appealed to the most progressive theologians who had not been condemned. But Newman's ideas had to be adapted by the modernists before they could serve to protect the flank of the radical plan with which these reformers aimed to release the tension between static orthodoxy and the dynamic contemporary situation.

Bibliography

The general context of Catholic theology in the nineteenth century has been well summarised in A. Dru's attractive book *The Church in the Nineteenth Century: Germany 1800–1918* ('Faith and Fact' series, 103), London 1963, and in more detail in E.E.Y. Hales, *The Catholic Church in the Modern World: a Survey from the French Revolution to the Present*, New York and London 1958. Apart from these books, and, of course, the manuals on Church history, which are not entirely satisfactory for our purpose, there seems to be little contemporary literature in English, unfortunately. The most illuminating study on Catholic theology during this period is an article dating back to 1954 by the religious philosopher of Freiburg University, Bernhard Welte. It was the title of this article, 'Zum Strukturwandel der katholischen Theologie im 19. Jahrhundert', which provided the heading of the preceding section of this book. This article can most easily be found in Welte's collected essays *Auf der Spur des Ewigen*, published in 1965 by Herder of Freiburg. The broad outline of Welte's interpretation has also been followed by L. Scheffczyk in an anthology selected with imagination and expert knowledge: *Theologie in Aufbruch und Widerstreit* (Bremen 1965). His general introduction to, and more detailed presentation of, individual theologians undoubtedly form the most easily accessible survey of this period, in German, that is. Among the texts that Scheffczyk has chosen will be found the essence of von Drey's programme as set out in the Tübingen *Theologische Quartalschrift*, several of Hermes' typically unattractive passages, a fascinating argument by Günther about faith and knowledge and a sizeable extract from von Döllinger's manifesto of 1863 at Munich. There is also E. Hocedez' classic work in three volumes on the theology of the nineteenth-century Catholic Church, *Histoire de la théologie au XIXe siècle* (Brussels and Paris 1947–52), which contains abundant material on theology in language areas other than the German, all, however, seen in a strongly neo-scholastic light. B. Reardon's anthology, *Religious Thought in the Nineteenth Century* (Cambridge 1966), includes only two Catholic authors, Newman and Lamennais, but does also provide extracts from the writings of such great figures as Schleiermacher, Hegel, Feuerbach, Ritschl, Harnack, Kierkegaard and William James, without whom Catholic thought in the nineteenth century would remain in a vacuum. For the influence of the life of the Church and politics on theology, two books must be mentioned. The first is the classic work of R. Aubert, *Le pontificat de Pie IX (1846–1878)* (Paris 1952), which forms the twenty-first volume of a history of the Church edited by A. Flitche and V. Martin. The second is the fascinating Pelican book, *The Church in an Age of Revolution*, in which the Anglican historian of theology A.R. Vidler made his specialised studies, in particular of French Catholic liberalism, available to a wider public in 1961.

More specific information about the Catholic school of Tübingen can be traced via the articles 'Tübingen School' by Elmar Klinger in *Sacramentum Mundi*, VI (London 1970), and 'Möhler' by R.H. Nienaltowski in the New Catholic Encyclopedia, IX. For the history of this school, we are most of all indebted to J.R. Geiselmann, a Tübingen theologian himself who is now almost eighty years old and who has written several standard works on the subject, none of which, unfortunately, have been translated into English. He has also edited a new and critical text of Möhler's work with commentary (Cologne 1957—). There is an early translation of Möhler's *Symbolik* in English: *Symbolism*, London 1843, 2 volumes, but not of *Die Einheit*. Congar included a new French translation in his series 'Unam Sanctam': *L'unité dans l'Eglise* (Paris 1938). O. Chadwick's *From Bossuet to Newman* (Cambridge 1957), has a section on the Tübingen theologians. On Döllinger the *New Catholic Encyclopedia* contains a fairly extensive article in volume IV, with further references, among others to Lord Acton's work.

Chadwick's book mentioned above is, of course, mostly about Newman, but anyone wishing to know more about him should consult the attractive book by C. Hollis, *Newman and the Modern World* (London 1967), which relates Newman as a person and as a thinker to his own and to our times. Rather more specialised are the various contributions in *The Rediscovery of Newman: an Oxford Symposion*, edited by John Coulson and A.M. Allchin (London 1967). A work by A.J. Boekraad, *The Personal Conquest of Truth According to J.H. Newman* (Louvain 1955) can also be recommended. Studies on Newman's ideas on development, which also contain more general information, will be mentioned in a later section. Newman's own works, almost unique in theology for their beauty of language, are, of course, easily available, even in various paperback editions.

The Hope of the 'Modernists'

When a surprise attack by the Germans in 1940 banished all Dutch hopes that the Netherlands would, as in 1914, remain in safety and not be involved in the war, a mood of fear and panic quickly developed and was expressed in paralysing rumours and nervous exaggerations. People thought that enemies and traitors were lurking everywhere. In the general confusion, Colonel Mussert, the brother of the leader of the Dutch National Socialist Movement but himself not a member of it, was arrested and shot without any form of trial. Even now, there are still many Dutch people who refuse to believe that there were not thirty to forty thousand victims of the German bombing of Rotterdam, but barely a thousand.

Similar reactions were caused by the appearance of the modernists in the Catholic Church at the beginning of the twentieth century. The very fact that these men, who had scarcely any contact with each other and very divergent ideas and aims, were given the collective name of 'modernists' — in its narrower sense, this name derives from their condemnation—can be seen as an attempt to localise this fifth column within the fortress of the Catholic Church and thus make it easier to render it harmless. The modernists themselves made use of pseudonyms and obscure formulae, which their opponents in turn quickly interpreted as camouflage, hiding a fatal attack on the Church. Especially after they had been condemned, opposition to them deteriorated into a shameful heresy hunt, complete with a cunning system of espionage, a secret code and a campaign of slander. This resulted in the emergence, in the vocabulary of the Church, of another tabu word, 'integralism', in opposition to 'modernism'.

It takes a certain amount of courage to look for the truth about this confused episode in the history of Catholic theology. The smoke screen that still covers this old battlefield is so thick that it is hardly beginning to lift even today.

Often, all that the person in search of truth has to go by are emotionally charged statements and interpretations which are reminiscent of the letters sent to the editors of today's newspapers on Vietnam or the 'holy war' of the state of Israel. In the past, Catholic writers dutifully took the side of the judge, whose verdict, 'the sum total of all heresies', was accepted submissively as the basis for research. At present, however, the fact of the condemnation of the modernists seems to be regarded rather as evidence for discharge and the fact that, for example, such a convinced sympathiser of the movement as Baron von Hügel accepted the verdict seems to be overlooked.

Difficult though it may be, however, it is vitally important to be really objective in describing the attempt made by the modernists, because this deep conflict between a theology in search of renewal and the traditional interpretation of the Church's teaching about faith has determined the position of Catholic theology until our own times.

The French Church in the nineteenth century

The situation of the Catholic Church in France had become very confused in various spheres by the end of the nineteenth century and this had repercussions on theology. The problem that had been debated ever since the restoration of the Bourbons, namely the attitude to be taken towards the 'principles of the Revolution', had still to be satisfactorily solved. The oldest and most influential form of French ultramontanism went back to an aristocrat of the *ancien régime*, J. de Maistre, who had, as the Sardinian envoy in St Petersburg, had years in which to foster his abhorrence of the French Revolution and had become convinced that only the papacy could provide a new foundation for order and authority and only absolute monarchy could provide the superstructure for this foundation. According to ancient custom, the French hierarchy was more convinced of the soundness of this second point of support than of papal authority. The reactionary Bourbons could be satisfied with the support of the bishops. It was therefore not surprising that the energetic group of Catholics gathered round Lamennais, who were seeking to renew the life of the Church through reconciliation with the ideas of the Revolution, received no encouragement from the episcopacy. They consequently appealed directly to the Pope, with the result that ultramontanism found itself with an unexpected offshoot in these Catholic liberals. Gregory XVI was not flattered by the trust of a group of men who advocated, as the basis of their plan to reform the Church, the separation of Church and state. This, after all, meant that the Church would have to give up her claims to supervise the Christian states. The Pope's condemnation of the Catholic 'liberals' in 1832 did not, however, put out the ultramontane fire. Both the liberals and the intransigent followers of Veuillot, who had become the most vociferous advocate of supreme papal authority in the most extreme sense, had, by about 1850, put all their hopes in Rome. The whole French Church was, however, by this time becoming less and less dependent on the authority of the state, as a result of various political upheavals. Those who supported the separation of Church and state were in any case helped in a rather rough way by the anti-clerical republicans who were in power. An important group of Catholics also continued to identify the cause of faith with that of one of the royalist pretenders and these men were ready to take part at any time in risky adventures to further their cause. In the midst of all this, another factor of social and economic origin was also beginning to play a part—under the impact of the industrial revolution and the socialist elements in the political revolution, a small but active group of Catholics in France had begun to tackle the social problem. This movement was to provide the impulse and the material for the later social encyclicals and to give French Catholic life a distinctive aspect which still lends it a certain fascination of its own, even today.

The Catholic Church in France, then, was characterised, towards the end of the nineteenth century, by a confused pattern of contrasts. After 1870, the Republic was determined to banish clericalism—with which the whole Church was identified—from the state. A series of drastic 'laicisation' laws, keenly felt in the sphere of education, and, on the other hand, a number of fiascos on the part of the royalists which seriously compromised the Church, brought this aim almost within reach. In addition to this, Leo XIII, who had been pressing for reconciliation with the Republic, was succeeded, almost at the climax of these difficulties, by Pius X, who was more opposed to reconciliation. Therefore, when, round about this time, various groups of theologians also began to show signs of unrest, very few people had the patience to listen to their problems or to those of the group of Catholics working for social renewal. There were, at this period of French history, numerous journals of a very high standard and the problems of faith that were discussed in these publications were not only of fundamental importance but had also been thrust aside by more urgent affairs in Church circles for far too long. However, they came to the surface at a most unfortunate moment—just when the final stage of the struggle between Church and state was beginning in France. The consequence of this was that a vociferous and bitter controversy flared up which, as it continued, grew more and more like an impatient indictment. The condemnation of modernism, when it followed, was one of the most violent ever pronounced by the Catholic Church.

The new attempts of these French theologians were made above all along two different routes, in which it is not difficult to recognise the two main routes of theological renewal which have already been outlined in this book—the way going back to the source of the real gospel of Christ and the way leading to renewed contact with contemporary experience. A striking characteristic of the situation of theology at this time, moreover, is that these new movements came about outside the quasi-official neo-scholastic theology of the period, were opposed to it and therefore almost automatically came under fire from this fortress. Loisy, who followed the way of going back to the source, was originally a specialist in biblical criticism, but began to explore the fields of systematic theology and religious philosophy only when the exegetical conclusions that he had reached compelled him to do so. The other impulse, with which modernism was in fact no more than indirectly involved, but without which it is impossible to form a true picture of these years, came from apologetics, that rather seedy offshoot of theology in which, unfortunately, basic concepts such as revelation, faith and the Church had, in the course of centuries, landed up. It was also there, however, that the facts of the historical sciences and of contemporary philosophy—data which are not directly theological—had the opportunity to fertilise theology.

Maurice Blondel

In reaction to the increasing dechristianisation of intellectuals brought about by anticlericalism, a movement emerged towards the end of the nineteenth century with the aim of renewing apologetics in such a way that it could make modern man capable of experiencing Christian faith again as an answer to his questions. Instead of concentrating on the external signs and arguments for Christ and his Church, the attempt was made to make man's quest for God conscious and thus, by following this path, to open his heart and mind to the Christian answer. By far the most original expression of the basic ideas of this new movement, some of which were derived from Newman's psychology of faith, was provided by the French philosopher, Maurice Blondel.

The word 'philosopher' was not simply added to Blondel's name in the preceding sentence as a decoration. He himself always continued to stress that he was a philosopher, not a theologian or even an apologist. He was also convinced that his strictly philosophical analysis inescapably led to the basic question about the meaning of life which would bring man to the threshold of Christian faith. Upholding this view cost him years of painful and laborious discussion, first with his university colleagues, to show that he was not practising theology, but later, with his fellow-believers especially, to prove that he was not attempting to make the Christian revelation accessible to purely 'natural' philosophical thought.

It was above all in confrontation with theologians that he continued to feel ill at ease. He came from an old, firmly Catholic family in the Burgundian town of Dijon, but his personal life gives little reason for us to regard him as a Burgundian figure. He described himself as 'scrupulous in character and excessively sensitive to the opinions of others'[22] and had an unshakeable, but strict and sombre faith, with an almost meticulous attention to mortification and asceticism. Brought up in a pious and sheltered environment, he had assimilated the Catholic faith into his life and spent the whole of his eighty-eight years without any serious doubts or crises in this sphere. For a time, he believed that he had a vocation to become a priest, but after a retreat he decided to become a philosopher, a task which he also regarded as a religious vocation. This caused a certain amount of embarrassment in university circles, where it was fashionable to regard Christianity as belonging to the past. The Sorbonne had, however, become used to the oddity of this 'provincial' since he had enrolled there in 1881 as a twenty-year old student. His family had, of course, objected to the 'dilettantism' and free-thinking environment of the state university, but Blondel had gone there consciously in order to present himself officially, as the first stage in the struggle in which he aimed 'to do better than our modern thinkers in the light of the gospel'.[23] The amused mockery changed into annoyance when he announced that he wanted to write a thesis on such an unphilosophical subject as action and, what is more, not on the concept of action, but on man's factual action. It was only in the face of considerable resistance that this subject was accepted and then mainly on the insistence of two professors, Emile Boutroux and Léon Ollé-Laprune. The latter had come under the influence of Newman and believed that Blondel's thought was similar to his own. It was only after Blondel had, according to the usual practice, spent some time in teaching that his graduation took place in 1893. It was looked forward to with a certain amount of tension. In the meantime, Blondel had built up around himself a circle of kindred spirits and these were understandably curious to know how a thesis which quoted, as its most important source, the author's own diary and which, as far as its contents were concerned, offered such a challenge to the university would be received. The book contained a detailed and penetrating analysis in which Blondel fathomed man's life as far as the source of all activity and the communal, dynamic origin of all thought and will. On the basis of this, he had come to the conclusion that human action was impelled by an inner, creative orientation which inevitably resulted in a powerless cry for the transcendent and a quest for a transcendental reality which came to man from history as a religion 'from outside' and imposed dogmas and a rule of life.

In a crowded hall, Blondel defended his thesis with success and it was well received by the Catholics, but the university as a whole remained very reserved. Because his work had come to 'Christian conclusions' and was therefore thought to be not philosophy, but apologetics, he was excluded from the Sorbonne and, for two years, even from all teaching at university level. Blondel realised that he had missed his mark. He therefore published, three years later, a series of articles, which were later collected and published together under the simple title of *Lettre*, on the demands that had to be made of apologetics in the modern age and on the method that philosophers could use to study the religious phenomenon. In the four years that he had spent working at *L'action* he had come to understand that only a strictly philosophical treatise would be really convincing and therefore also apostolic. He had consequently gradually eliminated all 'apologetical' undertones from his text. Now he once again postulated, in opposition to non-believers, his explicitly rational intention and method and his acceptance of the concept of immanence which they 'regard with jealous susceptibility as the condition of philosophy'—he too was of the opinion that 'nothing can enter man unless it proceeds from him and in one way or another corresponds to a need for development'.[24] On the other hand, he also made it clear to his fellow-Christians that the current methods of apologetics were very inadequate at the philosophical level. He said that the philosopher who was concerned with action could also criticise and assimilate the supernatural without the transcendent aspect being compromised or 'tainted' by the natural values within which it was contained.

This exposition of his principles brought about a surprising change on the part of his opponents. The Sorbonne philosophers lost their reservations and recognised Blondel as a promising colleague. But, to the consternation of Blondel himself, who believed that he had performed an apostolic service for the Church, the theologians now began to discover a number of equivocal and dangerous elements in his philosophy of action. They accused him of undermining the real value of truth by making it dependent on action and of failing to do full justice to the objective data of faith and the transcendence of the supernatural by placing too much emphasis on their inner acceptance and assimilation. The consequence of this was a long struggle, at times quite bitter, with traditional theology, and in fact this lasted until the Second World War. In this conflict, Blondel was accused, for example, of subjectivism, naturalism and fideism.

He was not at his best in these debates. He was above all inhibited by his rather overwrought piety and felt, as a layman without any real theological training, constrained to be extremely modest. This modesty contrasted sharply with his boldness at the Sorbonne and also with the self-assurance of most of his theological opponents, whose scholastic terminology and way of thinking were hardly able

to grasp Blondel's more subtle language. The constant need
to explain his ideas exhausted him and, indeed, he was often
far from consistent, thus creating a thicker and thicker fog
around his real intentions. His later great works were written
with an enervating caution. Duméry has observed that he
was diverted from his true course by this conflict.[25] His
major work therefore came thirty years too late, when he
had gradually come to be accepted as a lay theologian who
was no longer listened to by atheists. Now that more than
three quarters of a century separate us from his first appearance, it is easier to see how strikingly his basic ideas anticipated later thought and especially French existentialism.
The word 'existence' could almost be substituted for 'action'
in his writings, although Blondel certainly did not mean the
same as Sartre when he wrote: 'the substance of man is
action—he is what he makes himself'.[26]

His influence, however, was decisive on the theology of
renewal in the French-speaking countries. He always had a
devoted group of followers—he was able to arouse the sort
of enthusiasm that made men copy out, word for word, the
hundreds of pages of *L'action* during the many years when
the printed work was no longer obtainable. But his influence
extended far beyond this circle of kindred spirits. It is often
not possible to point out clearly the lines along which his
thought was developed, because his ideas acted more as a
catalyst. The various themes in his philosophy are, however,
met with again and again especially in the sphere of speculation about the problems of the historicity of revelation and
of faith as a personal response to revelation which are
fundamental to theology. Now that German and English
translations of his work have recently been published, it
would seem that Duméry's prediction that he would be
explicitly rehabilitated is beginning to come true.[27]

The difficult path of Alfred Loisy

At about the same time as Blondel was a centre of interest,

Loisy was beginning to follow a different and spectacular course of renewal. Taking the results of historical research and biblical exegesis as his point of departure, he aimed above all to 'go back to the source'.

Although the historical and philological approach to Scripture and the writings of the early Church had flourished in the Catholic Church since the time of humanism, it had never had any marked influence on late scholastic theology or on preaching. It is true that Richard Simon had caused a stir in the Church as early as the second half of the seventeenth century, not only by drawing attention to various literary levels in the Pentateuch, but also by attempting to incorporate this discovery into the Church's teaching about faith. Simon's efforts had, however, only resulted in increasing tension between Catholic theology and the historical sciences, mainly because he himself was disposed to controversy and had aroused the eloquent indignation of Bossuet in particular. Later, towards the end of the eighteenth century, positive theology began to flourish anew in Protestant circles and the results of the work of these theologians were taken over by the Catholic school of Tübingen. Round about the middle of the nineteenth century, however, the sensational reconstructions of David Strauss' *Leben Jesu* and of F.C. Baur of the Protestant faculty at Tübingen were greeted with increasing reservation by Catholics. Their historical approach was clearly tinged with Hegel's doctrine of evolution and was also increasingly criticised by their Protestant colleagues. In the second half of the century, in which theology tended more towards positivism, Protestant theologians moved farther and farther away from 'metaphysics' and were more and more drawn to the natural sciences and to the data of religious history which were becoming increasingly available. A. Ritschl led a crusade in systematic theology itself against all 'metaphysics' in the science of faith, insisting that faith was not a matter of intellectual consent to historical facts or philosophical arguments, but a personal decision in which the will had a greater part to play than thought. Historians welcomed this tendency, not only because it gave them the opportunity to practise their science without fear, but also because it made it possible for them, through their science, to expose irrelevant historical deposits of personal faith. Many people looked forward to such a restatement of the gospel, as was proved by the unheard-of success of the popular synthesis written by Adolf von Harnack, the most striking figure to emerge from Ritschl's school. In his book, Harnack, who, as a librarian, had once said to his assistant that he could classify dogmatic theology under *belles lettres*,[28] had not been afraid to analyse the consequences which the historical sciences had for the Christian faith. On the other hand, it is no less surprising that the most penetrating reply to Harnack's book was written by a French Catholic priest, Alfred Loisy.

It is surprising for two reasons—firstly, that the reaction came from France and secondly that it came from a Catholic. It was not that Catholics simply held themselves aloof from the historical sciences at this time. The intellectual climate acted as a powerful stimulus to research into positive theology. This tradition had in no sense been terminated in the German-speaking countries after von Döllinger, but it did remain aloof from theology and preaching and did not venture, as Harnack had done, to tread on the thin ice of direct relevance. In this aloofness, there was also an understandable element of hesitation on the part of Catholic positive theologians in Germany simply to accept the assumptions of their Protestant colleagues along with their historical approach. In France, however, historical studies and biblical criticism as such had hardly got into their stride within the Catholic Church. The two great language areas were at this time far more mutually exclusive with regard to each other's scientific achievements than might be imagined. The German language has, for example, always been a formidable barrier for France. Ernest Renan was virtually the only writer who attempted, in his book on the life of Jesus, which was written for a large public, to bring the French sharply face to face with what had been accomplished in Germany during the first half of the nineteenth century. The gulf was too great to bridge, however, and Renan was simply not taken seriously. Such an attitude towards him was, moreover, relatively easy, not only because he had for years been considered an apostate from the Church, but also because his book bore clear traces of his talent as a novelist. In 1858, an apologist predicted that Renan would be totally forgotten in twenty years' time[29] rather imprudently, as it transpired, because Renan was elected to the Académie Française just twenty years after this prediction had been made and began to achieve more and more fame as an orientalist. Among those who heard him teach at the Collège de France from 1882 onwards was Alfred Loisy, who had just been ordained a priest.

This fact alone was enough to disqualify Loisy in the eyes of many of those who later opposed him. This is one of the simplifications to which the heat of the conflict gave rise. Loisy never met Renan personally and attended his lectures simply 'in the hope of proving to him that what was true in his science could be made to agree with a sound view of Catholicism'.[30] On the other hand, however, it cannot be denied that Loisy's manner and personality were particularly well suited to emotional simplifications. In many respects, he reminds one of Abélard—he too was a brilliant scholar who was, not without good reason, convinced that the new biblical studies, which he was one of the first in France to have mastered, could be a great blessing to the Church's thinking and preaching. He also took very little trouble to conceal this conviction and consequently antagonised an increasing number of less flexible colleagues, partly because of his ability to write unwelcome things in a very cool and effective way—things which were all the more unwelcome because they were so difficult to refute. There was, however, nothing in Loisy's life that was comparable to the scandal of Héloise. His leading opponents all testify, somewhat, it would seem, to their surprise, that his personal life was beyond reproach. What is more, it is even now not difficult to admire his courage, perspicacity and integrity, although it is less easy to admire his sense of reality and relativity. Even anyone who recognises that sufficient restitution has still to be made in the Catholic Church for the injury done to his memory cannot overlook a certain fanaticism usually peculiar to more intellectual pioneers. Loisy clearly lacked openness to the views of others, such as Blondel, and seemed to be lamentably incapable of laughing at himself. Because of this professional blindness, he led a lonely life. Even now, hardly anyone would unhesitatingly call him likeable or sympathetic, as Tyrrell and von Hügel certainly were.

He came from a peasant family, but lacked the good health that is usually associated with this background. Fortunately, however, he proved to be extremely intelligent and, after having decided, from personal conviction, to become a priest, gladly took advantage of the opportunity to specialise in Hebrew and biblical criticism. After his ordination in 1879, he therefore did not hesitate to accept Louis Duchesne's invitation to join him at the Institut Catholique at Paris (Catholic institutions of higher learning were, at that time, still forbidden by law to call themselves universities). The historian Duchesne, who was then in the process of building up a circle of young and promising specialists around himself at the Institut Catholique, had already become notorious for his strictly scientific and fearless practice of historical research with modern critical methods. He was a man with great personal powers of attraction who hoped to initiate a progressive theological movement and he believed that such a movement stood a real chance of succeeding in the Church of those days. This was more realistic than it might at first sight seem. Pius IX had been succeeded in 1878 by Pope Leo XIII. Towards the end of his life, Pius had admitted, 'My system and my policy have had their day, but I am too old to change my course. That will be the task of my successor.'[31] It would be an exaggeration to say that Leo's pontificate marked a sudden break with the years that had gone before. He certainly did not throw the gates of the Catholic fortress wide open. Many years spent as a diplomat in the Church had taught him the value of moderation. On the other hand, he did at least aim, in the political and social sphere, at co-existence between the Church and the modern world. He relieved the tension brought about in Germany by the *Kulturkampf*, instructed the French Catholics to become reconciled to the Republic and gave his explicit sanction to the endeavours of the Catholic progressives in the social sphere. A year after his election, he made the mistrusted 'liberal' theologian Newman a cardinal and, a little later, opened the Vatican archives for historical research.

It is especially easy to understand Duchesne's optimism in the light of this last action. Loisy had learnt the technique of historical criticism from Duchesne but, encouraged by him, decided to concentrate on the Bible and attended Renan's lectures. As he himself said, he regarded it as his vocation to use historical criticism to save the essence of the Christian faith from the outdated forms that it had assumed in the Church's teaching of that time. His attempt to carry out this plan occupied him for some twenty years. What sustained him in the face of all difficulties was an almost naïve hope—even many years after Duchesne had felt compelled to adopt a more realistic attitude—that the Church would admit that he was right or at least tolerate his ideas. He was, however, aware of the increasing suspicion that he aroused among conservative theologians and worked with great caution, partly on the advice of the exegete and rector of the Institut Catholique, Mgr d'Hulst. A maladroit publication by d'Hulst also involved Loisy in 1893 in a controversy about 'free exegesis' which ended in the restraining encyclical *Providentissimus Deus* and, in order to save the Institut, Loisy's dismissal.

The loss of his professorship meant that he also lost his most readily available followers On the other hand, however, his new post as spiritual director at a girls' boarding school gave him plenty of time for study and, perhaps even more important, extended his sphere of interest—giving religious instruction to his pupils now brought him face to face with the ordinary reality of the life of the Church. He began to think about incorporating the results of his specialised biblical studies into a work which would reformulate the whole deposit of faith for people of his own time. He also felt the need of an orientation of this kind for himself as well. Later, he wrote about this period in his life, saying that the only statement that he still accepted in the twelve articles of faith was 'Jesus was crucified under Pontius Pilate'. This confession did not mean what was all too easily accepted in the later polemics, that is, that Loisy had lost his faith and was acting as a hypocrite by deliberately continuing his work of undermining the faith of others within the Church. It is quite clear from all kinds of data that he only doubted the current interpretations of scholastic theology. He became increasingly preoccupied with the fundamental problem of the historical development of revelation. This in turn led him to Newman, whom he began to read enthusiastically at the suggestion of Baron von Hügel. This sympathetic, tireless confidant of so many progressive Catholics, whose greatness lay, according to Duméry, in his constant readiness to give more than simply moral support to friends who were again and again exposed to suspicion, was one of the two men with whom Loisy came into close contact at this time.[32] The other was the remarkably open Archbishop Mignot. As early as 1860, while he was still at the seminary, Mignot had come under the spell of Newman's theology of development and, as a bishop, he never ceased to stress the importance of study and in particular of exegesis. Despite the risk to himself, he continued to support Loisy and to defend him in Rome.

As time passed, however, unease and uncertainty increased. Loisy went on writing, sometimes under a pseudonym, and measures were taken in the Church against certain of his articles. He finished his synthesis of re-interpretation in its broad outline, but continued to hesitate for years as to whether he should publish it. It was, in the end, never published. In 1902, the French Church was startled when the abbé Marcel Hébert, one of Duchesne's circle, left the Church and when A. Houtin published an embarrassing book in which he exposed, in a way that was difficult to refute, the impotence of French Catholic exegesis.[33] The French translation of Harnack's best seller, *Das Wesen des Christentums*, appeared the same year, a book which evoked a reply from Loisy in the course of which he also hoped to gain the Church's recognition of his own attempts to reformulate the gospel.

The temptation to ask for a hearing in this form must have been almost irresistible. Harnack's book called for a Catholic response and Loisy indisputably had very effective means of defence at his disposal. Harnack's basic idea was that the essence of Christianity, God's universal fatherhood and the 'infinite value of the human soul'[34] in its personal relationship with God and other men had, since the time of the very early Church, been gradually buried under many different historical deposits. He was able to justify this view convincingly with the help of his incredible erudition. His conclusion was that Christianity now had to return to its original essence. The public response to Harnack's surprising reconstruction exceeded all expectations and was in fact a foretaste of the reception given, in our own times, the age of paperback editions, to Robinson's *Honest to God*. *Das Wesen des Christentums* was translated into fifteen languages and was reprinted more than seventy times in the original German. The book was obviously a challenge to the Catholic Church, which placed so much emphasis on visible structures and the external mediation of salvation and traced these back directly to Christ's institution of the Church. A realistic response based on the current theology or apologetics of the Church was, however, hardly conceivable.

Loisy, on the other hand, believed that he could prove

that the most important biblical texts on which Harnack based his arguments were, from the point of view of textual criticism, later interpolations and that Harnack had wrongly eliminated the eschatological element from Christ's teaching. He also went further than this, by outlining a much more satisfactory positive alternative, which he believed was in accordance with the Catholic tradition in its emphasis on the visible Church. The main argument of his book was that the gospel of Christ was *destined* to grow into the Church of today. It was in no sense a diminution, but a fulfilment of the biblical message that it had developed along with history and that it had continued to take on new forms. Loisy did not take long to finish the book, to which he gave the characteristic title of *L'Évangile et l'Église*, because he incorporated long sections of his unpublished synthesis into it. The book appeared in 1902, mainly on the urgent advice of Mgr Mignot, who was of the opinion that the Church could not allow herself to condemn such a convincing refutation of Harnack's views. Von Hügel was also in agreement with this decision to publish, believing that it was the only possible reply to Harnack and that the Church was realistic enough to overlook the more audacious points in Loisy's argument.[35]

The book, however, had a very sobering reception in the Catholic Church. Looking back now to the beginning of the century, we realise that it was hardly to be expected that the Church of that period would simply pass benevolently over various comments made by Loisy in passing, for example, that the gospels were not historical documents, but testimonies of faith, that the later development of the Church had not been anticipated by Christ and that constant reinterpretation of the ancient formulae was necessary to the discovery of the essence of faith, because the dogmas of the Church were 'not truths come down to us from heaven and preserved by religious tradition in the exact form in which they were first presented to us'.[36] In any case, the book was greeted by a storm of criticism, so much of it simply stupid and embarrassing abuse that it comes as a relief to read this perspicacious comment by the Jesuit, B. Gaudeau: 'The Catholic Church has shut herself up in a far corner of a deserted country and now we think that we are invincible because no one worries about us or even knows us.'[37] The main impression that one is left with is that the Church could only interpret such a disclosure of the fact that she had been determined by history as relativism. Loisy himself had in any case to admit to his critics that the development of dogma was not explicitly accepted in the Church, although this had, in his opinion, to be modified by saying that the Church had not yet come *consciously* to this conviction. But it was after all hardly realistic to expect the Church of the beginning of the present century, with her closed mind, to be able to recognise the case for a 'development' in the *near future*, an essential reform—of the kind that Loisy was clearly proposing—of her interpretation of the gospel, of her quasi-official theology and—perhaps the most painful proposal of all—of her hierarchy.

The book was quickly condemned by Cardinal Richard, the Archbishop of Paris, though this condemnation was endorsed by only seven of the French bishops. With the encouragement of Mignot and von Hügel and also of Tyrrell, with whom he had come into contact for the first time, Loisy published, during the course of the following year, another book, *Autour d'un petit livre,* in which he set out to clarify his argument in the previous book and to reply to his critics, the more competent and to some extent sympathetic of whom— in particular Lagrange, Batiffol and de Grandmaison—had asked for the points at issue to be made clearer. The second book did in fact throw a little more light on the problem for these critics, but it only made things far worse for Loisy himself and for his cause. Almost everyone had by now lost sight of the original purpose of the first book—a refutation of Harnack's thesis—and Loisy's attitude seemed to become more rigid under pressure from those who were opposing him. He based his defence of his own position on a drastic division between faith or dogma on the one hand and historical and biblical criticism on the other, preferring to confine himself to biblical exegesis. This made Blondel enter the arena, putting forward, in a fascinating way, the tradition of the Church as the essential link. Blondel, however, was not a professional exegete and Loisy was not disposed to regard history as 'metaphysics in action'. Somewhat irritably, he could not refrain from adding that Blondel was eminently suited to the writing of encyclicals.[38]

If only he had had the chance, one is inclined to think after the event, for in addition to this debate at the scientific level, which will be discussed in greater detail later in this book, there were more and more official interventions on the part of the Church, each revealing a shameful lack of understanding of the fundamental problems at stake. After the death of Leo XIII in 1903, the last signs of any attempt on the part of the Church to go forward to meet the world began to disappear. The saintly Pope Pius X returned to the policy of Leo's predecessor. He felt so ill at ease in the presence of all learning that the Holy Office were given a free hand. Loisy submitted to the discipline of the Church, but did not believe that he could or should renounce his convictions in the sphere of historical and biblical criticism. On the other hand, he offered to give up the lectureship at the Sorbonne that he had held for some time and to publish no more books or articles. The Vatican's reply to this offer, which had been so difficult for Loisy to make, was a cool order to submit unconditionally to the Church's judgement on his writings. His confidence in the Church was exhausted. The Church's official condemnation and excommunication of Loisy was delayed only by various political entanglements —the more simple of his opponents had always given him a place with the Catholics working for social renewal, with the supporters of Blondel and the 'democratic priests' who were seeking a *rapprochement* with the lay Republic.

In his most recent book on Catholic modernism, Vidler

has two important things to say about Loisy. The first is that Loisy explicitly chose to become a 'modernist' instead of shutting himself off in a peaceful academic environment and following a career, for example, in the field of philology, and that he did this for genuinely pastoral reasons.[39] In other words, he regarded re-interpretation in the light of modern knowledge of the Bible as his vocation in the Church of his own times. Vidler's second observation, which is closely connected with his first, is that Loisy abandoned this aim as soon as it had been rejected by the Church and thus showed himself, in his consciousness of the Church, to be a typically Catholic Christian.[40] He was not playing a part when he reacted against Harnack's liberal Protestantism. Even years after his condemnation, he was still convinced of the validity of his criticism. It is worth while mentioning this in passing, because certain characteristics of Catholic theology are clearly revealed in the figure of Loisy.

George Tyrrell

The two ways along which a renewal of theology was sought round about the beginning of the twentieth century were best illustrated in the work of Blondel and Loisy. There were, of course, various other important representatives, some of whom have already been mentioned in passing. Several theologians were at work in Italy, especially those grouped around R. Murri, E. Buonaiuti and the novelist A. Fogazzaro, who also had practical and above all social interests. In France, E. le Roy, the philosopher, who was as convinced a Catholic as Blondel, tried to outline a system of modern apologetics in the tradition of Bergson in which the Church's teaching about faith was regarded above all as the valid expression of fellowship with God and the way to it. George Tyrrell, the most striking 'modernist' after Loisy, also looked in this direction.

In the first place, he sought to establish renewed contact with contemporary Christian experience and thus followed the path of Blondel, although the word 'follow' is not sufficiently dynamic to be applied to Tyrrell, who was more of a prophet than a theologian. All that he said and wrote had that sort of intensity which the English are prepared to admire, but which they nonetheless find rather embarrassing. But Tyrrell was born in Dublin and, although he came from an old English family on his father's side, he had an Irish temperament—sincere, magnanimous, restlessly energetic and not without a trace of impatient obstinacy. He had an intuitive mind and was very open to all kinds of new ideas and impressions in his environment which he was able to incorporate into a surprising and original synthesis expressed in compelling language. He was extremely well read, extending his studies over a very wide field and even, for example, reading works of biblical criticism written in German. Yet one does not have the impression that he was a typical scholar—he seemed to lack the necessary temperament for patient and persistent analysis. His background and interests and the circle of readers that he aimed to reach were certainly theological, but his voice was not that of a scientific theologian. With his delicate sensitivity to religious experience he was above all gifted for spiritual guidance. Did circumstances perhaps lead to his development taking place outside the sphere where his greatest possibilities lay? His work gives the impression of brilliance, but not of having been fully thought out to its ultimate conclusion.

Tyrrell changed course several times during the course of his life. He was brought up in the low Church of England, but when he reached maturity this rather pietistic atmosphere no longer satisfied him and his search for intellectual certainty led him, via the high Church of England, to Catholicism in its sharpest form, the Church of Rome and the Society of Jesus which he joined, convinced of the society's total commitment to 'the cause of Roman Catholicism'.[41] It was while he was studying for the priesthood that Leo XIII urged a renewed study of Thomas Aquinas and Tyrrell was strongly attracted to the 'simplicity, directness and universality'[42] of Thomas' thought. In fact, he became such a passionate Thomist and this conviction was in such sharp contrast to the Jesuit tradition that his superiors kept him, a brilliant teacher, out of their seminary. They had also come to realise that Tyrrell was unable to be as docile and obedient as a Jesuit was at that time expected to be almost as a matter of course. For his part, Tyrrell became increasingly disappointed with the Society, although he continued for many years to devote his energies to Jesuit activities in the sphere of publicity and pastoral work.

Even as a student, however, he had begun to question the objective value of Thomism. This doubt had been caused by his reading of Newman and especially the *Grammar of Assent*, in which the certainty of faith was so strongly linked to personal experience and 'real knowledge'. His thinking came more and more under the influence not only of Newman's ideas, but also of William James' work in the field of religious psychology and of the 'liberal' Anglican theology of the period. He did not think of it as a sudden conversion when, after a period of about ten years, Baron von Hügel—Tyrrell regarded his meeting with this inspiring thinker in 1897 as a decisive date in his life—introduced him to the new apologetics of Blondel and Laberthonnière. It was also at about this time that von Hügel advised him to go to another and quite different source of inspiration, that of the new science of biblical criticism, in other words, Loisy and the leading German exegetes. Round about the turn of the century, then, he became more and more explicitly associated with the theologians who were looking forward to an opportunity of bringing theology up to date. His own contribution to this theological renewal was to emphasise that Christian experience was more important than theological statements and to insist on the radical adaptation of theology under the pressure of this new Christian experience, an adaptation in which the new findings of biblical exegesis were absolutely indispensable.

He published these ideas with great energy and far less

caution than his friends and supporters regarded as healthy. This inevitably led to difficulties with the Church—firstly, only with his Society, but later with the Vatican. After Pius X's condemnation of modernism and Tyrrell's prophetic reaction to this in *The Times*, his break with the Catholic Church was complete. He still continued, however, to devote his energies to the 'Catholic' branch of Christianity, regarding its institutions, its liturgy and sacraments, its ascetic and mystical traditions, its moral teaching and even its dogma as providing the norms for Christian thought. He continued, as before, to reject the ideal of progress and the interpretation of Christ of liberal Protestantism, convinced that this had been effectively refuted by the most recent biblical criticism (of Loisy among others) with its emphasis on the eschatological element. During the last years of his life, he became the prophet of a radically transformed Catholicism which had to be purged of 'Vatican' narrowness. Death overtook him, however, in 1909, when he was putting the finishing touches to his last book, *Christianity at the Crossroads*, a vision of the Christianity of the future. His funeral was marred by certain manoeuvres on the part of the Church which revealed how seriously his challenge had been taken.

Condemnation as the end and the beginning

Two years before Tyrrell's death, the hope of the modernists had already died. In two papal documents, *Lamentabili* and *Pascendi*, modernism had been built up into a well constructed system and had then been rejected as the 'sum total of all heresies'.[43] It is impossible not to agree with Vidler's opinion that the theologians who were working for renewal were not given any chance to discuss their developing ideas seriously within the Church.[44] The moment that they chose to attempt to do this proved to be extremely unfortunate. But, as Vidler has observed elsewhere, the setting up of supervisory bodies in every diocese which were bound to secrecy, the imposition of an anti-modernist oath on all members of the clergy and the reign of terror that was the consequence of these two measures all reveal a panic that was unworthy of a Church which makes such high claims as the Church of Rome.[45] Equally depressing is the definition of the aims of the modernists in the encyclical, written in the traditional curial style of harsh invective developed in the course of centuries of condemnation, as a deliberate plot against the Church, inspired purely by curiosity and pride and 'leading to the destruction of all religion . . . the first step was made by Protestantism, the second has been made by modernism, the third will plunge us all into atheism'.[46]

Loisy and Tyrrell soon disappeared from sight and those who remained, Blondel and the 'critics' Batiffol, de Grandmaison, Lagrange and others, together with other members of the theological intelligentsia, faced a difficult future. Laypeople were far less vulnerable, but, apart from a few individuals like Baron von Hügel, there were almost no active lay members of the modernist movement. Even priests engaged in pastoral work were, according to Miss Petre, Tyrrell's confidante, so frightened of being bitten by the sheep dogs that they hardly had time to look after the sheep. Certainly her own bishop never found time to answer her question as to whether, in his opinion, everything contained in the documents condemning modernism was and would continue to be of faith, and without such an answer she felt that she could not, in conscience, give her assent to the decrees.[47] What was really ominous, however, was not only that neo-scholasticism was confirmed in theory as *the* theology of the Church, but also that merely to suggest an alternative theology or to question neo-scholasticism became subject to ecclesiastical sanctions.

The only signs of theological life that were to be found in the Church after the defeat of modernism, then, were those within neo-scholasticism itself. Even before the final condemnation of modernism, two creative sources had arisen as a result of critical reflection on the scholastic heritage. The

Dominican A. Gardeil, the impulse behind the centre of theological studies which was later to produce, among others, Chenu and Congar, had already begun to direct neo-scholastic apologetics to some extent and with caution towards the ideas of Blondel and to formulate a plan of theology in which historical research and contemporary Christian experience could both find a place. Even more remarkable, however, was the plan envisaged by the Jesuit Pierre Rousselot, a man whose granite Breton solidity was fortunately balanced by a more gracious West Indian background on his mother's side. His own reading had convinced him that modernism had posed a real problem and he set out consciously to look for a satisfactory answer in medieval theology itself in the light of modern thought. The result was a surprising and entirely new interpretation of Thomas, especially in an application of his teaching to the way towards faith.

This, the discussion about Blondel and rearguard actions against modernism were the main preoccupations of theologians in the Catholic Church until the First World War put everything else out of their minds. Rousselot himself died in battle in 1915 when he was only thirty-six. After the war, the centre of new theological impulses shifted to the German-speaking countries.

Bibliography

A. Latreille has written a skilful and very comprehensive description of the historical background of modernism in the third volume of the *Histoire de catholicisme en France* (Paris, 1962). A summary and reference to further literature can be found in A. Dansette's article 'France' in the *New Catholic Encyclopaedia VI*, especially pages 15–24. There are various general accounts of modernism as a theological movement, most of which also deal with Blondel. R. Aubert's in *Sacramentum Mundi IV* (1969) is brief, but very balanced. He has also provided an instructive outline of the recent bibliography on modernism in *Concilium* (2/7), 1966, p. 47 ff, and a rather more extensive outline in *La Revue nouvelle* (44) of the same year, 1966, p. 95 ff. The 'classic' Catholic presentation and interpretation of modernism, which is of course biased, but not really unfair, was provided by J. Rivière in *Le modernisme dans l'Église* (Paris 1929). The author wrote a summary of his book under the heading 'Modernisme' in the *Dictionnaire de Théologie catholique* X (1929). To counterbalance this account, I would recommend A. Vidler's fascinating and very well-documented study, *The Modernist Movement in the Roman Church* (Cambridge 1934). I am greatly indebted to this book for my outline of modernism in the preceding section. Summaries of the ideas contained in this book and some additions will be found in the Pelican book by Vidler on recent Church history to which I have already referred, and in his *Twentieth Century Defenders of the Faith* (London 1965). A new work by Vidler was recently announced, containing the Sarum Lectures of 1969. A detailed survey of the early discussions about Loisy's work will be found in E. Poulat's favourably reviewed book, *Histoire, dogme et critique dans la crise moderniste* (Casterman 1962). H. Duméry throws valuable light on the historical, theological and philosophical backgrounds to the modernist movement in his contribution, 'Le modernisme', in *Les grands courants de la pensée mondiale contemporaine. Les tendances principales* (Paris 1961). The work of M. Ranchetti, *The Catholic Modernists*, is now available in English (London 1969; original Italian edition 1963). Its emphasis is, naturally, on the Italian modernists. An attractive American study has also been published recently: John Ratté, *Three Modernists: A. Loisy, George Tyrrell, William L. Sullivan* (New York 1967). The recently published memoirs of M.J. Lagrange throw an interesting light on the exegetical problems that arose at the turn of the century: *Le Père Lagrange. Au service de la bible* (Paris 1967).

A good introduction to Blondel's thought will be found in the studies of A. Dru and I. Trethowan which are included in Maurice Blondel, *The Letter on Apologetics and History and Dogma* (London 1964). More specifically philosophical, but very enlightening is J. Lacroix' *Maurice Blondel, sa vie, son oeuvre* (Paris 1963), available in English as *Maurice Blondel: an Introduction to the Man and his Philosophy* (New York 1968). Blondel's significance for theology can best be understood by reading H. Bouillard's *Blondel et le christianisme* (Paris 1961) and the contributions by H. Duméry on Blondel and by R. Jolivet on 'Le courant néoaugustinien' in the encyclopedia *Les grands courants* referred to above.

A biography of Loisy written some time ago by A. Houtin and F. Sartiaux and prepared for publication by E. Poulat was published in Paris in 1960 under the title of *Alfred Loisy, sa vie, son oeuvre*. Loisy's 'modernist' work is very difficult to obtain nowadays, but E. Poulat has presented it in considerable detail and with many quotations in his *Histoire* mentioned above. Harnack's *Das Wesen des Christentums* is published in an English translation with the title *What is Christianity?* (5th ed. London 1958).

M. Nédoncelle (Paris 1935) and M. de la Bedoyère (London 1951) have written good introductions to the thought and life of Baron von Hügel. A good approach to Tyrrell is provided by F.M. O'Connor's contribution in the *New Catholic Encyclopedia*, XIV, which in its bibliography lists no books on Tyrrell apart from the *Autobiography and Life* presented by M.D. Petre, and the objective Dutch thesis by the Protestant theologian J.J. Stam, *George Tyrrell (1861–1909)* (Utrecht 1938). On the occasion of the sixtieth anniversary of his death, however, a memorial number on Tyrrell was published by *The Heythrop Journal* (10/3) 1969, containing 'Post-Vatican-II Impressions', a character sketch, a short unpublished study by Tyrrell himself and a most valuable bibliography of his printed works—as a whole, a very welcome gesture by a Jesuit journal. There seems to be a new interest in Tyrrell's theology, as witness various unpublished dissertations. Tyrrell's *Christianity at the Crossroads* was republished in London in 1963 under the editorship of

A. Vidler and this book provides a very good introduction to the author's fascinating thought and writing. The *New Catholic Encyclopedia* contains two balanced and factual notes on integralism, one under this heading in volume VII, another under 'Sodalitium Pianum' in volume XIII, both by G.J. O'Brien. Recently E. Poulat has presented the documents and facts of this shameful episode in his *Intégrisme et catholicisme intégral* (Tournai 1969).

An introduction to the ideas of A. Gardeil will be found in two studies by M.D. Chenu published in his *La foi dans l'intelligence* (Paris 1964). L. de Grandmaison wrote a very vivid account of P. Rousselot in his introduction to the second edition of Rousselot's *L'intellectualisme de Saint Thomas* (Paris 1924), which, unfortunately, was not included in the English translation, *The Intellectualism of St Thomas* (London 1935).

Germany in Movement

Herman Schell and 'Reform Catholicism'

It may have struck the reader that none of the 'modernists' mentioned in the previous section were from the German-speaking countries. It is, however, equally striking that it was precisely Catholic thinkers in these countries who resisted the papal measures most firmly, with the remarkable result that the practical conclusions were not enforced in Germany and that university professors there were not obliged to take the anti-modernist oath. The fortunate consequence of this was that Catholic thought was able to continue to develop more freely in Germany. German Catholic thinkers were above all concerned with the standing of Catholic scholarship in relation to the 'free research' of their non-Catholic colleagues. In Rome, this was regarded as hypersensitivity and was not really understood, but long experience had taught the Vatican that it was better to give way to some extent to the Germans. What is more, modernism proper had not been discovered to any great extent in the German-speaking countries by the most suspicious integralist sleuths.[48]

The probable reason for this is, rather paradoxically, that theology was still much more open and therefore more up to date in the German-speaking countries than, for example, in France or Italy. A radical reaction such as modernism was consequently less urgent. Germany had certainly been in a state of turmoil since the First Vatican Council, but not primarily in the strictly theological sphere. This period, from the end of the nineteenth century until the Second World War, was above all significant for the much wider unrest in the German Catholic Church, within which it is possible to discern the broad outline of the ideas that began to take shape more clearly in the theological revival after 1945. Herman Schell, who certainly dreamed of a new synthesis, was hardly able to arouse any interest in his strictly theological plans. The creative contributions of, for example, Karl Adam, Romano Guardini and the theologians of 'kerygmatic' theology were also outside theology proper, because they were in opposition to the established theology of neo-scholasticism.

Bismarck's *Kulturkampf*, which was in itself a reaction against the 'fortress' mentality of the Roman Church that had been raised to the level of a principle by Pius IX, and the consequences of the resulting controversy, which were not favourable to the Chancellor, had made the Catholic population of Germany more conscious of itself. This resulted in the kind of triumphant emancipation that is all too well known today, notably among the Dutch Catholics. Within the Catholic Church in the Germany of the period under review, small but influential groups, in various spheres, reacted against this mentality. With different motives, they followed a single direction in their criticism of ultramontanism, the central authority of Rome and all the many expressions of this, including neo-scholasticism. One example of the results of this movement was the founding of *Hochland* at the turn of the century. Karl Muth, a student with a passion for controversy, had asked whether Catholic writing was really at the same level as other writing of the period[49]—

a question which no one, now, with even a superficial knowledge of the Catholic literature of that time would answer in the affirmative. This challenge led to *Hochland*, a periodical devoted to dialogue with modern society and culture in its widest sense, which, when it first appeared, broke entirely new ground and has always continued to maintain a very high level, both in the diversity of the subjects discussed in it and in the quality of its articles, which have, in the past, been contributed by such great figures as Schell, Scheler, Adam and Guardini. More directly associated with the Church was the movement that is known by the rather too general and all-embracing name of 'reform Catholicism'. The term was first used by the priest Joseph Müller, whose ideas for the reform of the Church, which were more vociferous than important, were honoured by condemnation on the part of the Church in 1901. That the same term is also applied to the profound and scientific thought of Schell is proof of the fact that the same label is all too frequently used for very different contents.

An authority on Schell has said that he specialised in theology 'with tough, unceasing industry'.[50] He also had an apostolic fervour which had been intensified by ten years spent in pastoral work. He was born in 1850 and studied theology in Germany and later in Rome. It goes without saying that this was, of course, neo-scholastic theology, but he had ample opportunity in the universities of Freiburg and Würzburg to become acquainted with contemporary thought, including that of Nietzsche. He also had direct links with the theology of Günther and J.E. Kuhn, the last representative of the 'classic' Catholic school of Tübingen. In 1888, he began to teach his own, highly distinctive and dynamic theology at Würzburg. This theology had a strongly 'apologetic' flavour and was expressed in compelling language. He also published a number of extensive works, among them a book on dogmatics consisting of some 1,800 pages and all of them displaying not only deep personal commitment, but also scientific originality. He wrote in fact 'missionary' theology. He was only too well aware of the fact that real apologetics had to be strictly scientific—this is not the only aspect that his work has in common with that of Blondel, who was writing at about the same time.

It caused no little surprise, then, when this widely recognised theologian was drawn, after his inaugural speech as vice-chancellor of the university in 1896, into writing several books on the reform of the Church which were directly related to the contemporary situation and in which he was not always entirely fortunate in his choice of practical points of departure and in the conclusions that he drew from his proposals. The quasi-official neo-scholastic theologians had never been very enthusiastic about the speculations that Schell expressed in his poetical language, but now that his books on the reform of the Church were being reprinted again and again, their complaints resulted not only in these later books, but also in his dogmatics and apologetics being placed on the Index in 1898. It was only much later that Schell heard that there were also difficulties in connection with his dynamic doctrine of God and his ideas of sin and hell. The question that we might ask now is whether it was not his view that Catholicism had to be understood and experienced as universality—the underlying principle for his reforms—which had given rise to the greatest anxiety. Schell himself could not believe that he had deviated in any way from the tradition of the Church, but nonetheless made his submission with grief in his heart. While the controversy continued to rage around him, he rewrote his apologetics after further profound study of the Bible and it is interesting to note that he also published a reply to Harnack at almost exactly the same time as Loisy. His immersion in Scripture gave a new dimension to his last works and his great book, *Christ, the Gospel and its Relevance to World History*, written five years after his condemnation, made an especially profound impression. A year after this inspiring theologian had died, quite suddenly and at the height of his powers, in 1906, another detailed refutation of his ideas appeared. It is only recently that his ideas have begun to be considered again and the importance of his synthesis rediscovered.

Another scholar, the historian A. Ehrhard, who was for some time a friend of Schell but who, unlike Schell, was always very cautious in the position that he took up in public, is generally included among the 'reform Catholics' because of the character of his published writings. Schell frankly supported progress and evolution, but this expert in the field of history always kept many qualifications in reserve before venturing to express an opinion. His programmatic book, *Catholicism and the Twentieth Century*, however, was a great success, partly because it was—no doubt to the great joy of the publisher—provided with a spectacular *imprimatur* (in German!) in which Bishop Keppler of Rottenburg stated that, although he disagreed with the author in many respects, he was glad to give his permission for the book to be printed because it had clearly been written with such moral seriousness and such warm love for the Church. Keppler's approval kept the book from being placed on the Index despite the unflagging attempts made by Ehrhard's opponents, although the impulsive bishop did later, under the influence of Langbehn, rather rudely accuse Ehrhard of deceit.[51] As time went by, however, such a confused controversy arose in connection with reform Catholicism, in which practical questions such as the celibacy of the priesthood, the Index, monastic life and the Catholic attitude towards politics became more and more prominent, that the movement gradually became a negative slogan which obscured the original and fundamental issue of renewal in the Church and theology. After the catastrophe of 1918, the renewal movement, which had continued to have its centre in the periodical *Hochland*, began to take a more positive form.

The 'movements' between the two World Wars

The period between the two World Wars was particularly confused in Germany, or is at least extremely difficult for an outsider to understand now. A Dutchman approaching the problem of Germany at this time is frequently struck by remarkable parallels with the same period in his own country, which were, of course, often echoes of the events in the German-speaking world. But again and again he finds himself going astray in the multiplicity of directions and changes of emphasis. The reader must not expect anything more than a few indications, none of them very original, but a few such indications are indispensable as helping to provide a background to the theology of the period.

The year 1933 is, of course, an obvious dividing line, but it would perhaps be more realistic to go back a few years before Hitler's coming to power to look for the change in Catholic life. Contemporary writers even point to a crisis and a transition round about 1926. In the first ten years or so between the wars, there was certainly a clear, perhaps even disconcerting, Catholic revival, coming from below and hardly able to find sufficient outlet in the many 'movements' of the time. After about ten years, however, this mountain stream seemed to be more and more in search of the deeper river bed of the organised life of the Church, a process which came to an end with the struggle against National Socialism, even though this crisis also caused sporadic breaches in the dykes. The situation of the Church at this period was reflected, as it always is, in theology.

The First World War caused a dramatic change in many different spheres. A whole vision of the world seemed to have crumbled to pieces with the collapse of the German Empire that had grown up with such close bonds with official Lutheranism. Everyone talked of a 'change of direction', a change from the subjective to the objective, from the individual to the community, from society to an eschatologically tinged religiosity. While a way out of the chaos which immediately followed the war was being sought with great difficulty in the political sphere, the rise of 'dialectical' theology confirmed the obvious decline of humanitarian or liberal Protestantism. The war and its violence had put a harsh end to the optimistic spirit of progress and the civilised individualism with which the liberal theologians had associated Christianity. Increasing interest was now being shown in the uncompromising teaching of a group of theologians who were inspired by the rebel Kierkegaard and insisted on the total impotence of man and the decisive supremacy of God's Word—Barth, Gogarten, Brunner and Bultmann. In philosophy too, there was a strong tendency to turn away from neo-Kantian concentration on subjective categories and towards the object via the phenomenological method, the leading protagonists of this movement being Husserl, Scheler and Heidegger. In 1929, Erich Przywara, a sagacious observer of the Catholic scene and himself a great thinker and an equal partner in dialogue with all the great figures of his time, summarised this whole event in the two concepts of 'movement' and 'essence'.[52] There was a constant search for the essence, a search which took place with almost enervating vigour, the Catholics looking with perhaps even more 'movement' than the others.

German Catholics had been made even more conscious of themselves as Catholics by the fall of the 'Protestant' Empire. They realised that the change of direction towards the objective and communal aspects also gave emphasis to typical elements of the Catholic tradition. They translated the change almost automatically into turning towards the community of the Church, the liturgy and the objective, dogmatic content of faith and believed that this process could also be observed in Protestant Christianity. Overoptimistic prophets in Germany, like the exuberant van Ginneken in the Netherlands, were already predicting that all Christians would soon be converted to Roman Catholicism. Even a more cautious man like Przywara was aware of hopeful parallels in the theology of the Reformed Churches, not only in the objective tendency of the otherwise rather 'anti-Catholic' dialectic theologians, but also in the Catholicising, High Church group gathered around R. Otto and F. Heiler, who had been advocating an 'evangelical

In Search of an Explanation in History

Catholicity' since leaving the Catholic Church and going over to the Lutheran Church. Nonetheless, it was clearly realised that there was a need for a Catholic concentration, from which an ecumenical offer of peace might perhaps emerge, though it would be an offer based on clear and well-defended positions. There was certainly no question of simply aiming at the creation of a Catholic ghetto. When the philosopher Peter Wust, with a great deal of support, called on German Catholics to return from their exile in 1924,[53] what he had in mind was an appeal to the Catholic conscience, which in the new situation had so much to contribute to the christianisation of the world. This was the real reason for concentrating on the specifically Catholic heritage, from modern times and the Counter-Reformation as far back as the great period of Catholic life and thought in the Middle Ages, in the firm expectation that this traditional inheritance would once again exert a dominant influence on Western life. Seen in this light, frequently repeated expressions such as Guardini's 'Catholic man', 'the Catholic idea' and 'the Catholic view of the world', and Adam's 'essence of Catholicism' are far less restricted than they might seem to be at first sight. This concentration on the Catholic heritage also implied a movement towards 'integrally Catholic' experience and a rather too serious rejection of compromise of any kind. This eschatologically tinged war against all irresolute half-measures was a frequent feature of the cells, particularly those of young Catholics, within the 'movements' of this period.

Fifty years later, it is not easy to grasp the enthusiasm that emanated from the German 'youth movement' from the beginning of the present century onwards and perhaps it is even less easy for someone who is not a German and who is bound to find it the more difficult to see through and beyond the later distortions of this youth movement, such as the *Führer* principle and worship of nature. A common misunderstanding has to be cleared up at once in connection with the term 'youth movement' as applied to Germany of this period. Unlike the idea of youth movement that is current today and in the Netherlands, the equivalent at that time in Germany—and to some extent also in the Netherlands, under the influence of her neighbour—was above all a phenomenon which manifested itself among young men and women, had originated with them and was in no way an organised structure that had been imposed upon them from above. They wanted to create something in opposition to the pressure of school and home which was undoubtedly heavier in the Germany of that time than, for example, in the Netherlands and elsewhere, and in opposition to the middle-class mentality in general. The image that has, of course, remained in the popular imagination of these young *Wandervögel* is that of strenuous excursions in the freedom of nature and abstinence from smoking and drinking, but their real aim was deeper and quite positive. They wanted to be independent, inwardly true to themselves and to develop freely as persons and thus to penetrate through the stale patterns of contemporary society and behaviour to the real essence beneath and in this way create a new way of life. The general revival that followed the First World War strengthened these positive impulses and made the movement look towards society as a whole. A great sense of social responsibility was evident, particularly among the soldiers who had returned from the war.

A specifically Catholic youth movement which gave expression to many of the impulses initiated by the group associated with the journal *Hochland* began to take shape after the war. A distinctively 'Catholic' emphasis was given to the general desire within the youth movement as a whole for free personal development in inward truth by a deeply felt and serious preoccupation with the religious question. The philosophy of 'values', particularly as expounded by Max Scheler, who was for a time a Catholic, acted as a source of inspiration for personal thought and action among the members of this Catholic branch of the youth movement, who tended to use phrases like 'greatness of mind' and 'personality' with a predilection which now seems rather exaggerated. Even more influential was the movement's sense of social purpose, which had its origin in an increasing orientation towards the Church and the liturgy of the Church, seen not as an institution but above all as a community. The Catholic youth movement thus almost automatically overflowed into a liturgical movement and, partly under the influence of this, into a biblical movement, a lay movement and—a very characteristic formation—a 'university' movement. This involvement of these various Catholic movements in Germany during the nineteen-twenties was ultimately responsible for, among other things, the beginning of a renewal in the sphere of moral theology, a spectacular change in theological thinking about such various aspects of the Church as the rediscovery of the Mystical Body, of the role of the laity and of the liturgy as a 'celebration in mystery', a renewal of Christology and, perhaps the most fundamental aspect of all, a renewed reflection about the ultimate meaning of faith. In the light of this renewed experience, theology was sent back again to its sources, a trend which was at the same time influenced by the beginning of dialogue with the other Christian Churches.

Romano Guardini and Karl Adam

When, bearing this background in mind, one thinks of the men who gave direction and clear expression to thought and action in the Catholic Church at that time, the figure of Romano Guardini comes to mind again and again. Glowing panegyrics have been written about this man by many different admirers. Although the youngest generation has not come directly under the spell of his writings, very many people—and especially students—continued to be drawn by his spoken words to his weekly sermon and celebration of the Eucharist even after his retirement in 1963, when he was seventy-eight years old. Strangely enough, however, this kind of popularity makes one instinctively suspicious. The theologians who write about Guardini are so emphatic in their claim that he really belongs to their rather exclusive club that they manage admirably to impart their scepticism. What, then, is the theological significance of this man, who seems to write far too well for a 'serious' thinker, who was, for years, a leader of the 'youth movement', who helped to give new content to the liturgy and who also published penetrating studies of Socrates, Plato, Dante, Hölderlin, Dostoevski, Mörike and Rilke as well as studies of Pascal, Kierkegaard and Augustine?

Almost automatically, one places Guardini within the sphere of Augustine, together with Newman, with whom he had a great deal in common—not only a similar ability to write, a deep sensitivity of spirit and a rather reserved manner of expressing himself, as though he were still seeking, but also a clear awareness of the 'living concrete', of 'real' rather than merely 'notional' knowledge and of 'phenomenological' description. His concrete and, even today, still fascinating approach to the symbolism of the liturgy, based on the movement, the gesture, the elements of play in worship, makes the link with Augustine even more direct. To this we may perhaps add his remarkable emphasis, for all his openness to the present age, on the antithesis between Christianity and the world—an antithesis in which there are perhaps also echoes of Bonhoeffer's contrast between religion and revelation—and his fervent hope for a renewed Christian Europe in which humanity and Christianity might grow together in accordance with the medieval example.

Guardini's preference for Europe, however, had a surprisingly concrete background. Although he was by birth an Italian, he was brought up almost entirely in Germany, so that an Italian home environment went together in his case with a German education at school and university. To judge by what he himself has said later, this was for him the source of a real conflict and his choice of subjects as a student reveals a remarkable uncertainty—first of all mathematics and physics, then economics and social and political science and finally theology. He had ultimately to choose, before his ordination as a priest, and could only decide in favour of Germany, in the consciousness of being a European.[54] This episode may perhaps be regarded as summing up Guardini's attitude to life—his quite remarkable balance is a synthesis of contrasts, the existential basis of what he himself called, in philosophy, the 'antithesis view'. In other spheres too, Guardini's life and ideas were determined by concrete circumstances. Intellectually, he was exceptionally well fitted to specialise in theology, but he felt emotionally called to the apostolate and this quickly led to close contacts with the centre of the youth movement and its new experience of the Church, especially in the liturgy. In the heyday of neo-scholasticism, it was almost impossible not to choose a medieval figure as the subject of one's thesis, but Guardini twice refused to consider Thomas Aquinas and instead chose his opponent Bonaventure who was the medieval representative of the stricter Augustinian tradition. He must have felt inspired by the tireless Bishop of Hippo in his pastoral work and it was Augustine's commitment to life, his 'wisdom' which allowed room for intuition and feeling and his concrete unity of science and the experience of faith which impressed him so much in his thinking.

His published works and his work as a university lecturer in the sphere of dogmatics rapidly attracted attention and when in 1923 a chair in Catholic philosophy was set up in the faculty of philosophy of the state university of Berlin, which had no faculty of Catholic theology (this was at the time clearly a compromise), Guardini was invited to occupy it. Once again he was faced with a difficult choice—this time between systematic theology and 'the world'. But it is difficult to escape the impression that the choice between Germany and Italy caused him greater tension. It is not surprising that he found his life's work in Berlin—taking Christ and his gospel, as it lives in the Church, to the intellectual summit of the world of his own time. This was confirmed by the almost sensational success of his lectures. Apart from a period of silence during the time of National Socialism, he was to continue to teach 'his subject' after the war in Tübingen and Munich until he retired.

Is not most of Guardini's work, then, outside the sphere of 'systematic theology'? In the strict sense of the word, one is bound to agree with Guardini's own answer 'yes' to this question. But this was by no means a bad thing. For it is true that, even within the sphere of systematic theology, a start had already been made at that time to renew Catholic thought and to exchange ideas with contemporary philosophers and Protestant theologians, especially in the field of the knowledge of God and the basis of religion, but a really comprehensive renewal was held back, at least for the time being, by the pressure exerted by neo-scholastic thinking. By virtue of his special position, however, Guardini was able to keep clear of the scholastic tradition and to prepare the way for the breakthrough to which Catholic theologians were looking forward, in his apparently 'merely' literary or popular writings. Later conciliar theology about the Church, the liturgy, Christ and Christian faith in the modern world is in fact deeply indebted to Guardini, far more than it is possible to point out in detail.

This also applies to the work of Karl Adam, the other name that appears again and again from the end of the First World War onwards. His activity was confined to a rather more limited sphere than that of Guardini—the faculty of theology at Tübingen—but it still remains to be seen whether this resulted in his influence being less deep or extensive.

The son of a schoolteacher, he was one of a family of eleven children and grew up in a little place in Bavaria. Perhaps for this reason he seems to have been more robust and 'closer to the soil' than Guardini, liking walking in the open air and climbing mountains, and all his life he felt quite at home in the easy-going atmosphere of *Gemütlichkeit* in south Germany. His lectures were given in straightforward though careful language, accompanied by lively gestures—a testimony to his own uncomplicated faith and personal involvement in it. This does not mean, however, that he was unscientific in his approach or uncritically naïve. While he was in Munich, he had specialised in the history of the Church and of dogma and had studied the Latin Fathers especially deeply, publishing several important writings on this subject. Nonetheless, it soon became clear to him that a scholar as vital as he was and as open to the real problems of his own age could not remain preoccupied with purely historical reconstruction. He embarked upon a profound study of the philosophy of his own times, especially the philosophy of religion of Scheler and his circle, and followed sympathetically the more recent Protestant theology. He was one of the first to introduce Karl Barth to a wider circle of Catholic readers in the journal *Hochland*.

In 1919, when he was about forty, he became a professor at Tübingen. It was then that the various courses that he had pursued in his life began to converge and it became clear to him that, following von Drey, Möhler and Kuhn, his task, too, was to achieve unity in the historical findings and the thought of his own period, in dialogue with his colleagues in the Protestant faculty of the university. He felt that there were great possibilities, just after the First World War, for a synthesis of this kind. In his inaugural lecture at Tübingen, he went straight to the heart of the basic problems both of the practice of theology and of the function of faith and philosophy. In the spirit of the contemporary philosophy and psychology of religion, his lecture was a creative reaction to the current narrowly rational views of neo-scholasticism. The protagonists of neo-scholasticism consequently criticised him sharply for attempting to undermine the rational basis of faith as defined at the First Vatican Council, but Adam received widespread and very encouraging support from other scholars. He became, almost overnight, the most discussed Catholic theologian in Germany and the continuing debate about faith and theology, which had many striking points of contact with the attempts made by Barth and his school, had a very deep influence on Catholic thought.

Did Adam's work in fact reach the peak that was attained by the greatest of his predecessors at the Catholic faculty of Tübingen? There can, of course, be no doubt about his potentialities and his intentions or about his far-reaching personal influence, but it does seem as though he was inhibited in his own synthesis by the environment that prevailed while he was alive and working. Since his death in 1966, when he was almost ninety years old, a few data have become available concerning the difficulties with the Church which Adam experienced during the period shortly after the heyday of modernism. According to Heiler, it was only the intervention of the Crown Prince of Bavaria, whose two sons received religious instruction from Adam, which prevented him from being deprived of his priestly office.[55] It also appears that accusations were laid against him several times after this. Neo-scholasticism had become more cautious than ever since the condemnation of modernism and many of Adam's colleagues confined themselves, for this reason, to strictly historical research, though this did, it should be pointed out, help to provide a point of departure for the breakthrough of theology at a later stage. Although he certainly wanted to shape a renewed dogmatic theology, Adam himself seems, after the polemics about faith and theology, to have avoided a direct confrontation by turning to a wider public than that of professional theologians alone. At this level, to be accused of using 'concepts inaccurately'[56] was not so very serious—and his inaccurate use of concepts meant, in fact, that he avoided the neo-scholastic terminology and aimed at a direct 'theology of life'. There was clearly no place in neo-scholasticism, with its tendency to objectivise and, so to speak, transcend time, for dynamic realities and categories determined by history. Adam was therefore obliged to express his theology, which took as its point of departure Möhler and Augustine (Augustine seems to have inspired many 'renewers' at this time—he was clearly a refuge from neo-scholasticism!), outside professional theological circles.

His book on the Church, which was published in 1924 and was at that time little less than revolutionary because of its emphasis on the inner principle of life—Christ's continuing life in the Church—was an admirable contrast to Heiler's tempting attack on the inner division within the Catholic Church.[57] Was this perhaps a repetition, on a small scale, of Loisy's desire, that of making his own ideas more digestible by defending the Church? In any case, Adam's work was astonishingly successful and was even translated into Chinese and Japanese. His fame throughout the world as a theologian who appealed to countless people was finally established by his books about Christ, which he regarded as the logical consequence of his ecclesiology. His concentration on Christ's humanity, in the wake of the New Testament, satisfied a widely felt need, but Adam never descended to a consideration of the more deeply rooted theological problems and when he did make use of Protestant exegesis he seemed always to go on tiptoe, preferring to let sleeping dogs lie. Like Guardini, he worked in a different sphere, simply laying a broad foundation for the future. His greatness was that he recognised this possibility; his sorrow, that he could do no more.

The last ten years before the Second World War

It should be to some extent clear from the life and work of Guardini and Adam—the activity of many other theologians whom I have not mentioned here should not, of course, be forgotten—how the turmoil during the years between the two world wars in Germany formed the positive basis for a renewed theology later. The first ten years were the most fruitful in this respect. Regression became visible from 1925 onwards. The quest for the 'essence', the 'inner' aspect of the Church as a community, became lost at times in purely charismatic activity or even, as Przywara has observed, resulted in a new kind of withdrawal into the ghetto of 'ideal Catholicism', which remained unproductive in the presence of the ordinary, day-to-day Church.[58] The not unexpected consequence of this was a reaction on the part of the institutional Church. This, moreover, went together with a parallel counter-movement in German life as a whole, especially after the economic crisis of 1929. This collapse of German society meant the end of free initiative and spontaneous ordering from below. The only possible answer seemed to be tighter organisation from above and firmer leadership. The movements became associations and the youth movement became welfare of the young. The 'leader' increasingly became a dictator and the terrible consequences of all this soon began to appear in the ascendant National Socialist movement.

During the last ten years before the outbreak of the Second World War, this constantly increasing threat had its effects on the image of the Catholic Church and on Catholic theology. To begin with, there were certainly, in Church circles, ideas which were closely related to particular points in the Nazi programme, one of these being, for example, the notion that the national community ought to form the basis of the saving community of the Church. Even a man who was as little concerned with politics as Karl Adam, following his predecessors at Tübingen and influenced, as they were, by Romanticism, believed that the 'spirit of the people' was a pillar of the Church and hoped, together with many others, that the Nazis would be able to exert a healthy influence. After seizing power, Hitler carefully nourished this hope by drawing a thick smokescreen round his ultimate intentions. Unfortunately, so long as the 'rights of the Church' were safeguarded, the Catholic Church was then, as in the past, fairly quick to make concessions and, when an official concordat had been concluded in 1933, even Catholics who had at first been sceptical were ready to give the Nazi régime a chance. But those who had recognised the danger from the very beginning and had continued to warn the people against National Socialism were very soon proved right. Resistance to the régime, including resistance by the Catholic Church, became increasingly open and explicit and one reprisal that was made, with the cooperation of certain bishops, was to remove Guardini, Adam and several other theologians from their chairs and even to close whole faculties of theology. The Catholic Church was obliged to become more and more preoccupied with purely ecclesiastical matters. Her own movements had, in any case, already been canalised into the well regulated form of lay apostolate which had become known, since the time of Pius XI, as 'Catholic Action' in the narrower sense and this was such an obviously Church form of activity that Seyss-Inquart, for example, was apparently able to combine it with political support for National Socialism.[59]

Energy thus confined found an outlet especially in liturgical life and two remarkable theological impulses resulted from this. The first came above all from the Benedictine Abbot Odo Casel, a man who combined the classical remoteness from the world of a monk with a remarkable awareness of the signs of the times and the charismatic gift of being able to convey his ideas to others in an infectious manner. After a period of about ten years of preparatory study, he published in 1932 his great synthesis of the Christian cult-mystery, in which he provided a theology rooted in his experience of the liturgical event, especially the mystery of Easter, a theology in which he interpreted the liturgy, in the light of Scripture and the Church Fathers, as a renewed presence of Christ's saving action. With the passage of time, this idea was seen to contain unexpected riches for the experience of the liturgy and the theology of the Church and the sacraments, especially the eucharist. This does not mean that Casel's view remained unchallenged, but he defended it fervently and not without a certain acrimony, especially against those who wanted to 'explain' the mystery or to minimise the primacy of God's activity in the liturgy. It is clear from the constitution on the liturgy formulated by the Second Vatican Council that the basic outline of his ideas has survived all attacks.

The second of these theological impulses in fact had only its origin in the liturgy and the liturgist who first expressed the basic ideas of this movement in 1936, the Jesuit J.A. Jungmann, can be regarded, because of the emphasis that he placed on the catechetical aspect of worship, as Casel's direct opposite. On the basis of the clear discrepancy between the Church's proclamation of the gospel and the then current theology of the Church, Jungmann argued in favour of a separate branch of theology alongside neo-scholasticism, in which God's revelation could be presented as a call and a living value, as a message which could be proclaimed, in other words, a 'theology of proclamation' or 'kerygmatic theology'. This theology had, Jungmann argued, necessarily to be based on an appeal to the imaginative language of Scripture and the Fathers and on the central position of Christ and his saving work. Now, more than thirty years later, this new attempt to break through neo-scholasticism in the Church's theology looks rather a forlorn hope. It was, in theory, not difficult to refute the project and full use was consequently made of this opportunity. Strictly speaking, the movement remained confined to the Jesuit faculty at Innsbruck, where F. Lakner and Hugo Rahner, Karl's elder brother, were especially responsible for its further development. It was, however, as an impulse that it continued to have a profound effect. It caused the official theologians to examine their gnawing consciences and this was the first step towards making the affirmation that theology is reflection about our salvation as a practical reality.

Protest against the concrete form of the Church and her teaching about faith was, however, not limited to the more indirect criticism of the theologians of Innsbruck. The pressure exerted during the period of National Socialism seems also to have resulted in a sharpening of the contrasts within the more immediate sphere of the Church herself. During the nineteen-thirties, three startling books were published anonymously and each of these reiterated, in a manner which was adapted to the situation prevailing at that time, the more negative demands of reform Catholicism —the need to break through the influence of the Vatican, to achieve freedom in theological investigation and to reanimate the liturgy and the life of the Church and make these less remote and alien, to overcome the tyranny of canon law and to strive towards the abolition of the Index and of the obligatory celibacy of the priesthood. There was also criticism from the other side—in a letter to all the bishops of Greater Germany, sent at the beginning of 1943, Archbishop Gröber of Freiburg im Breisgau complained about the increasing pressure exerted by the younger theologians. In this criticism he referred, among other things, to their underestimation of scholasticism and natural theology, their pastoral and liturgical experiments, their newfangled concept of the Church (the mystical body of Christ), their extravagantly mystical relationship to Christ and their obscuring of the differences between the Churches and of the distinction between the clergy and the laity.[60] Almost in spite of itself, this astonishing list of criticisms bears witness to the success of the new movements within the Church at this time in the German-speaking countries. One remarkable aspect of this whole affair is that the young theologian Karl Rahner, who had, together with authorities like Karl Adam, opposed one of the books of the revived 'reform Catholicism' in 1938,[61] was now ordered by the Viennese Cardinal Innitzer to compose a reply to Archbishop Gröber's letter of complaint. In the new beginning made by German theologians after the end of the Second World War and the long period during which they had been scattered and oppressed, it was Karl Rahner who was to become the most important force.

Bibliography

In the absence of specialised English literature on this particular period in Germany, I can only refer to the more general works already mentioned, in particular those of Dru and Hales. Background information can also be found in

A.R. Vidler, *A Century of Social Catholicism 1820–1920* (London 1964), and in W. von Loewenich, *Modern Catholicism* (London 1959). The *New Catholic Encyclopedia* contains articles on 'Muth, Carl' (vol. X, O.B. Roegele), and 'Reformkatholizismus' (vol. XII, E.J. Dunne). See also V. Conzemius' extensive contribution 'Reform' in *Sacramentum Mundi* V (London 1970). There are, of course, several studies in German. Two of them ought to be mentioned, the very personal account by W. Spael, who, as a publicist and editor, was an active witness during much of the period described in this section: *Das katholische Deutschland im 20. Jahrhundert* (Würzburg 1964), and G. Maron's article 'Reformkatholizismus' in *Religion in Geschichte und Gegenwart* V (3rd ed. 1961), which is an able summary of the theological and religious background, although not everyone would wish to classify modernism and the 'new theology', for example, under the heading of reform Catholicism. Herman Schell has found a devoted advocate in J. Hasenfuss, whose principal work, *Herman Schell als existentieller Denker und Theologe*, was published in 1956 in Würzburg. With P.W. Scheele, Hasenfuss is editing a critical edition of Schell's *Katholische Dogmatik* (vol. I, Munich 1968). The interest in Schell is clearly gaining ground once more.

E. Przywara's most important chronicles and critical studies of the period between the two world wars have been recently collected and republished in *Katholische Krise* (Düsseldorf 1967), but, strangely enough, one of his most enlightening studies in French, which appeared in 1929 in the *Nouvelle Revue Théologique* (56), is not included in this collection. A satisfactory introduction to Guardini's life and work is the French book *Romano Guardini* by H. Engelmann and F. Ferrier (Paris 1966). The suggestive 'portrait' of Guardini in *Tendenzen der Theologie im 20. Jahrhundert* (see the bibliographical reference given on page 21) is written by Walter Dirks, himself one of the German progressives of recent times. Perhaps the best introduction to Guardini himself is his book *The Lord* (London 1956), in which,

In Search of an Explanation in History 93

however, the pre-war origin (1937) is clearly discernible in the exegesis.

This also applies to Karl Adam's first two books on Christ, which are even earlier than Guardini's book. When they appeared, they were, because of the emphasis which Adam placed on the humanity of Christ, acclaimed by Vidler as the first Catholic approach to modern biblical criticism since the condemnation of modernism (see *The Modernist Movement in the Roman Church, op. cit.*, p. 230). R. Aubert's portrait of Karl Adam in *Tendenzen* is written with the care that characterises all his work.

An extensive and penetrating study of the relations between the Catholic Church and Hitler's National Socialism has been written by G. Lewy, *The Catholic Church and Nazi Germany* (New York 1964). A good survey of Casel's life and theology is given by various authors in the French liturgical journal *La Maison-Dieu* (14) 1948. More specialised studies will be found in B. Neunheuser's contribution in the *New Catholic Encyclopaedia* III, under the heading 'Casel'. His main work is translated as *The Mystery of Christian Worship* (Westminster, Md. 1962). A very good introduction to the 'theology of proclamation' was provided by Hugo Rahner in his *A Theology of Proclamation* (New York 1968); the second German edition of this was prepared with the 'advice and help' of his brother Karl and published in Freiburg in 1939. Jungmann has recently adapted his early book, *Die Frohbotschaft und unsere Glaubensverkündigung*, which was published in Ratisbon in 1936, and republished it under the title *Glaubensverkündigung im Lichte der Frohbotschaft* (Innsbruck 1963) of which the English version is *Announcing the Word of God* (London 1967).

The Challenge of the 'World' in France

'Laicism' and the Church

The movement which had taken root in the German-speaking countries round about the time of the First World War had also gained a foothold in other parts of Europe and especially in France, where the Catholic Church had been inspired by the German tendency to such an extent that there are, at first sight, a number of parallels to be seen between the two linguistic zones. On closer inspection, however, there are just as many striking differences. This is, of course, partly attributable to a difference in temperament. It is perhaps possible to contrast the active commitment of the Germans with the dynamic suppleness of the French. When one passes from a consideration of the German mind to a study of the French spirit, one misses something of the Germans' thorough and scientific spadework and determined struggle to reach the ultimate foundations, but it is possible to overcome this sense of loss without much compunction when one is confronted by the great gain in generosity, impetuosity, clarity and characteristic *esprit* of the Church. One should, of course, be prepared to accept a certain carelessness or even hardness into the bargain.

More important for the difference in the development of Catholic life and thought in the two countries, however, is a difference in historical background. This difference will be seen to be very significant in the period to be considered now. France has always been what is called a 'Catholic' country and the concrete result of this has been, as we have already seen, that the 'state', to use this rather vague word, has always been a very special concern of the Catholic Church in France, whose loyalty has always had to be divided between the papal centre in Rome and the more immediately apparent government in France. The changing tensions between these three poles, Rome, the French Church and the French state, has for a long time been made concrete in a number of conflicts. I have already indicated that the Catholic Church in France had some difficulty in finding the right attitude towards the new state after the Revolution and this resulted, for example, in Lamennais' call—which was in fact an appeal to the Pope and the beginning of a new ultramontanism—for a separation of Church and state, a desire which was unexpectedly fulfilled by a succession of 'laicist' governments. One has the impression that this semi-religious, semi-political development—with a counterpoint of papal interventions—has taken up most of the energy of the French Church. The Catholics in the German-speaking countries have had anxieties about their own emancipation, but these have not occurred everywhere and at all times, and they do seem to have been able to achieve the freedom to study the theological problems that have arisen from their religious experience. These problems were also present in France and it would be an exaggeration to say that theologians simply overlooked them, even under the pressure exerted during the period following modernism. But hardly any serious attention was given even to the real problems of the modernists. In the prevailing confusion, political labels were pinned on to the modernists in France, which made the situation more difficult, while above all the violent dislocation of the structures of the Church caused by the anti-clerical governments of France—the liquidation of Church finances, the suppression of Catholic education and the banishment of monastic communities—left very little opportunity for theologians to consider any other questions. They went on working, especially in the sphere of positive research, but they had to wait for a sounding board, a hearing both inside and outside the Church, before they could achieve a creative breakthrough. In fact, the religious and theological revival in France occurred about ten years later than that in Germany. The struggle between the Church and the state in France was beginning to abate at about the same time as the rise of National Socialism in Germany and as soon as French Catholics became relatively free to consider other problems, they became suddenly aware of the magnitude of the phenomenon of France's dechristianisation. This challenge evoked an immediate response in the form of a revival of Catholic life, which bore a great deal of very varied fruit, but was at the same time also characterised by the historical background of French Catholicism.

This is, of course, a simplification of the situation, which was in fact far more complicated. In the first place, it must be said at once that there was no simple antithesis between Church and state in France. Far more decisive for the Church, probably, was the antithesis existing within the Church itself and among its various members with regard to the question of the Church's attitude towards the Republic. A natural complication here was that this attitude was to a very great extent determined by motives which were not purely religious. The principal representatives of this non-religious attitude of opposition to the state were the Catholic members of the French aristocracy and the army, many of whom had, almost as a matter of course, become active supporters of the traditionalist movement founded by Maurras, *Action française*, which advocated a return to the 'old values' of France—the monarchy, the Graeco-Roman culture and the Catholic religion. During the First World War, this last point of Maurras' programme, which he himself regarded simply as a principle of national order, received a powerful impulse—faced with the unsparing attack of 'Protestant' Germany, French patriotism began to express itself more openly in favour of the Catholic traditions of France. In addition, French Catholics, among them some tens of thousands of priests, went to the front with such deep conviction to fight for the Republic that, when the war ended, the attitude of the 'laicists' had become more flexible. Approaches were made to Rome and found a sympathetic hearing with Benedict XV and Pius XI. There was an exchange of official envoys and an arrangement was made for the regulation of the finances of the Church and the appointment of bishops. After a final outburst of apparently irreconcilable opposition, both on the part of the anti-clericals and of certain bishops, Pius XI made a decision which previous popes had been afraid to make—in 1926, he condemned *Action française* and, following Leo XIII, pointed to the realistic path of Catholic support for the Republic and its structures. It hardly needs to be said that this condemnation had a shattering effect on many French Catholics and caused a deep crisis in the French Church. It was only after the passage of several years that the conviction began to gain ground that the Church had in this way freed herself of an oppressive weight, or rather that she had laid down at long last a burden which she had in fact for a very long time suspected to be ballast. The overwhelming experience of this new situation in which the previously close links with the state were officially broken was that there was now a great liberation of energy for other and more important work, now that 'laicisation'—which would be called 'secularisation' today—could be treated as 'laicity', with all the freedom that this implied.

Round about the year 1930, a long delayed spring seemed suddenly to have burst upon France after a change in the climate. What had been brewing there in the preceding years has clear parallels with the revival in Germany—the Catholic literary revival, with origins going back long before 1914 and with figures such as Charles Péguy, Renan's grandson Psichari, Paul Claudel and later H. Ghéon, G. Bernanos and F. Mauriac, the developing religious consciousness of the younger generation, who gave 'hiking' the characteristically French form of a new kind of pilgrimage, especially to Chartres, the vision of a rebirth of the Middle Ages with its Christian thought and social order, Gothic architecture and Gregorian chant and even a new form of chivalry—the French Catholic interpretation of the English boy scout movement, *scoutisme*. As in the German-speaking countries, tendencies towards an integral Catholicism emerged in France too, but again in a typically French way, especially among the 'converts', in particular a number of prominent men such as Péguy, Claudel, Jacques Maritain and Maritain's spiritual father, Léon Bloy. These men gave a very special appearance to the French Church; their radical attitude and refusal to compromise deeply disturbed their more traditional fellow-Catholics, but they gained more and more supporters. Initially, the emergence and growth of this Catholic intellectual élite aroused great hopes of a rechristianisation of the French people, only a 'small remnant' of which still took any real part in the life of the Church, but it gradually became clear that the social barriers were too great for this new way of experiencing life in the Church to filter through spontaneously. It was therefore with gratitude that the French made use of the initiative taken by the Flemish priest, Cardijn, to create a special movement for young Catholic workers, with the primary aim of conducting an apostolate among other young people in their own environment, and transplanted it in French soil. The basic inspiration of this young Catholic workers' movement, *Jeunesse ouvrière chrétienne* (J.O.C.) as it became known in France, was in turn taken over by four other, similar movements directed towards other groups of the population. It proved to be one of the most powerful forces leading to the revival after 1930.

The condemnation of *Action française* suddenly confronted all these partly conflicting initiatives with the reality of French Catholicism. The prominent conservative Catholics who exerted an inhibiting influence saw themselves abruptly discredited. The progressives, on the other hand, now had a clear field and gradually developed a new attitude of personal responsibility for the Church and society. The dechristianisation of France presented itself as a serious challenge and politics as a means of apostolate had clearly had its day. A realistic attitude was adopted and the 'small remnant' of French Catholicism decided to make use of scientific means, namely the pastoral or 'religious' sociological method elaborated by G. le Bras, to ascertain the facts and then, on the basis of these data, to plan a concrete strategy which would transcend the juridical approach. The fact that these men only formed a 'small remnant' seemed to act as a stimulus rather than as a discouragement. With an almost too daring dynamism, they began consciously to introduce the gospel not only into the personal sphere of life, but also into the social and public sphere. Christian commitment, *engagement*, even in laicised political life, *présence* and *incarnation* became the favourite slogans and they even attacked, with not too much concern, those forms of Christian life which had previously been regarded as inviolable—for example, the 'established disorder' of contemporary capitalism, thus continuing the work which had already been carried out for almost a century in France by the 'socialist' priests. Even religious experience was focused almost exclusively on the community and the religious renewals in Germany were accepted with alacrity. Finally, a stream of publications helped to complete the 'miracle of the *Jocistes*' and within ten years the Catholics were able to substantiate their creative efforts for the country as a whole.

The Second World War made their unity with the French people even deeper. After some hesitation, they decided on their attitude towards the tempting offer of a new, specially privileged position by Pétain's Vichy government and their conscious and active support for the Resistance was greatly to their credit in the eyes of their fellow-countrymen when the war was over. This was especially true of the progressive Catholics who had been members of the *Jeunesse ouvrière chrétienne*, since the Catholics of the 'establishment' had compromised themselves during the war with Pétain. The development that had taken place before the war continued afterwards at greatly increased speed and the need to 'join the world evangelically' was expressed even more forcibly. Years later, Congar was to write: 'Anyone who did not live through the years 1946 and 1947 in the history of French Catholicism has missed one of the finest moments in the life of the Church.'[62] The laicity of the state was experienced more and more as the guarantee of genuine pluralism and even progressive Catholics themselves went in different directions. The most controversial of these Catholics were the extremely left-wing group advocating explicit collaboration with their Communist partners in the Resistance movement. At the more directly ecclesiastical level, this aspiration coincided partly with the initiative of the worker-priests, a movement which bore clear witness to genuine French radicalism. This almost desperate attempt to make the Church, still far too closely identified with the middle classes, acceptable to the working classes was the most far-reaching expression of the *Mission de France*, the specialised apostolate in France, which was becoming more and more a 'mission territory'. Cardinal Suhard of Paris devoted all his energies to the success of this venture, among other things by writing prophetic Lenten letters which were read all over the world. It was certainly not pure coincidence that, shortly after the death of this undaunted renewer in 1949, the reactionaries, who had for a long time been seriously alarmed and had been actively engaged with the authorities in Rome without consulting the bishops, began to achieve concrete results which shrouded the French revival for years in obscurity.

The French theologians thus worked towards a renewal within the context of dialogue between the Church and the contemporary world. The tradition within which they were working, and indeed still work, is rather different from that of the Germans—the philosophical ideas which surround them have a lighter specific gravity and even German thought seems to lose some of its heaviness when it crosses the frontier into France. This is quite apparent in the case of modernism and it is equally apparent in the case of later theologians in the two linguistic zones—there is a clear difference between, for example, Chenu, Congar or de Lubac and Karl Rahner, J.B. Metz or even theologians such as G. Söhngen and E. Przywara, who are still closer to the scholastic tradition. In France, contemporary experience was above all to lead to an exploration of the Christian past, a quest through the historical life of the Church to the original inspiration of the gospel. Since Loisy, the relationship between faith and history (history both in the sense of the historically reconstructed past and of the dynamic present) has been seen by the French as the basic theological problem. The way to conduct the dialogue both with the contemporary world and with our ancestors in the faith, had already become clear during the aftermath of modernism, in the attempts of Gardeil and Rousselot. It was a new and tactically very effective method of attacking the prevailing neo-scholasticism which was to be successfully worked out in France—a creative re-interpretation of scholasticism itself, on the basis of its scriptural, patristic and historically medieval background. It is important to mention here that the real basic questions of the modern age were raised for discussion behind the scholastic presentation—one is almost tempted to say, beneath the mask of scholasticism. The debates about the relationship between nature and the supernatural and about an 'incarnational' or an 'eschatological' attitude towards history—will the kingdom of God be realised through the agency of man and his efforts or simply by a transcendent act of God?—are ultimately concerned with secularisation or laicisation and the background to these discussions is to be found in the antithesis between the acceptance of the Republic by French Catholics and *Action française* or between Christian humanism and integral Catholicism. Naturally the Thomistic philosophy of Sertillanges, Gilson and Maritain, which itself had gone back to the sources under the pressure of the ideas of Blondel and Bergson and later of existentialism, was to play an important part in this re-interpretation of scholasticism.

It was in two centres, one Dominican and the other Jesuit, that this new attempt to bring Catholic thought up to date was to reach completion. The first of these two centres had been in Paris since 1937, but it still bears the name of the house of studies in Belgium that had been used during the long period of exile—Le Saulchoir. The basic formula for work that was used in this faculty had been established by Gardeil round about the beginning of the century, but its real fruitfulness did not become fully apparent until the modern historical method of the exegete Lagrange and the Louvain historians, among others P. Mandonnet, was also applied to the study of medieval theology. This broad historical approach was almost personified in M.D. Chenu, who was for years practically responsible for the planning of the strategy of the faculty and was its official leader from 1932 until 1942.

Marie-Dominique Chenu

Chenu is one of the few people who seems to survive even the most extreme praise that his friends lavish on him—anyone reading about him is bound to want to meet him. His spontaneous and generous openness even to only half-formed plans or ideas, his humanity and his irrepressible vitality—he talks with unmistakable pride about the Roman prelate who, when he was himself already sixty years old, called him, in connection with something that he had written which was considered unorthodox, 'that young theologian'—make him the most irresistible theologian of the present day. He is also one of the most paradoxical. When he began to teach in 1920, at the age of twenty-five, he quickly developed into a great and well-known medievalist, but he clearly did not have the temperament simply to remain a reconstructor. For him, working historically has always meant practising theology with the world and man in mind—the present world and modern man in order to know what questions to ask of the past, the world and man of the past in order to recognise the constructive and creative answer that these can give to the present. In the tradition of the faculty, it has always been his practice to lay as broad a foundation as possible, even in his own speciality, and to build up on this basis a new interpretation of medieval theology, especially that of Thomas, both from the evangelical revival that underlies it and from a background of Scripture, patristics and Greek philosophy. In so doing, Chenu has succeeded in burrowing through the later 'baroque' commentaries and neo-scholasticism to the original intuition of Thomas himself. This he has done explicitly in answer to the difficulties raised by modernism with regard to history and faith. Theology is thus seen to be humanly integrated faith; it is an attentive study of the historical event of Christ and its historical 'incarnation' through the centuries as far as the contemporary Church, with the aim of giving what is learnt from this study a place within the present-day world by continual reflection.

Chenu has not, however, simply professed this in theory. It is at first sight certainly rather difficult to recognise the subtle, pioneering historian when one encounters him engaged in animated conversation with, for example, young members of the *Jeunesse ouvrière chrétienne* or leaders of the *Mission de France*. On reflection, however, one is bound to agree with his own testimony, namely that he has always needed these living contacts with the Church and the world for his theology and his history because they have supplied him with the questions which he had to ask of history. In a mysterious way, then, Chenu has been involved in most of the risky experiments in the French Church and has often taken the initiative in them. He has certainly also experienced many set-backs and has had his share of condemnations, especially in connection with the worker-priest movement, to which he was totally committed. Even in 1933, he sent Dominican students into the mines as workers. The worker-priests, in turn, regarded Chenu as 'their' theologian. It has in fact always been one of Chenu's deepest convictions that the Church of today is confronted with the workers as she was confronted with the 'barbarians' of the West in the fifth and sixth centuries—the workers are her only hope of radical and life-giving transformation now that the Constantinian period is irrevocably past.

The result of all this activity can be found in numerous articles, which together form a theological commentary on many different contemporary problems in the world and the Church, especially in connection with the world of work and which also include more general studies, for example, of pastoral sociology, 'the Church in a state of mission', the priesthood and work, Marxism and 'a new type of Christian in the world'. What is fascinating in this connection is that, when one examines all that he has written, this 'committed' theology seems to alternate at random with detailed medieval studies. Chenu himself has given the best explanation of this apparent paradox: 'It might be thought that there are two Chenus. One is an old medievalist, not without a certain reputation, entirely absorbed in his reading of ancient texts, full of learning and attached to the early centuries of Christianity, a tradition to which he clings in the middle of the present century. Then there is the other Chenu, young, energetic, almost frivolous, caught up in the bustle of the modern world, very sensitive to its demands, quick to commit himself to the most critical problems in the world and the Church and for some time now a controversial figure who is suspect in certain quarters. But this is not true —there is only one Chenu. The unity of theology is revealed in this paradoxical unity of two personalities and two commitments—the word of God *in* the world, where the Spirit even *now* still continues and realises the meaning of Christ's incarnation in human thinking both individually and collectively.'[63]

On the one hand, the whole life of the Church in the world, a life that is in constant movement, has always been for Chenu the source of theology. This apparently modernistic recognition of historicity and human experience within theology is probably the reason why—to the unbelieving dismay of his students and disciples—Chenu's private edition on the theology of Le Saulchoir[64] was placed on the Index in 1942, with the result that he had to leave the faculty. On the other hand, however, he still calls the theology of Thomas his 'daily food' and 'a better instrument than any other for understanding the modern world', regarding it not as 'a completed, permanently closed system, but as a way of grasping the human and Christian reality'.[65] In this way, Chenu affirmed that Thomas' attention to the independence of man and the world was the beginning of a liberating 'laicisation' or secularisation. But who urged him to put this question to his medieval predecessor? It is precisely this tension between the present and the past which makes a study of Chenu's theology so fascinating and so rewarding.

Yves Congar

Chenu's plan bore fruit in quite a distinctive way in the work of his colleague Congar, his junior by almost ten years. Chenu and Congar are in many ways very similar, both sharing the same basic convictions, the same working formula and the same interest in the present and the past. Congar too is to be found in the front line. He also believes in the value of realistic dialogue and has always been fascinated by Chenu's historical method in the practice of theology.

In 1931, immediately after he had been appointed, on the conclusion of his studies, to a teaching post in Le Saulchoir, he was obliged, by pure chance, to take over Chenu's basic introductory course in theology. This put him at once in contact with modernistic ideas and he became convinced that the task of theologians of his generation was to integrate their attempts to apply critical methods to the Christian data and to approach the religious reality from subjective experience in Christian thought. The problem of the historical condition of the basic Christian data never ceased to preoccupy him. Because of this, Chenu and Congar are often found together.

This does not mean that the two theologians are like twin brothers—there are, on closer inspection, many differences between them. In his recent biography, J.P. Jossua has said that Congar is more withdrawn than Chenu, that he tends to obstinacy and, working for thirty-five years and until very recently without an assistant from seven o'clock in the morning until ten every evening, has never spared himself, that he is, according to his own admission, a 'Celt of the

Ardennes' without any skill in negotiation, that he lacks Chenu's charismatic gift for personal contacts and that he is a teacher rather than a pastor and a prophet rather than a doctor.[66] On the other hand, however, he takes a spontaneous joy in living, is engagingly ordinary and is averse to all posing, 'idealism' and supernaturalism—these characteristics make him comment, in an account of his difficulties, that he lacks the patience to wait for a bus or that he likes England, even though he is quickly bored there.[67]

More important, however, is an explicit difference in orientation which Congar traces back to an experience in youth. He was born and brought up in Sedan, which was a centre of French Protestantism in the sixteenth and seventeenth centuries and still has a very 'mixed' population. The Calvinist minister placed his chapel at the disposal of the Catholics of Congar's parish for six years when their church was burnt down by the Germans. It was here that Congar prayed during the years when he was growing up from boyhood to young manhood and, when he concluded his theological studies, he made a definitive choice in favour of ecumenism. This was at first a disappointment to Chenu, until he realised that Congar, who had an explicitly 'doctrinaire' ecumenism in mind, intended to apply his own quest for a truly contemporary theology which had developed from the past to a new and broader field.

In the first place, however, he had to listen to what was being said in other circles. Le Saulchoir had never been satisfied with data at second hand. Yet even there a certain amount of anxiety was caused by the young Dominican's declared intention of attending classes and lectures in the faculty of Protestant theology at Paris. Congar himself, however, has never shrunk from difficulties and has always read as much non-Catholic theology as possible and visited and associated with non-Catholic theologians. He came into contact with Orthodox Christians in Paris, Amay and Chevetogne, visited Anglicans in England and very early in his career made a pilgrimage to various Lutheran centres in

Germany. He conversed with Catholic pioneers in the ecumenical field such as Beauduin, Couturier, Gratieux and Portal, introduced Karl Barth, whose work he recognised to be vital for the future of Protestant theology, to one of his many ecumenical groups in Paris and visited Oscar Cullmann, to the consternation of Cullmann's deeply traditional Protestant housekeeper. Congar became more and more convinced that the other Christian Churches obliged him constantly to enlarge his own categories of thought in his continuing search for truth. He went more and more deeply into the historical origins of the divisions in Christianity, felt increasingly 'conformed to the gospel'[68] and concluded that his contribution to Christian unity had to consist of providing the doctrinal basis for a reform of his own Church: 'to rotate the Catholic Church through a few degrees on its own axis'.[69] Consciously and without fear, he chose a course which seemed to and did in fact lead to inevitable difficulties with the Church.

Partly as the result of numerous lectures, speeches and dialogues, he has published, in addition to a great number of articles and specialised historical studies, various great works. After his pioneering work, *Chrétiens désunis* (1937), the first part of his well-known series 'Unam Sanctam', there followed, after the interruption of the war and a delay caused by increasing difficulties with the Church, his great works on the reform of the Church, on the laity in the Church and the world and on tradition and development. His difficulties with the Church became concrete after 1939, when he was called, together with Chenu, to justify 'Unam Sanctam', and they lasted up to the Second Vatican Council. Congar's attitude towards these difficulties—a shameful succession of petty criticisms—was impressively calm and accommodating. He himself called it an attitude of 'active patience' and remained hopeful and convinced of the truth of Lacordaire's belief that 'the most favourable moments for sowing and planting' were 'times of trouble and storm'.[70] Under this pressure, Congar tended to place the main stress in his work rather more on ecclesiology, although this was no more than a shift of emphasis, since ecclesiology and ecumenism have always been practically identical in his case. Under the increasing influence of biblical theology in the Catholic Church since the war, and above all of Cullmann's theology of the history of salvation, Congar began to see the close connection between development and reform more and more clearly in the light of an increasing unity which is at the same time a 'conversion to Christ' and a 'service to the world'.[71] Not only as a historical specialist, but also in his almost scrupulous search for the 'liberating truth' in the past as the creative basis for the present, Congar has, like Chenu, given a very personal form to the tradition of Le Saulchoir.

The 'new' theology

Far more widely known than the Dominican centre of Le Saulchoir is the Jesuit theological faculty at Lyons, Fourvière, which acquired the reputation of being the place where the so-called 'new' theology originated and developed (*nouvelle théologie* in the strict sense, because this name is often applied to the work of Chenu and Congar as well and even to almost all pastoral initiatives in the French Church). Apart from modernism, this attempt at renewal within the Church has in fact been the only movement to attract considerable attention outside the circle of those directly concerned in it. This is above all attributable to one of the leading theologians in Rome at the time, the French Dominican R. Garrigou-Lagrange, who began in 1946 to write articles in the otherwise unemotional journal *Angelicum* with an almost medieval gusto and with a remarkably abundant use of italics, not only exposing a number of Jesuit theologians by name, but also revealing the existence of a kind of private and anonymous dispatch service for risky theological ideas which he ascribed indirectly to two other members of the society—Y. de Montcheuil and P. Teilhard de Chardin. Claiming that these ideas were directly derived from Blondel (a claim that he was, despite all his attempts, unable to substantiate), he concluded by reducing the movement quite simply to modernism.[72] This word, which was, of course, still tabu in the Church, aroused an unusually emotional response among certain theologians. In the ensuing theological discussion, opposition between Dominicans and Jesuits (or at least between a group of each order) also played an obvious part. One of those who joined in the debate was even able to catch Garrigou-Lagrange out—he had used Pius XII's address to the Jesuits as a weapon, but had suppressed the Pope's warning, given at almost exactly the same time, to the Dominicans.[73] Mgr Bruno de Solages, an outsider in the debate, also revealed, in a praiseworthy attempt to break through the secrecy, that the Dominican Chenu also belonged to the group of theologians attacked by Garrigou-Lagrange.[74] Chenu was no more directly involved in this debate than Blondel and Teilhard de Chardin, but, so it was ingeniously suggested, these three would bring further suspicion upon the theologians of Fourvière because of their earlier difficulties with the Church.

What the school of Fourvière was really aiming at, however, is even now less easy to establish than, for example, the basic intentions of Le Saulchoir. This is perhaps what made the critics of Fourvière so nervous. Chronologically, the first attack against the school—delivered even before Garrigou-Lagrange's list of accusations—was made by M. Labourdette in the *Revue Thomiste*, the journal of the Dominicans of Toulouse.[75] In this article, Labourdette challenged certain assumptions made in two theological series, *Théologie*, a series edited by the faculty of Fourvière, and *Sources chrétiennes*, a series edited by H. de Lubac and J. Daniélou. The author also attacked the alleged expression of these views in various volumes in both series and in a programmatic essay published by Daniélou at the beginning of 1946 in the journal *Études* on 'present-day trends in religious thought'.

This article—which expressed very characteristically not only the prevailing mood in theology during the dynamic years immediately following the Second World War, but also the brilliance and turbulent spirit of its author— proposed quite bluntly that the time had come to heal the breach between theology and life and to undertake the work of reconstruction with the help of the material that had been brought together by earlier generations of theologians. Daniélou, who has never been afraid of wide and all-embracing perspectives, outlined in this article the three possibilities that were open to theologians in this context: a return to the sources—to the Bible, the patristic texts and the liturgy, closer contact with Marxism and existentialism, which provided the basic ideas of 'historicity' and 'subjectivity', and an apostolic commitment to Christian life, both individual and social. Daniélou also made very suggestive and surprising cross-connections between these various levels, in which not only Karl Marx and the Church Fathers, but also Kierkegaard, Bergson, Karl Barth and Teilhard de Chardin played a part. The categories of thought of the Church Fathers and especially their typological exegesis were recommended by Daniélou as extremely suitable means of expressing the modern historical and social (Marxist!) consciousness and of making the gospel incarnate not only in Western society, but also in those of India, China and Africa. Daniélou also composed a number of variations in a minor key on this theme, expressing the failure of scholasticism to cope with and find a satisfactory solution to the problem of modernism which was still very much alive, despite the fact that it had been a useful defence against modernism in the past.

The rather staggering associations expressed in this article did not impress the more cold-blooded critics very much. It is, in any case, not difficult to understand why they reacted quite sharply to it and to similar judgements made, more in passing, by such theologians as H. Bouillard, G. Fessard and H. Urs von Balthasar. What is, however, still questionable is the extent to which Daniélou's manifesto was in fact a programme for Fourvière. There was an unmistakable orientation in this faculty generally towards patristic thought and this was particularly so in the case of de Lubac, who was later to publish a detailed study of Origen's understanding of Scripture—Origen who was himself regarded as 'quite ambiguous enough already'.[76] It is, however, not likely that all the members of the school of Fourvière simply accepted every detail in Daniélou's article. In a joint reply to Labourdette's attack—the first official indication that the 'new' theologians were making a common stand—this article by 'one of us' was called 'a broadly informative article containing sometimes rather hastily formulated statements'.[77] Was this a reservation on the part of de Lubac? It is, in any case, certainly worth while examining the theological attitude of this most balanced and—viewed in retrospect—most substantial representative of the 'new' theology more closely.

Henri de Lubac

De Lubac has never been a rebellious leader of the type that exists in the popular imagination. In comparison with Chenu, for example, or even Congar, he is in no sense spectacular, but rather the classical type of professor who is at the same time a gentleman, impressively and patriarchally courteous—certainly now that he has passed seventy. A wide circle of friends with whom he is constantly in contact bears witness to the fact that he is not, however, a remote figure. This goes right back to the time when he was seventeen years old and first joined the Jesuits in 1913. It was then that he became friendly with Auguste Valensin who was himself very close to Blondel and, with his charismatic gift for establishing human relationships, introduced his younger fellow Jesuit not only to Blondel, but also to Rousselot, Teilhard de Chardin and others. Since the death of these older men, de Lubac, who is certainly not really in need of work, has spent a great deal of his time patiently editing volume after volume of the unpublished work left by, for example, Blondel, Valensin and Teilhard.

The theological problem which preoccupied Blondel and Rousselot had more or less as a matter of course begun to fascinate de Lubac quite early in his career and, while he was recovering from a serious injury sustained at the front in the First World War, he followed Rousselot in a search into the most ancient tradition of the Church for illumination in the relationships between the awareness of God, grace, faith and human life. Once again almost as a matter of course, when he had completed his studies in England, where the French Society of Jesus, exiled from France, had found a temporary home, he began in 1929 to teach fundamental theology and the history of religion in Lyons. The importance of this branch of theology, which had developed from apologetics and in which revelation, faith, the Church and man's response to these were discussed, has already emerged in the case of Blondel and it was certainly not by pure chance that not only Chenu and Congar, for example, but also de Lubac's important supporter, H. Bouillard, also belonged to this circle of specialists.

In the years that followed, de Lubac systematically built up an impressive store of knowledge in the sphere of positive theology. This not only covered the whole of Christian tradition, with a clear preference for the Fathers of the Church and only slightly less interest in the whole of medieval theology, in de Bay and Jansen and many others up to the present, but also included the great authors and traditions of other religions, especially of Buddhism, and many different thinkers who have considered the religious question, if only negatively. It is clear from the great number of articles that he published that he was quite sensitive to the movements of his own times, but that what preoccupied him more than anything else and in his opinion merited a carefully considered answer were the fundamental questions of theology. These were man's quest for God and the consequences of God's answer for his existence in the world and his development, the concrete relationship between the impotence of this quest and the grace of God's answer, and the function of the very human community which is the Church, where God in fact offers to every man salvation realised in Christ. De Lubac clearly had the gift of being able to lay bare the living roots of the scholastic disputes which were concerned with these problems—about the relationship between nature and the supernatural, about the possibility of a Christian philosophy, about the relationship between theology and apologetics—by using his phenomenal learning to give scholasticism a place in the perspective of the underlying patristic tradition. This close parallel with the aims of Le Saulchoir did not escape Congar, who asked de Lubac to write one of the first volumes in his series 'Unam Sanctam'. De Lubac responded to this invitation by sending him his first book, *Catholicisme*, to which he gave the significant subtitle 'On the social aspects of dogma' and which was in fact a theological blueprint for the dynamic French Church of the period.

In 1942, during the German occupation of France, de Lubac interrupted his life of study to join the Resistance as a 'chaplain' and was, like so many of his colleagues, at once brought into contact with what he had hitherto only known from his reading—the deep conviction of those who adhered to Communism. This gave a new urgency to his thinking about modern man's quest for God and inspired him to study Proudhon, Feuerbach and Marx, Nietzsche and Comte. This resulted in various books on Marxism and atheistic humanism. Shortly after the war, his *Surnaturel* was ultimately published. This book was the result of years of study and in it he adopted a new position in a historical debate, but at the same time laid the foundation of a Christian humanism—by virtue of creation, that is, on the basis of his being, man is effectively called to community with God, the transcendent fulfilment of his longing for happiness. Obviously, in this, de Lubac's position was not entirely uninfluenced by Blondel. Garrigou-Lagrange was not mistaken on all points. The controversy that raged around this book was an advance-guard engagement fought over the 'new' theology. Whereas the more objective critics, even those who belonged to the Society of Jesus, thought that there was too much emphasis on humanism and too little on God's grace, the stricter Thomists were disconcerted primarily because the position of Thomas was discredited.

It would seem that J.M. Connolly was right when he said that the discussions about the 'new' theology were ultimately no more than a dispute between different schools of Thomists about the limits of their presumed submissiveness.[78] Earlier discussions about theological method were also taken up from time to time in this debate. The Belgian Dominican L. Charlier, whose writings were, with those of Chenu, placed on the Index, had played a conspicuous part in those discussions, especially by his rejection of the strictly rational character of the science of faith. It is, moreover, significant that this debate on Thomism could cause such a nervous reaction. The 'rebels' liked to make use of a quotation from Péguy that Thomism had been considered, praised, canonised and then buried,[79] while Garrigou-Lagrange nervously placed his guns—the papal instructions about following Thomas—in position on the first page of his first attack.[80] Fourvière was realistic enough not to want anything more, basically, than to return to the sources of neoscholasticism itself and to reconstruct a system on the resulting basis in contemporary terms. Congar recognised this affinity with the aims of Chenu's followers and referred to it openly, but his action hardly helped their cause, of course. Their opponents clearly realised that the historical approach, even if this were limited simply to scholasticism, would result in the introduction of the Trojan horse of relativisation. One line of argument in the debate was already concerned, as a result of a comment made more or less in passing by Bouillard, with the 'durability' of the (scholastically formulated) decisions of earlier councils.

Those who followed the prevailing scholastic theology could hardly avoid seeing the spectre of modernism in every attempt to detract from the unchangeable character of the 'eternal truth' even in the form in which it appeared here on earth. Pius XII confirmed this point of view in his encyclical *Humani Generis* in 1950.

No one and nothing were directly condemned in this document, but it contained distinct allusions to the work of the 'new' theologians, and de Lubac, the most defenceless of all of them, was advised to give up teaching for the time being. He began to revise several of his books, including *Surnaturel*, and, after professing his faith in the Church in his impressive book, *Méditations sur l'Eglise* (E. tr. *The Splendour of the Church*), devoted himself to the task of writing a book on Buddhism and an enormous study of medieval exegesis. Only his book on the equally suspect Teilhard de Chardin seems to go against the grain.

Pierre Teilhard de Chardin

Does Teilhard really fit into this discussion? In fact, this fascinating man was, as if by chance, in France from 1946 until 1950 and while he was there he was able not only to confront the scholars of Paris with his visionary ideas, but also to establish contact with the worker-priests. When Garrigou-Lagrange dismissed his ideas as 'fantastic', he was not particularly impressed, because he himself had used this qualification.[81] He was only too well aware of the fact that he had 'walked around like an elephant in the most carefully raked flower-beds of scholasticism'[82] and this was no doubt one of the few views which Garrigou-Lagrange shared with him. Of all the thinkers mentioned here, the life and work of Teilhard de Chardin is probably the most generally known and it is clearly important to say something about his 'theological' attitude.

When he returned to Paris in 1946, he was already sixty-five, fifteen years older than de Lubac and Chenu, and he had become world famous as a paleontologist during long years of work in China. He had been fascinated by stones since childhood and his teacher, Henri Bremond, ascribed his 'desperately good behaviour'[83] as a schoolboy to this obsession. During his years of study as a Jesuit, he went to three different places outside France and found in each of them the opportunity to do geological and paleontological work. It was therefore to some extent inevitable that his superiors should have decided to let him turn this hobby into a specialised study. After a few years, however, this study was interrupted by military service in the First World War. Even in the trenches he still looked for 'stones', but after a little time his experience at the front brought about a great change in his hitherto protected life and it was during these years that his ideas about the world, man and God acquired their basic shape. When he made his quite sensational discoveries in the scientific sphere between the two world wars, this progress was in his case almost as a matter of course accompanied by a similar development in his religious views. His faith and apostolic ideal even inspired his scientific thinking. He wanted both his fellow-scientists and his fellow-believers to share in his joy about the structures that he had discovered in the world of phenomena—the inner cohesion of the universe which is growing towards a divine fulfilment in Christ. He was only too clearly aware of the fact that both scientists and Christians were looking for a harmony—an orientation for their science and a sphere of experience on earth for their faith. In this, he did not aim to practise theology or philosophy, but simply wished to obtain a clear view of the whole pattern of phenomena, with the 'phenomenon of man' in the centre, and to present this in its connected orientation. He regarded this as a kind of 'meta-biology' which, on the basis of discovered data, resulted in a task for the present and in a religious, Christian vision of the future—God as the future of man.

Teilhard's work changed the lives of thousands of people for ever. Both scientists and theologians, however, felt lost amid views in which Teilhard, according to P. Smulders' telling assessment, spoke 'in virtually the same breath about the atom and man's striving towards eternity, about the evolution of life and the law of the love of one's neighbour and even the love of God'.[84] What is more, he did this in a torrent of poetic phrases which expressed something of his own enthusiasm. A certain amount of alarm was caused in the Church by the apparent lack of concern with which Teilhard wrote about the evolution of the universe as though it were an established fact and also, for example, about a particular interpretation of original sin which he linked to this. There were difficulties with the Church. Teilhard was always prepared to promise to confine himself to his science, but his 'phenomenology' had elements which others tended to regard as philosophical or theological.

Teilhard's thought clearly represents a very special development in recent theology. Because he approached the problems of theology from the unusual vantage-point of the exact sciences, there is always a danger that his efforts will be disregarded by professional theologians, just as an inventor without professional qualifications is seldom listened to seriously. An incident concerning the *Osservatore Romano* is typical in this context. In 1948, the Vatican newspaper published a report about lectures in Paris by, among others, the 'leading theologian' Teilhard de Chardin. A few weeks later, however, this statement was corrected 'by request', the newspaper saying that 'this religious, as everyone knows' had not distinguished himself in the sphere of theology.[85] It is in fact true to say that Teilhard's arguments did contain theological ideas which had outlived their usefulness. His thought was, like that of every 'visionary', attractive, but it was as relative as every vision is. Once interest had been aroused, however, there were seen to be many points of contact between Teilhard's vision and the life of the Church and theology in France at the time—especially the preoccupation with the dynamic element, with the Christian meaning of history and with the relationships between man's task on earth and his transcendent fulfilment, or between humanism and Christianity. In the debate about the meaning of history, Teilhard's optimism is very much inclined towards the view of an 'incarnational' thinker such as de Lubac. His ideas about the cosmic role of Christ, for example, would seem to go back to the Fathers of the Church, especially Origen—something which was acclaimed by Daniélou who was then almost as audacious in his thinking, but which was regarded with suspicion by Teilhard's opponents. De Solages actively defended Teilhard against the attacks of Garrigou-Lagrange, but the encyclical *Humani Generis* contained clear allusions to his ideas.

When he died in 1955, the French attempt at a realistic dialogue with the 'world' seemed to have failed. Even an extension of scholastic thought carefully based on tradition had not been able to achieve it and another group of adventurous spirits was recalled to the strengthened fortress of the Church. Ten years later, however, their ideas were to find their way into the conciliar documents on the Church and the world.

Bibliography

For the historical background to French Catholic thought of this period, I have relied a great deal on A. Latreille's *Histoire* (see the bibliography following the section on modernism). To this can be added W. Bosworth's informative account of *French Catholic Groups at the Threshold of the Fifth Republic*, Princeton, N.J. 1962. The first work, as far as I know, to have been written which deals specifically with this period of theological renewal in France is by an American author, J.M. Connolly, whose book, *The Voices of France*, was published in New York in 1961. It was recently translated into French and published in Paris in 1966 with the title *Le renouveau théologique dans la France contemporaine*. The author provides useful surveys and a good analysis of the work of de Lubac, but rather unsatisfactory analyses of the work of A. Dondeyne, the Louvain philosopher and theologian, Congar, Teilhard de Chardin and Daniélou. He concludes with a description of the clashes between the the French theologians and the 'teaching Church'—a chapter which might have been fascinating if it had not been written with a pre-conciliar concern for Church reactions, especially in the United States. P.A. Martin, in his introduction to the French edition, correctly but rather embarrassingly points out a number of omissions—that the book contains, for example, practically nothing at all about Chenu or any of the philosophers, even Blondel.

The German *Tendenzen der Theologie im 20. Jahrhundert* (see the bibliography on p. 21) contains a portrait of Chenu written with almost perfect sensitivity by Maurice Barth. An example of Chenu's fiery way of speaking can be found in an interview held on the occasion of his seventieth birthday in *Informations catholiques internationales* (233) 1 Feb. 1965 —the interview which contains the passage quoted in the preceding section on the 'two Chenus'. The first volume of his collected articles, *La foi dans l'intelligence* (Paris 1964), contains a bibliography of his writings up to 1963. The book that he likes most of all himself, however, is a collection of his articles on 'contemporary' themes—*L'évangile dans le temps* (Paris 1964). A selection of articles from these two books has been translated and published under the title *Faith and Theology*, Dublin 1968. An example of his 'actual' theology is *The Theology of Work*, Dublin 1963.

J.P. Jossua has written an excellent study of Congar, full of characteristic quotations and containing a bibliography which is complete almost up to the moment of publication: *Le père Congar* (Paris 1967). Congar himself has written an autobiographical introduction of sixty-four pages to his collected ecumenical essays, *Chrétiens en dialogue*, Paris 1964 (E. tr. *Dialogue between Christians*, London and Dublin 1966), a document which is moving because it is so direct. (The change that has taken place in relationships between Christians during the past twenty-five or so years is at once perceptible simply when the title of this, the fiftieth volume of the series 'Unam Sanctam' is compared with that of the first volume—*Chrétiens désunis*.) Any reference to other studies of Congar in addition to these two sources would seem to be rather superfluous. Congar's portrait of himself is also a good way of making acquaintance with the man's theological attitude—most of his books require a good measure of time and patience.

The 'new' theology has been described in a rather half-hearted contribution by H. Rondet in *Sacramentum Mundi* IV (London 1969), to which a representative bibliography is added. Useful and balanced information is provided by two articles of G. Weigel, 'The Historical Background of the Encyclical *Humani Generis*', *Theological Studies* (12) 1951, pp. 208–30, and 'Gleanings from the Commentaries on *Humani Generis*', *ibid.* pp. 520–49, where one also finds an extensive international bibliography. A perceptive exposition will also be found in G. Thils' *Orientations de la théologie* (Louvain 1958), p. 57 ff., in which the author has rightly pointed to the discussions resulting from L. Charlier's book *Essai sur le problème théologique*, Thuilles 1938.

A rather untidy but informative book on Daniélou has been written by P. Lebeau (Paris 1967), who, strangely enough, has nothing to say about the 'new' theology. Important facts about de Lubac are contained in H. Vorgrimler's portrait in *Tendenzen*, in W.C. Russell's more detailed survey in *Modern Theologians: Christians and Jews* (see the bibliography on p. 21) and in the interview published in *Informations catholiques internationales* (215) 1 May 1964, but it would seem as though no one can provide a sharp enough picture of this theologian. A bibliography of his publications up to 1963 will be found in volume 3 of the commemorative collection of essays written in his honour, *L'homme devant Dieu*, Paris 1964 (Part 58 of the series 'Théologie'). Of his works which have been translated into English, his *Discovery of God* (London 1960; originally published in 1956) is a good point at which to begin reading de Lubac.

In Search of an Explanation in History 121

An obvious choice as far as Teilhard de Chardin is concerned is de Lubac's *La pensée religieuse du père Teilhard de Chardin*, Paris 1962 (E. tr. *The Religion of Teilhard de Chardin*, London 1967) and finally P. Smulders' widely praised book —of which I have made grateful use—*The Design of Teilhard de Chardin* (New York and Westminster Md., n.d.). This author also provides a very clearly defined portrait of Teilhard in his introduction. The study by C. Mooney, *Teilhard de Chardin and the Mystery of Christ* (London 1964) is also to be recommended.

After the War in Germany and the Netherlands

Germany after the war

A few months after the capitulation of Germany in 1945, Romano Guardini was once again able to lecture. It is clear that he was only too well aware of the position of those who came to hear him: 'Our young people have been injured, seriously injured, by this terrible conflict. We have to speak to them calmly, as we would speak to people who have returned from a distant country. For twelve years, they have been handed over, without any defence, to leaders whose only ambition has been to prevent them from thinking. We now have the task of giving back to these young people their mental and spiritual dynamism.'[86] The end of the war did not have the same significance in Germany as it did in France or the Netherlands, for example, where it meant a real liberation, resulting in a sudden upsurge of new mental and spiritual energy, despite all the destruction and dislocation of society. The collapse of Nazism ought perhaps to have given rise to this reaction in Germany as well, but it could hardly be expected that the Germans would regard the military defeat, the economic chaos and the occupation of their country as a new beginning. At the most it meant a slow awakening from anaesthesia after a serious operation —the fact that this action had been necessary did not make it any easier to bear. It was only after several years, when normal conditions had gradually returned, that Germany—or the western part of the country at least—began to recover her dynamism. The country was restored within a miraculously short time to the same level as the rest of Europe by a reconstruction planned and carried out with typical German thoroughness, in which the demand for personal welfare, which had been held in check during the Nazi era, could be fulfilled. This provided the foundation for what we in Western Europe call the 'modern world'—an urbanised welfare society which is dominated by science and technology and which expresses itself at the level of religion as a call to 'secularisation'.

In the German-speaking countries and also, for example, in the Netherlands, the friction between the Church and the world seems to have been very different, at least in its origin, from that in France. There is not and seldom has been any really violent conflict betwen Church and state in Germany—on the contrary, they seem to be able to get on too well together. In the Second German Empire, it was the Lutheran Church which played such an important part in Church-state relationships. Since the Second World War, the Catholic Church has had a far greater influence because the government has been in the hands of the predominantly Catholic Christian Democratic Union. The obligatory Church tax—which is not, of course, simply for the Catholic Church—seems almost to indicate a return to the idea of a state Church and ultimately even a form of 'secularisation', although a different kind of secularisation from that which is usually meant by this word. This Church 'established in the world' is, however, also undergoing an inner change. For a very long time now this Church has been closely tied to the middle-class environment with the result that the changes in that environment are now being clearly reflected in a decline in active Church membership and attendance. Increasing industrialisation and urbanisation and the migration within Germany of some twelve million refugees torn out of their native environments have led to a much

In Search of an Explanation in History 123

more rapid discovery by and influence on the 'cradle' Catholics of Germany of new secular values than in the past. The traditional structures of the Church as an institution seem to be falling farther and farther behind the constantly expanding and progressing structures of secular society—indeed what has been taking place has been aptly called 'the Church's emigration from society'.[87] The quasi-official 'people's' Church seems to be falling apart and there would at first sight seem to be no remedy for this.

Silent lapsing has, however, not been the only reaction to the people's Church's loss of social function. The revival of the various 'movements' had become more vigorous in confrontation with Nazism—active cells of resistance had arisen and the members of these were quickly faced with the inevitable need to make personal decisions, because the hierarchy was either unable to or simply did not give any clear guidance in many instances. Because of external pressure, these groups concentrated on personal commitment and on the 'inner Church', the community nourished by a suitably adapted liturgical celebration. These groups were also frequently politically committed and this meant that they were subject to persecution by the Nazis, but also that they enjoyed considerable prestige—comparable to that enjoyed by the French Resistance—when the war ended. They knew that they would be listened to if they advocated breaking out of the Catholic ghetto and replacing the older attitude of uncritical obedience to the authority of the Church by a more critical sense of personal responsibility. As in the case of French Catholicism, the influence of this progressive minority was in no sense decisive, but it did lead to the gradual suppression of the ideal of a people's Church and the emergence of a 'community' Church, a Church purified of all functions not strictly religious, and to which people freely chose to belong because of their convictions.

In addition to these rather more superficial reactions to the course of events outside the Church, a change of attitude also took place at a deeper level. Looking back at this period, it seems as though the Catholic precursors in the 'change of direction' that became noticeable after the First World War were too ready to see a parallel between what they were working towards and elements of 'objective' tradition in the Catholic Church. Within the Church, it is true that the result had been a religious and theological revival of interest in Christ, the Church and the liturgy, which had been sanctioned in broad outline in two papal documents, *Mystici Corporis* and *Mediator Dei*. But when, after about ten years or so, the 'objective' character of the various movements had, to a very great extent, become solidified in external organisations—the National Socialist organisations soon became a particularly repellent example of these—this aspect of the change of direction acquired a permanently bitter taste. Insufficient emphasis was given initially in Catholic circles to the fact that this change, which was inspired by Kierkegaard especially, had also led, both in the dialectic theology of Reformed Christianity and in the philosophy of such men as M. Heidegger, to a re-orientated interest in personal decision and commitment. As the originally objective orientation of society in general degenerated more and more, however, the interest among Catholics shifted similarly.

This continued even more noticeably after the Second World War, when science and technology came more and more to be seen as a threat to human values and there was an increasing tendency in the Churches of the Reformation to withdraw into an existentialistic interpretation of the Christian data and to concentrate on a personal existential decision with regard to the gospel presented in this way— the enormous response to Bultmann's theology in Protestant circles is evidence of this. When Guardini said in 1950 that man had felt since the nineteen-thirties that he was threatened by nature, by man himself and by the technological society that man himself had evolved and that he had experienced the reality that surrounded him as something requiring a radical decision, he was only repeating what Heidegger had described, from 1927 onwards, as the

In Search of an Explanation in History 125

fundamental 'fear' and 'care' of man's existence. A. Kolping —to whom I am indebted for this remarkable parallel—has commented sourly in this context that Catholic theology has 'revelled' in the elaboration of personalistic flights of thought.[88] 'Personalistic' is, however, too confusing a word. Guardini himself had, from the very beginning, focused his attention on concrete, personal realities rather than on objective, present, given and factual realities and the Catholic revival was obviously intent on breaking through the purely objective aspect. But this emphasis on the personal aspect was almost at once absorbed by an interest in the social aspect—the living community of the Church *within which* we are personally responsible. It was only when the ideal of a christianisation of the world around a renewed Catholic Church began to fade after the Second World War that this personalism came to concentrate directly on individual man in the world planning his life freely within history. This does not mean that no further interest was taken in the community or that ecumenical openness and the creative practice of going back to biblical and traditional sources were pushed into the background in post-war Catholic theology in Germany. Catholic theology in the new Germany is certainly no less dynamic than it was in pre-war Germany—one has only to think for example, of such figures as Hans Urs von Balthasar, the literary and sometimes rather prolix originator of a 'contemplating' theology, the imperturbable exegete H. Schlier and his younger colleague A. Vögtle, with their constant recourse to speculative theology, the brilliant ecumenical theologian Hans Küng, who astonished even Karl Barth, and his venerable colleague at Tübingen, J. Geiselmann, who played havoc with the older ideas of Scripture and tradition.

Nonetheless, the most ambitious and all-embracing project was that of Karl Rahner and his 'school', which made use of the basic human datum itself, as revealed by Heidegger, with the aim of completely restoring the whole of theology from its foundations upwards.

Karl Rahner

A few years ago, Karl Rahner's elder brother Hugo revealed that both of them offered their father a private commemorative collection of essays in 1928 on the occasion of his sixtieth birthday and that Karl, who was then twenty-four, contributed one essay on 'history and man's understanding of history in the light of Thomist metaphysics'.[89] Did his father, who no doubt felt highly honoured when he read this contribution, remember, one wonders, his exclamation of incredulity six years before this, when his turbulent son had told him that he also wanted to become a Jesuit?[90] This may perhaps seem to be a rather frivolous point of departure for an outline of the man who is regarded as the most penetrating Catholic theologian of the moment. Nonetheless the picture that it calls to mind is an authentic one. The animation and intense involvement are no less now than they were then. These characteristics were perhaps less in evidence at school, where Karl was bored, but outside school he was an enthusiastic member of the Catholic 'youth movement' and an admirer of Guardini. His energetic spirit has, in later life, probably been most in evidence in personal contacts, but it is frequently discernible even in the inordinately long sentences of his articles, even though these sometimes give the first impression of being as impossible to penetrate as the contribution to the commemorative collection unintentionally was, one imagines, for his father. The theme of this contribution does, anyway, express something of the apparent ease with which Karl Rahner has always been able to move deep below the surface of concrete thought. It also brings together two poles which—so it had always been believed—inevitably repelled each other, namely history and Thomist metaphysics, an antithesis to which Rahner did not want to resign himself. Finally, it is also clear that he wanted to travel along the well-known path of a creative interpretation of scholasticism—he asked the modern question of historicity of medieval philosophy.

When Rahner wrote this study, he had already completed the usual three years of philosophy at the faculty of his order, but his contact with modern thought had been relatively indirect. What was remarkable, however, was that he carried out his own course of study of Kant and the Louvain philosopher J. Maréchal during his period of scholastic training. (One of the writers who is responsible for this story even reports that Rahner had to do this in secret.[91]) It is worth noting in this context that—probably partly under the influence of Blondel—Maréchal succeeded, in a very personal way, in integrating Kant's ideas into neo-Thomism, by placing all emphasis in human thought on its dynamic orientation towards reality and by basing a realistic metaphysics on this. Talking recently about those who had most influenced his thinking, Rahner mentioned first of all this fellow Jesuit who in any case had a considerable following among theologians and secondly Rousselot, the most striking figure in neo-scholastic circles who had engaged in open dialogue with other trends of thought, including, for example, that of Blondel.[92] The most decisive confrontation, however, occurred when Rahner had completed his normal course of studies. His superiors sent him back to the town where he had been born and brought up, Freiburg im Breisgau, so that he could specialise in the history of philosophy at the university there. But Freiburg meant Heidegger and Rahner succeeded in getting into his exclusive seminar. It is clear that there was a great affinity between them—Rahner absorbed Heidegger's ideas with gratitude and fascination and twenty years later the philosopher, who was by then almost seventy years old, made one of his sporadic journeys to Innsbruck to visit his ex-student.

Rahner did not achieve his immediate aim in Freiburg. His professor did not accept the thesis that he had written on Thomas' doctrine of knowledge, because it was not, in his opinion, a historical interpretation, but a piece of philosophising by the author himself. In the introduction to his thesis, Rahner had written significantly enough that 'he did not know why he should concern himself with Thomas if it were not for the sake of those questions which affected his own philosophy and that of his own times'.[93] The same theme, expressed in a more directly theological context, is also to be found in a discussion of de Lubac's *Catholicisme* which Rahner wrote at about the same time (that is, just before the Second World War). De Lubac had, in Rahner's opinion, translated the ideas of the Church Fathers into real, present-day theology.[94] In the meantime, Rahner had also acquired a broad background of positive theology, especially in the sphere in which his brother Hugo specialised, that of patristics. He graduated at Innsbruck in 1936 with a thesis in this subject. During the last years before the Second World War, the different threads began to be knitted more and more closely together in his courses and lectures, in his apostolate of 'proclamation' and in the theological discussions that he organised with his professional colleagues. It was within the framework of these discussions that his new plan for the study of theology, which was later to have such an influence, and the idea of a new series of publications which would make these new theological views available for public debate (an unheard-of idea in those days) were first born.

He was therefore not unprepared when, during his 'exile' in Vienna in the war, he replied, at the request of the Viennese cardinal, to Archbishop Gröber's complaint against the 'newfangled' theology. In his report he diagnosed the situation and on this basis stated that Catholic theologians in the German-speaking countries had not yet really begun on their true task of scientifically confronting contemporary problems. An enormous amount of work had still to be done, he maintained, not only in the field of positive theology, but above all in that of systematic theology, before the real problems were reached, not only in non-commital 'essays', but also in a strictly scientific attempt to deal with them.[95] After a few moves, Rahner was able to undertake this great task from 1948 onwards in Innsbruck.

Anyone looking back at the results of this undertaking will probably be impressed above all by the great quantity of work done by Rahner, who recently gave a striking indication of his almost discouraging productivity in a laconic remark during an interview: 'Some days I write nothing.'[96] A constant questioning of the concrete situation underlies the rich variety of his themes. And indeed Rahner, who is so feared and respected because of the profundity of his thought, does speak and write about almost every conceivable subject, many of them not strictly theological, such as public opinion in the Church, laughter, illness and sleep, work and free time, the songs of the abbé Duval and television broadcasts of the Mass. In the main, however, what he deals with are the urgent problems of theology—the inspiration of Scripture, the question of 'many Masses and the one sacrifice of the cross', the people's Church and the new Christian diaspora, monogenism and evolution, sin in the Church, charismatic dynamism in relation to the hierarchical leadership of the Church, the position of the bishops in relation to the pope, the restoration of the diaconate, the need for a new form of theological training, and so on. When he writes about more concrete subjects, Rahner's normally laborious style acquires a certain evocative, even poetic element which can give new life and meaning to even the most ordinary things.

In the last resort, however, the most impressive aspect of Rahner's work is not the great amount of his writing or even the range and universal nature of his thought, but the depths to which he is again and again able to descend. This is apparent in the astonishing and methodical way in which he is able, after delving deeply into tradition, cautiously to reveal and to give a central place in his own synthesis to what is really valuable in that tradition for men today. He does this, as H. Asmussen has said, 'without a trace of compromise'[97] and with a remarkable capacity, reminiscent of that of Thomas, for incorporating numerous partial insights into his thought in a most balanced way.

J.B. Metz, his original follower, has observed pointedly that it was this 'conservative' aspect of Rahner's theology, his creative affirmation of tradition, which caused his pioneering ideas to be accepted so quickly—on closer inspection, the essentially traditional ideas could be discovered in a rejuvenated form in his writings.[98]

Thematically, the depth of Rahner's thought is most strikingly revealed in the anthropological insights which again and again emerge as the basis of his ideas. The only two 'real' books which Rahner has written are, characteristically enough, both concerned with man in the world and his relationship with God. Rahner frankly calls his theology 'anthropocentric' and does not believe that this is in any way opposed to God's claim to be the centre of theology. Man is, according to Rahner, absolute transcendence towards God and it is impossible to speak about man without at the same time involving God and nothing can be said about God unless man is also discussed. With this theology which is centred in man and his possibilities and which has been 'cut out of the rock of scholastic objectivism'[99] Rahner has not only taken on the fundamental questions of the post-war Church, which is so conscious of having been thrown back on personal decision, but has also provided Christian theologians with a new basis for dialogue with non-Christian believers and with Marxist atheists.

This does not mean that Rahner's ideas have been received everywhere with equal enthusiasm. Certainly a 'Rahnerian' school has developed with a number of important followers and a series of theological projects of impressive consistency, including especially the new edition of the *Lexikon für Theologie und Kirche*, the modern *Summa* of salvation-history, *Mysterium Salutis*, *Sacramentum Salutis* and the *Handbuch der Pastoraltheologie*. But not all Rahner's fellow theologians have been equally deeply impressed by the metaphysical power of the more obscure passages, and penetrating questions have been asked about many details. Not only Roman authorities but also theological circles in the 'misty North' successfully requested just before the Council that Rahner's articles should be examined by seven censors before being published. Rahner's re-interpretation of neo-scholasticism resulted in the neo-scholastic point of departure becoming hardly distinguishable from the conceptual system of traditional theologians who were in any case unable to understand why the 'eternal truth' had to be 'adapted' to the continuing life of the Church and (above all) of the world. The controversial points in Rahner's writings provided a natural point of departure for a long series of warnings and prohibitions, although there was no open condemnation—perhaps because there was some apprehension about German feelings.

The Netherlands

When in 1953, Rahner recommended a book which was, to his regret, 'only obtainable with great difficulty for us poor non-Dutchmen',[100] he was only one of several theologians who believed that it might be possible to discover in the Dutch-speaking countries a theological world which could be reached only with difficulty and was therefore all the more fascinating and which was able, they imagined, to exist in an almost paradisiacal state, ignored by the central authorities because of the isolation of the Dutch language. The natives living in the Netherlands, however, and certainly their theologians, had to shatter this idyllic picture. In the first place, uneasiness on the part of the 'authorities' had, at about this time, come to a head in the form of a sensational visitation resulting in a change of working environment for three progressive theologians. Secondly—and more importantly in this context—there had simply not been enough time to build up in the Netherlands a firmly established theological tradition like that in France or Germany.

J. Rivière, the 'official' Catholic specialist in modernism, was clearly well informed when he stated that the Netherlands remained almost entirely immune to modernism and he was not so very wide of the mark in his explanation of this—that Dutchmen were entirely concerned with practical activities and were hardly interested at all in intellectual questions.[101] The fact is that Dutch Catholics were at that time actively engaged in the task of securing a place for themselves in society. That there was indeed talk of integralistic reactions indicated above all that every countertendency, however weak, was regarded by most of the solidly ultramontane Dutch Catholics of that period as a waste of energy which might otherwise have been devoted to the vitally necessary task of Catholic social emancipation. Throughout the course of this century, however, and particularly since the end of the Second World War, the situation in the Netherlands has undergone a gradual change.

The various movements and reactions which had originated in France or Germany were now to be found, in a suitably adapted form, in the Netherlands. Dutch theologians were also beginning to find more and more freedom to think creatively, especially at the Catholic University of Nijmegen, which was founded in 1923, and Dutch theological articles and books were also being increasingly discussed internationally. Nonetheless, it does rather seem as though the Netherlands prefer, even in the theological sphere, to remain 'concerned with practical activities', with concrete experience. Thus, after years of rigidity lasting until the first years after the Second World War, dialogue with Christians of the Reformed Churches quite suddenly accelerated and resulted in several remarkable theological studies. Dutch scholars were also inspired by the post-war revival of biblical theology which flourished especially in the French-speaking countries. In fact, there has always been great interest among Dutch scholars in concrete research especially in spheres that are so concerned with life as Scripture, the liturgy and the history of the Church. The faithful and yet personal interpretation of the neo-scholastic tradition which had been established for a long time in the

Netherlands had also developed more and more into a 'theology of life' of the type practised by Guardini and Karl Adam, whose works have long been widely read in Dutch Catholic circles. It would, however, be very difficult to maintain that, seen within the context of the whole Catholic Church, all this has given rise to any really new theological movement. This has certainly not happened in the stricter sense in which the idea of a *theological* tendency has so far been understood in this book. In any case, a Dutch theologian of 'renewal' would be more inclined to look to man's concrete experience and to follow the practice of going back to biblical and traditional sources than to consult philosophy in the strict sense of the word. This interpretation may to some extent be illustrated by examining the theological attitude of P. Schoonenberg, one of the two dogmatic theologians at Nijmegen.

Schoonenberg completed his theological education only a few years after Karl Rahner, his fellow Jesuit, and at a place only about six miles away. But whereas Rahner gained a life-long aversion to 'theological positivism' in the German Jesuit house at Valkenburg, where the course of studies had a rather one-sided historical bias, Schoonenberg on the other hand became aware of the need for a historical basis to all theological reflection because of the excessive emphasis in the Dutch faculty of Maastricht on speculative theology (in the neo-scholastic tradition). When the war was over, after having taught theology for several years, Schoonenberg was at last given the chance to do special studies in Rome and chose to study at the Biblical Institute under, among other scholars, the inspiring French exegete, S. Lyonnet. In dialogue with contemporary views in the French-speaking countries, his thesis dealt with the structure and aim of theology and in particular the function of historical research, the affirmations made by the Church's teaching authority and their philosophical content (in other words, their neo-scholastic content). He graduated in Maastricht, but, perhaps because he was clearly too much inclined towards the view that a strictly rational argument was not possible in theology and had to give way to a more descriptive interpretation of the Church's experience of faith and preaching—he never ascertained the exact reason for this—his thesis *Theologie als geloofsvertolking* (*Theology as Interpretation of Faith*) was never published. He subsequently taught for some years at Maastricht, but when it became clear that he was not, as he put it himself, 'orthodox' enough, he moved first to the city where he was born and brought up, Amsterdam, and then, after teaching there for a few years, to the Higher Catechetical Institute at Nijmegen. In 1964, when he was about fifty years old, he became a professor at the University of Nijmegen.

Schoonenberg's theological interests are in many ways very similar to those of Karl Rahner. He too is fascinated by the complex relationships between God and man and the consequences of these for man's freely chosen pattern of life in the world. 'God is not in competition with man' is the title—and a very significant one—of one of his many articles. 'God or man—a false dilemma' was the subject of his inaugural speech at Nijmegen. He has elaborated this basic theme in many surprising studies, not only of man's life in the world, of sin, original sin, death and eschatological fulfilment, but also of the mystery of God and man as manifested in Christ. Under the inspiration of Teilhard de Chardin, he has, in recent years especially, given a new depth to these themes by explicitly revealing them as facets of evolving reality.

His style of writing and his way of thinking are, however, not at all similar to those of Rahner. This difference would in the first place seem to be a reflection of Schoonenberg's less outspoken nature and even perhaps rather awkward, professorial manner and of his discretion with regard to the accepted structures of his language. Just as one has to listen very carefully in conversation with him if one does not want to miss his aphorisms, which are usually made in passing and in a spirit of self-ridicule, so too one has to remember that he is inclined to understatement in his writings, with the result that the essence is easily missed if one reads too quickly. His presentation is entirely lacking in the sensational or spectacular, an element which so often leads to misjudgement in the case of those less important authors who make use of it. This is also true of his work as a whole—his books are strongly influenced by the 'catechetical' environment in which he has lived and worked for so long, but they are based on a series of less well known scientific articles.

His characteristically Dutch approach—the practice of taking concrete human experience as his point of departure and of remaining in close contact with this—is also apparent in his theological writings. He obviously feels at home in his catechetical environment and seems hardly to need to descend to the extreme depths of a transcendental anthropology in his attempts to interpret man's contemporary experience. The other typically Dutch point of departure in approaching the problems of theology—that of going back to biblical sources—is also very much in evidence in Schoonenberg's writings. This is the course that he almost always follows before leading his readers on, in his unobtrusive way, to a new theological insight. Finally, although this practice of returning to the sources is closely associated with a sympathy for the theological orientation in France which has become no less since the time that he wrote his thesis, there is also a noticeable parallel with contemporary German theological practice in the case of Schoonenberg's particular interest in the evolving human forms which the interpretation of the gospel has taken in the course of history. The fact that this has led to his being warned more than once officially by the Church—even in the period preceding the Council—can surely only be a surprise to anyone who believed in the protective unobtrusiveness of the Dutch-speaking areas on the edge of France and Germany.

Flanders

In the first part of the preceding section, the reader may

have noticed that I tried, with a certain amount of manipulation of linguistic terminology, to make a distinction between the Netherlands (Holland) and the Dutch people on the one hand, and the Dutch-speaking countries and the Dutch language on the other, but have, in the second half of this section, outlined the career and work of a theologian who was brought up and is still active in the Netherlands, the northern Dutch-speaking country. It will be clear, then, that our quest for the Catholic theology of the Dutch-speaking linguistic zone is not yet over.

The southern part of the Low Countries, in which Dutch (Flemish) is spoken, has for centuries been separated, not only politically, but also culturally and ecclesiastically, from the northern 'Protestant' federation of states and has in that time acquired a distinct character, to such an extent that the northern Dutchmen and the Flemish southerners have no difficulty in catching each other out. There are also considerable differences between the two countries in the theological sphere. Catholic theology has been able to develop more freely in Flanders and a completely distinctive scientific tradition has been represented by the University of Louvain since the time when it sent important theologians to the Council of Trent and formed the context within which de Bay and Jansen appeared, even though this tradition can hardly be regarded as belonging simply to the Dutch-speaking linguistic zone. In modern times, the theology of Louvain has been mainly concerned with a fundamental return to biblical, patristic and liturgical sources, but Louvain has also been the centre of important philosophical movements. A theologian whose work was praised by Rahner in 1953 is remarkable because he has succeeded in merging all these different elements into a new synthesis.

This theologian, Edward Schillebeeckx, is in many ways similar to Karl Rahner, his senior by ten years, but the resemblance is more in temperament and in their way of thinking (which can perhaps be explained in the light of

In Search of an Explanation in History

their shared interest in and application of philosophy) than in the direction taken by their ideas. Schillebeeckx also comes from a large family (he was born in Kortenberg, between Brussels and Louvain) and he also has an elder brother who is a Jesuit. He studied at the Jesuit college at Turnhout, but what was expected did not materialise. He did not become a Jesuit but a Dominican. In a frank confession later in a television interview, he said that he began, during his last years at this school, to react inwardly against the education he was receiving there, with its exclusively classical bias (English and German, for example, were not taught there as they are in similar schools in the Netherlands) and the strict emphasis on the training of will-power and on acting 'on principle'. In any case, it is clear now that there was no need for Schillebeeckx himself to be strengthened in this way—as soon as he undertakes a task, he forgets almost everything else, a quality of the mind which is responsible not only for the synthetic character of his thought and the dense, all-embracing style of his writings, but also for the instability of his health.

By joining the Dominican order, his ideas were led along a different track from those of Rahner. During his philosophical training, he became deeply and permanently interested in the anthropology of the philosopher D. de Petter, whose personal synthesis of the best of the Thomist tradition and modern phenomenology, especially that of Husserl, was, in certain essential respects, quite different from the philosophy of J. Maréchal, which provided the point of departure for Rahner's interpretation of Thomism. Schillebeeckx also spent several years in specialised study after the war in France and this resulted in two extremely important and lasting influences in his life. In the first place, when he was at Le Saulchoir, he came under the spell of Chenu's historical approach to theology and of his creative interpretation of Thomas. When he arrived, he was still looking forward to collaborating with de Petter in the sphere of philosophy, but his study of Chenu's programme resulted in an inner conversion to theology. In the second place, he gladly let himself be carried away by the dynamic tendency in the French Church to turn towards the world and spent a good deal of his time attending lectures in Paris, not only in historical theology and philosophy, but also in modern philosophical thought, existentialism and personalism. Since then, he has been more and more intensely preoccupied with the relationship between the Church and the world—a concrete transposition of the ancient problem of the relationship between the natural and the supernatural, the theme which he chose to discuss in his thesis. He had, however, to teach sacramental theology prematurely at Louvain, with the result that his work on the Church and the world had to wait for the time being and he graduated by writing an elaboration of this course.

De sacramentęle heilseconomie (*The Sacramental Economy of Salvation*), the book which attracted Rahner's attention in 1953, was, quite frankly, an event in the Catholic theology of the Dutch-speaking countries. Almost seven hundred pages in length, it was in fact only the first, more historical part of a much longer work. But this freshly conceived approach to the sacramental element in the Church as a dynamic reality undeniably had all the characteristics of a new beginning. Even more impressive than the unbelievably magnificent knowledge of the whole tradition of the Church which Schillebeeckx displayed in the book, from Scripture down to recent times, were his presentation and interpretation of this tradition and the part played by modern anthropological and personalistic thought in this. As though they had been set out in ordered lines by an invisible magnet, the many tendencies and counter-tendencies in the tradition of the Church were related in this book to the burning contemporary question of man's personal encounter with the God who has shown himself in Christ as someone who also plays a part in our world. In Schillebeeckx' interpretation, an important place was also given to Casel's theology of the cultic mystery, grafted on to the basic christological ideas of Thomas. The synthesis, which in 1957 was abbreviated and published as *Christus, sacrament van de Godsontmoeting*,[102] was at the same time an expression of a basic Christian datum that Schillebeeckx had rediscovered in Thomas and an expression of the Christian experience, sustained by the liturgical movement and directed towards man, with which he, as one who was responsible for guiding the Dominican students and as editor-in-chief of the *Tijdschrift voor Geestelijk Leven* (*Journal for the Spiritual Life*), remained closely in touch.

Schillebeeckx also established his theological programme with his first book. According to the introduction, it was explicitly intended by him to be used by students of theology as an alternative to the manuals of neo-scholasticism which had become so barren. He was well aware of the fact that the technical, scientific nature of his book would repel many students, but he believed that the problems facing the Church were only suppressed by facile language and popular treatment. Schillebeeckx was furthermore convinced that faith itself called for as complete an integration with man's spiritual life as possible and that this reflection had to remain as closely as it could in touch with the *whole* of tradition, in other words, even with those elements which had been 'pushed into the background of the consciousness of faith' by polemics in the Church.[103] This scientific theology, springing from the contemporary life of faith and in turn serving this life, would have to make its way in the world.

In addition to this 'course' on the sacraments, which was published more or less by chance, his teaching at the Dominican house of studies in Louvain resulted in similar and hardly less comprehensive and surprising treatises on the introduction to theology, creation, Christology and eschatology, which found their way every now and then into the outside world in the form of concise articles. Optimistic fellow Dominicans began to think in terms of a new *Summa*, but the author himself seriously doubted whether an all-embracing synthesis of this kind would ever be possible to achieve in the constantly changing modern world. In any case, his appointment to the University of Nijmegen, which was obtained with great energy at the end of 1957, when he was forty-three, ended such speculations for the time being at least.

Schillebeeckx, who as a Fleming tends to be not in the least formal, was accustomed to the easy-going atmosphere of Louvain and did not feel immediately at home in the Netherlands but, once he had managed to see through the game of playing the professor—which was not difficult for one with so open a personality—he soon found fresh inspiration in the rather cooler environment of the north. He also quickly learned that the Dutchman is a *homo theologicus* who seldom lets the opportunity to talk about his religion or the absence of it go by. He thus discovered new perspectives for his theology in many new personal contacts (which often make him forget everything else, as he does during study, which he often does at night). It was the scientific approach to all study at Louvain which had really kept him from the direct implications of 'ordinary' life for theology until his move to the Netherlands, where he learned increasingly to take human experience as his point of departure, even though he refused, despite this grafting on to the Dutch 'tradition', to make any concessions to the scientific method. This meant that he extended the field of his research to include the behavioural sciences as well.

Schillebeeckx' rapid adaptation to the situation in the Netherlands can be attributed both to the fact that he was intensely fascinated by the living questions with which he came into contact and to his personal defencelessness, which prevents him from saying 'no' directly to the many requests for lectures and articles, unless circumstances force him to do so, in which case he does refuse although only with many apologies. These countless invitations are, of course, clear evidence that his work and aims have been recognised in the Netherlands. There is further proof of this recognition—the incredible response to the *Tijdschrift voor Theologie*, the working formula for which he originated—it was to be a journal that would accompany, in a scientifically theological manner, the urgent problems of today. This journal and to some extent *Concilium* later, which adopted the same formula, are the only approximations to anything like a 'school' of Schillebeeckx, because he simply does not possess the organising skill of, for example, Rahner. His scientific approach has from time to time raised in the minds of many Dutchmen the suspicion of ideology, but this is usually quickly dispelled on personal contact with Schillebeeckx himself, who at once shows himself to be incapable of the cross-grained tenacity that characterises most native Dutchmen. He is, on the contrary, always ready to consider every reasonable objection to his argument, however unpromising it may at first sight be, and to correct, adjust or modify his own view in accordance with it. This readiness to accommodate has always reminded me personally of the same characteristic in Anton Bruckner, who was similarly always so willing to change his musical compositions. This is not, by the way, the only characteristic that they have in common—Schillebeeckx also shares Bruckner's splendid breadth of vision, his intensity and his uncomplicated 'southern' attitude. Many of his writings too have the 'resounding' quality of Bruckner's music and full justice can often only be done to the repetitions, full of subtle changes of emphasis, that they contain, when they are rendered oratorically. Whether this comparison is accepted or not, one thing is certain—the development to which Schillebeeckx submits his ideas is in many ways astonishing. He has received several offers to have a book written about himself, but so far has rejected all of them, because he would feel this to be a 'freezing over' of his possibilities. It is significant that, in his most recent work, he looks for the hermeneutic key which has, despite all the progress that has been made and will go on being made in the interpretation of the gospel, to ensure continuity.

Since coming to the Netherlands, he has undertaken one

more comprehensive synthesis like that in his first book—
Het huwelijk, aardse werkelijkheid en heilsmysterie,[104] the very
title of which indicates the two poles of his thought. Up to
the present, only the first and more historical part of this
work on marriage has appeared, but the basic thesis clearly
emerges in the analyses of the data—the human reality
which is marriage is itself the mystery of salvation; in what
it is itself, this highest form of human togetherness also
manifests God's turning towards man. His ability—so
reminiscent of Rahner and indeed of Thomas—to extract
the essential aspect of the Church's tradition in modern
interpretation is once again very much in evidence in this
work. This quality that characterises Schillebeeckx' work—
one which inspires a certain confidence—is the probable
reason why he has been protected from direct confrontation
with the Church for longer than Rahner. The authorities
in Rome are aware of his intimate knowledge of the whole
scholastic tradition and have tended to turn a blind eye
to certain elements in his work which they found difficult
to reconcile with the 'eternal truth'. Or, it may be that
the central authorities have relied on the isolation of the
Dutch language and the possible consequent isolation of
Schillebeeckx' writings, since, as soon as he began to acquire
an international reputation at the time of the Council, he
ceased to be invulnerable. On the other hand, however, he
is, because of his rather disconcerting optimism, often able
to draw attention to unsuspected brighter aspects in the
more recent negative documents emanating from Rome.
Like Rahner and—perhaps even more especially—like his
colleagues and fellow Dominicans in France, he is not afraid
to take on the increasingly unpopular task of realistically
defending the Christian tradition that is seeking expression
in the whole Church, even in those fields that are often
regarded as theologically underdeveloped. Schillebeeckx has
gladly assumed the Dutch practice of approaching the
problems of the Church and the world in a practical and
direct way, but his historical studies and his knowledge of so

many different traditions have made him permanently suspicious of any claim to hold a monopoly of truth, especially of the truth of faith.

Bibliography

The situation of German Catholicism since the war, to which that of Dutch Catholicism is very comparable, is considered from many points of view in *Catholicisme allemand*, volume 56 of the series 'Rencontres' (Paris 1956), but a more contemporary survey is presented in the German book edited by N. Greinacher and H.T. Risse and published in 1966, *Bilanz des deutschen Katholizismus*. Greinacher's essay, 'Auf dem Weg zur Gemeindekirche', and Walter Dirks' contribution, 'Ein "anderer" Katholizismus', are especially worth reading. C. Amery's animated argument in his book, *Capitulation: an Analysis of Contemporary Catholicism* (London 1967; original ed. Reinbek and Hamburg 1964), can be felt in the background in almost all studies of the German situation. His argument has met with general agreement in its broad outlines. A very comprehensive survey of theology in the German-speaking countries, especially during the period that preceded the Council, is provided in *Fragen der Theologie heute* (Einsiedeln 1957). The French translation is *Questions theologiques d'aujourdhui*, Bruges and Paris 1964—; an American translation was started in 1965 under the title *Theology Today* (Milwaukee, Wis.). The German theology of renewal has become so extensive since the end of the Second World War that, in all justice, for the pre-conciliar period the reader must be referred to this comprehensive survey, which was the work of many scholars, and to the various portraits given in *Tendenzen der Theologie im 20. Jahrhundert* (see bibliography, p. 21), since I am prevented by lack of space from doing more than simply giving a brief outline of the life and work of a few dominant figures.

A book has been written about Karl Rahner by H.

Vorgrimler, a theologian who has collaborated with him for many years now: *Karl Rahner: his Life, Thought and Work* (London 1963). The French adaptation of this book which Vorgrimler prepared with C. Muller and which was published in Paris in 1965 is rather more substantial. J.B. Metz' creative interpretation in *Tendenzen* (*op. cit.*) is indispensable to an understanding of Rahner. Metz' essay had already appeared in a rather longer form in a commemorative collection in two volumes for Rahner entitled *Gott in Welt* (Freiburg 1964), which also included the 'Eucharisticon fratris' by Hugo Rahner and an enormous bibliography with a thematic index. One should also consult C. Ernst's introduction to his translation of Rahner's *Theological Investigations* I (London and Baltimore 1961).

As introductory reading of Rahner's own work, I would suggest, apart from the studies discussed later, 'Prospects for Dogmatic Theology' and 'A Scheme for a Treatise of Dogmatic Theology' in *Theological Investigations* I, the article 'Exegesis and Dogmatic Theology' in *Theological Investigations* V or one of his articles on 'contemporary' themes in *Mission and Grace*, 3 volumes, London 1963—. Most of his articles in German have been or will be published in one of the volumes of *Schriften zur Theologie*, Einsiedeln 1954—(E. tr. *Theological Investigations*). His *Kleines Theologisches Wörterbuch* (Freiburg 1961), which was written in collaboration with H. Vorgrimler and was published in an English translation as *Concise Theological Dictionary* (London 1965), provides a good insight into Rahner's ideas on many different subjects. In the smaller works of Rahner the English translation is not always trustworthy.

There is not much background literature dealing with Dutch theology. For those who can handle the language, some information can be obtained from A. Weiler's contribution 'The Netherlands' in the *New Catholic Encyclopedia*, X. The more recent developments are described in *Les catholiques hollandais* (Desclée De Brouwer 1969), which includes an interview with E. Schillebeeckx on theology. I would recommend several penetrating essays by W. Grossouw which have been collected together in his *Een overlevende uit de voortijd* (Hilversum 1967), and an article by W. van der Marck, 'Van orthodoxie naar vrijzinnigheid?' in *Annalen van het Thijmgenootschap* (54) 1966, p. 332 ff. Dutch theology itself can be caught wild, as it were, in annual volumes of the *Werkgenootschap van Katholieke Theologen in Nederland*, published by Gooi & Sticht of Hilversum, in the journal *Studia Catholica*, which was remodelled into the *Tijdschrift voor Theologie* in 1961, and in *Bijdragen*. Both the latter have Flemish as well as Dutch editors and summaries of the main articles in a major language. Information about Schoonenberg can only be found here and there, for example in his contribution in *Crucial Questions* (New York 1969). The general direction of his theology can be sampled by reading his *God's World in the Making* (Dublin 1965) and *Man and Sin: a Theological View* (London and Notre Dame U.S.A. 1965).

An idea can be gained of the ancient and fertile tradition of Louvain University by consulting the *New Catholic Encyclopaedia*, VIII, under 'Louvain', a contribution by V. Denis. A penetrating portrait has been published of Schillebeeckx in *Tendenzen* (*op. cit.*), written by B.A. Willems, and M.J. Houdijk has provided a more extensive account in *Modern Theologians: Christians and Jews* (see bibliography, p. 21). No complete bibliography has yet been published of either Schoonenberg's or Schillebeeckx' writings. A good introduction to Schillebeeckx' pre-conciliar theology will be found in 'The New Trends in Present-Day Dogmatic Theology', *The Concept of Truth and Theological Renewal*, London and Sydney 1968, pp. 106–154. Another possible introduction to Schillebeeckx' writings of about ten years ago will be found in the second volume of his collected articles, *God and Man* (London and Sydney 1969)—the two chapters 'God in Dry Dock' (1959) and 'The Search for the Living God', which is his inaugural speech at Nijmegen, first published in 1958.

Results of a Hundred Years of Neo-Scholasticism

Anyone who looks back at the development of Catholic theology since the early nineteenth century and tries to compile a balance sheet of the new impulses that have emerged during this time will certainly not be able to ignore one constantly recurring pattern. The most characteristic aspect of this development has not been that the pressure of concrete experience in the world and the Church has forced Catholic theologians to leave the well-trodden paths and to search in Scripture and the Church's tradition, in the theology of the other Christian Churches and in the writings of philosophers and others who have analysed contemporary human experience in order to make God's word heard again within this adapted context. This is certainly a regular pattern in theology as a whole, but it has not characterised Catholic theology. One could, indeed, point to typical variations in emphasis which are connected with the direction taken by the Catholic tradition as a whole. In the first place, greater importance seems to be attached to the tradition of the Church, especially with regard to the liturgy and the decisions of the Church's teaching office. Moreover, the Catholic tradition is more optimistic towards human thought and seems somewhat over-confident in its attitude towards the theology of the Reformed Churches. And, of course, it is possible to point to many different gradations in the common theological attitude within the whole tradition of the Catholic Church. I have, for example, already spoken in passing about the difference between German thoroughness and French clarity and impetuosity in theology. But I cannot pretend that all this constitutes an essential variant in Christian theology as a whole. If I have outlined in some detail both the context of the world and the Church and the theologians' response to this context as well as their personal reactions, which ultimately determine the character of this response, I have done this principally in order to demonstrate both the fact that Catholic theology has become increasingly open to the appeal of man's constantly changing experience, and the manner in which it has so become. I am convinced that the same questions have been and are still being asked in Catholic circles and also that the direction in which Catholic theologians have been looking for an answer has not been essentially different from the direction in which Christian theologians in general have been seeking. In this context, the question as to whether theologians have been acting as the prophetic pace-makers or whether they themselves have been impelled forward by members of the Church at the home front—or rather, perhaps, by active cells on that front—can really be left open. It often seems as though it is a result of interaction between these two groups.

If the credit balance in favour of a creative Catholic theology was less towards the end of the nineteen-fifties than had been anticipated and in any case below the level achieved by the greatest Protestant theologians, this would seem to be attributable to a factor which is indeed characteristic of the Catholic tradition but which in its effects is determined by historical circumstances or, one might even say, by chance events. Certain patterns to which I have pointed in the foregoing accounts may well have given rise to the expectation that this factor would have to be defined, quite summarily, as the functioning of the Church's teaching authority. But this would be too easy a way of localising responsibility and there is, after all, little point in simplifying the issue and making yet another attack on this much abused scapegoat. In view of the historical facts, however, it is very difficult to avoid taking this 'authority' (which, in its all too abstract form, is a safe alibi both for protagonists and for antagonists!) into account, if only as a key-word in the discussion. But, whenever this is done, further shades of meaning and emphases must be distinguished.

It is, for instance, possible to show that many of the themes developed in the theology of renewal have found the way into official documents of the Church, especially during the pontificate of Pius XI and the first part of the pontificate of Pius XII—themes such as the theology of the laity, the theology of the Church and her liturgy, and so on. Although it did not take place without some official restraint, biblical, patristic and liturgical studies were able to develop from apologetics and 'archeology' into theology and even speculative theology was also allowed to develop quite freely in many spheres. If, however, the official use in the Church of these adopted ideas is examined more closely and their obvious adaptation to the prevailing theology is observed, then it becomes all the more necessary to distinguish, as I have said above, further shades of meaning and emphases in the key-phrase 'teaching authority'. The factor to which the laborious progress of the theology of renewal can be attributed is not, on closer inspection, the *magisterium* as a regulating function within the Church and not even the historical, political concretisation of this function in the juridically determined institution of the Church, even though the coolness and the secrecy of this institution have caused much more personal unhappiness and suffering than has ever been described or even known and probably much more than the individuals working within this institution have ever been aware of or intended. No, the restraining factor is attributable to the fatal alliance between this teaching authority and neo-scholasticism, and even this statement has to be narrowed down—neo-scholasticism has not acted as a restraining factor so much because of its formal position of monopoly within the Church's thinking, a position from which any competition that might arise has been repressed (though it can hardly be disputed that this has frequently played a part), but rather because, as the system of thought which has in fact become inextricably involved with the tradition of the Church in recent years, it has hardly been able to regard any other possible approaches to the reality of faith as anything other than heresies.

History is to a very great extent responsible for this alliance between the teaching office of the Catholic Church and neo-scholasticism. The Church embodied scholastic theology in her definitions of dogma in the Middle Ages, when scholasticism was a distinctively modern mode of thought. By the time of the Council of Trent, however, scholasticism had fallen behind the development of the Church and the world and, in the centuries that followed the Council, it underwent drastic changes which resulted in its becoming a system of concepts alien to reality. Influenced by the polemics of the Reformation, however, the Church— in this instance, the Church as a whole and not simply the teaching office of the Church—began to regard this system as the incarnation of divine revelation guaranteed by the Church's infallibility and valid for ever. Later, especially in the nineteenth century, the unchangeable character of the Church's formulations came to be questioned more and more insistently in the light of historical study and of the historical experience of reality and the teaching office of the Church could only regard this as a direct frontal attack which had to be countered by a large-scale reinforcement of the old and somewhat ruinous positions. This was, in its essence, the origin of the modern neo-scholastic movement with its polemical bias. As it functioned within the fortress of the Church erected by Pius IX, it could hardly react to any theological system or idea which contradicted it in any other way than with indignant denial or rejection. The documents of the Church had, after all, used the language and the concepts of scholasticism for centuries and these had been sanctioned by many councils. The neo-scholastic theory of knowledge, lacking a sensitivity to time or history, could not place development or adaptation except within the logical relationships of formalised scholastic concepts.

The theologians who aimed at renewal had therefore to try to make their efforts acceptable to a teaching authority which believed firmly that this system of theological concepts was identical with the revelation of Christ, and which knew itself to be as one in this identification of a system of thought and revelation with the overwhelming majority in the

Church, in which 'confusion' was not to be allowed to prevail. These theologians of renewal thus had to show both that they too were fully part of the Church's traditional system of thinking and that they had not lost continuity with the gospel of Christ. In order to do this, they had to direct their attention to several aspects of the neo-scholastic system in particular. They went back to forgotten but indisputable elements of tradition which expressed a different interpretation of the gospel, demonstrating especially the extent to which basic data such as revelation, faith and tradition had been narrowed down in neo-scholasticism to concepts which were regarded as static, treated as things and almost separated from Christian experience. Over and against this, they stressed the whole traditional, dynamic and personal content of Christian experience and based a theology which was directed towards reality on this foundation—this is the background to the great part played by fundamental theology or 'apologetics' in the period that I have been describing. At the same time, these theologians developed a more sensitive insight into man's process of knowing in order to be able to convince the teaching authority of the Church that a departure from the neo-scholastic theory of knowledge with its emphasis on concepts and a relativisation of the concepts of faith that had become sanctioned by the Church did not necessarily imply relativism or a faithless betrayal of God's word. They above all tried to demonstrate that there is a dynamic form of continuity in man's knowing (and believing) and that only a recognition of this fact could do justice to the development of knowledge, experience and faith in the Church throughout the centuries.

This common basis of all attempts to renew Catholic theology certainly deserves to be considered separately at least in broad outline, as it is only in this way that light can be thrown on the precise and characteristic function within the Catholic Church of the teaching authority in the development of theology. It will already have become clear that this function is not only active in the case of the 'authority' of the

Church, for the theologians of renewal have, in principle, been clearly aware of the need to let themselves be guided and to let the free development of their ideas be ultimately corrected by the teaching office of the Church. This has, of course, led to great tensions, since both the Church's teaching authority, with its close ties with the neo-scholastic system, and the theologians of renewal have regarded their views as the representation of God's authentic revelation and thus as the essence of their personal relationship with God. All the same, the theologians who were looking for new ways of expressing the central elements of revelation, faith and tradition recognised the indispensable need to make their inner conviction acceptable to the teaching authority by a more and more subtly shaded presentation of their point of view. When it became apparent that this could not be done successfully from a position outside that of neo-scholasticism—the failure of the modernist movement is an example of this—an attempt was made to do it by going back to the sources of scholasticism itself. This dripping on the stone seems to have had an effect in the long run—eventually a change took place and again it was the Church's teaching office which brought it about, when this ultimately came to accept the direction in which the theologians of renewal had been moving and when the *magisterium* of the Church finally terminated its exclusive contract with neo-scholasticism at the Second Vatican Council.

NOTES

[1]See *The Critic* (XXV 6), June/July 1967, 5.

[2]'Falsa, temeraria, in scholas catholicas iniuriosa, debitae Apostolicis Constitutionibus oboedientiae derogans', Denz. 2679 (1579).

[3]See B. Welte, *Auf der Spur des Ewigen*, Freiburg 1965, 385.

[4]See O. Chadwick (who has preserved the curious verb *schleiermacherianisieren*), *From Bossuet to Newman*, Cambridge 1957, 110.

[5]'Im Rückspiegel der historischen Betrachtung nahe zusammentreten', L. Scheffczyk, *Theologie in Aufbruch und Widerstreit*, Bremen 1965, xxx.

[6]Quoted in A.R. Vidler, *The Church in an Age of Revolution* (Pelican History of the Church, volume 5), Harmondsworth 1961, 148.

[7]'Romanus Pontifex potest ac debet cum progressu, cum liberalismo et cum recenti civilitate sese reconciliare et componere', Praepositio 80, Denz. 2980 (1780).

[8]See A.R. Vidler, *The Church in an Age of Revolution, op. cit.*, 153.

[9]In this context, R. Aubert names two bishops, Mgr Bertaud and Mgr Mermillod; see *Le pontificat de Pie IX (1848–1878)*, vol. 21 in the series 'Histoire de l'Église' edited by A. Fliche and V. Martin, Paris 1952, 302–3; see also A.R. Vidler, *The Church in an Age of Revolution, op. cit.*, 154.

[10]See Wilfred Ward, *William George Ward and the Catholic Revival*, London and New York 1893, 14.

[11]J.D. Mansi, *Sacrorum conciliorum nova et amplissima collectio*, Florence etc. vol. 49, 10, 1757 f.

[12]J.D. Mansi, *op. cit.*, vol. 50, 166.

[13]See B. Welte, *Auf der Spur des Ewigen, op. cit.*, 395.

[14]'... Theologie des Trotzdem ... nicht ohne Nervosität bewahrten Orthodoxie'; see B. Welte, *op. cit.*, 397.

[15]Quoted by E. Poulat, *Histoire, dogme et critique dans la crise moderniste*, Tournai 1962, 205.

[16]Quoted from a letter by Kleutgen to the rector of the Germanicum in Rome, Gries. This revelation clearly applied in the first place to Günther and his school, but, in view of the date (6 June 1875), it also has a wider application. The quotation was unearthed by P. Wenzel, *Das wissenschaftliche Anliegen des Güntherianismus*, Essen 1961, p. 47, footnote 9. See also L. Scheffczyk, *Theologie in Aufbruch und Widerstreit, op. cit.*, 317.

[17]See J.J.I. von Döllinger, *Kleinere Schriften*, edited by F.H. Reusch, Stuttgart 1890, 184.

[18]Denz. 2912–2913 (1712–1713): 'Apostolicae Sedis Romanarumque Congregationum decreta liberum scientiae progressum impediunt.'

[19]'Den dogmatischen Stoff mit echter kritischer geläuterter Geschichte und philosophischer Spekulation verbinden'; von Döllinger, *Kleinere Schriften, op. cit.*, 194.

[20]O. Chadwick, *From Bossuet to Newman, op. cit.*, 111.

[21]A.R. Vidler, *The Modernist Movement in the Roman Church, op. cit.*, 54.

[22]'Un charactère naturellement timoré, ... une préoccupation excessive des jugements d'autrui'; *Mémoire à Monsieur R., Carnets intimes I*, Paris 1961, 549.

[23]See M. Seckler, *Tendenzen der Theologie im 20. Jahrhundert*, Stuttgart and Olten 1966, 76; see also *Carnets intimes I, op. cit.*, 551: 'What I really want to do is to present the gospel to contemporary man, to reply to the criticism that Catholic thought is sterile, to draw from the gospel the new light that is always present in it, to assimilate the unknown nourishment that it contains for the sake of coming generations and to derive a new human richness from its divine abundance . . .'

[24]'La pensée moderne avec une susceptibilité jalouse considère la notion *d'immanence* comme la condition même de la philosophie . . . rien ne peut entrer en l'homme qui ne sorte de lui et ne corresponde en quelque façon à un besoin d'expansion'; Lettre sur les exigences de la pensée contemporaine en matière d'apologétique, *Les premiers écrits de Maurice Blondel*, Paris 1956, 34.

[25]H. Duméry, 'Maurice Blondel', Portraits I, *Les grands courants de la pensée mondiale contemporaine*, edited by M.F. Sciacca, Paris 1961, 172.

[26]'La substance de l'homme, c'est l'action; il est ce qu'il se fait': J. Lacroix, *Maurice Blondel, sa vie, son oeuvre*, Paris 1963, 20.

[27]See H. Duméry, *Les grands courants, op. cit.*, 173.

[28]See T. Rendtorff, *Tendenzen der Theologie im 20. Jahrhundert, op. cit.*, 46.

[29]This prophecy was made by the Bishop of Poitiers, Mgr Pie; see A.R. Vidler, *The Modernist Movement in the Roman Church, op. cit.*, 30.

[30]'Ainsi je m'instruisais à son école, dans l'espoir de lui prouver un jour que tout ce qu'il y avait de vrai dans sa science était compatible avec le catholicisme sainement compris', A. Loisy, *Mémoires* I (1857–1900), Paris 1930, 118.

[31]See R. Aubert, *Le pontificat de Pie IX, op. cit.*, 498. The quotation is from D. Ferrata, *Mémoires*, I, Rome 1920, 32–3.

[32]See H. Duméry, *Les grands courants, op. cit.*, 144.

[33]A. Houtin, *La question biblique chez les catholiques de France au XIXe siècle*, Paris 1902.

[34]'Der unendliche Wert der Menschenseele'; see A. von Harnack, *Das Wesen des Christentums*, Munich and Hamburg 1964, 49.

[35]See A.R. Vidler, *The Modernist Movement in the Roman Church, op. cit.*, 99–101.

[36]'. . . ne sont pas des vérités tombées du ciel et gardées par la tradition religieuse dans la forme précise où elles ont paru d'abord'; A. Loisy, *L'Évangile et l'Église*, Paris 1902, 200.

[37]'Nous nous sommes enfermés dans un coin perdu d'un pays désert, où nous nous croyons imprenables parce qu'on ne s'occupe pas de nous et qu'on ne nous connaît pas'; quoted by E. Poulat, *Histoire, dogme et critique dans la crise moderniste, op. cit.*, 205.

[38]See *Au coeur de la crise moderniste*, edited by R. Marlé, Paris 1960, 96. In addition to this not entirely representative selection of letters, see also the extensive summary by E. Poulat, *Histoire, dogme et critique dans la crise moderniste, op. cit.*, 513–619, and the recent article by H. Bernard-Maitre, 'Un épisode significatif du modernisme. "Histoire et dogme" de Maurice Blondel d'après les papiers inédits d'Alfred Loisy (1897–1905)', *Recherches de science religieuse* (57) 1969, 49–74.

[39]A.R. Vidler, *Twentieth Century Defenders of the Faith*, London 1965, 38–9.

⁴⁰*Ibid.*, 46; see also A.R. Vidler, *The Modernist Movement in the Roman Church, op. cit.*, 180 ff.

⁴¹See *Autobiography and Life of George Tyrrell* I, arranged and supplemented by M.D. Petre, London 1912, 156.

⁴²G. Tyrrell, *Through Scylla and Charybdis*, London 1907, 311.

⁴³'Omnium haereseon collectum esse affirmemus'; see note 46 below.

⁴⁴A.R. Vidler, *Twentieth Century Defenders of the Faith, op. cit.*, 37.

⁴⁵A.R. Vidler, *The Church in an Age of Revolution, op. cit.*, 189.

⁴⁶'... Trahat ad ... religionem omnem abolendam. Equidem protestantium error primus hac via gradum iecit; sequitur medoernistarum error; proxime atheismus ingredietur.' In the official editions of the encyclical, this quotation, together with the other quotation given above ('omnium haereseon collectum esse affirmemus'), is to be found in art. 39. A fascinating historical and theological comment could be written about the gradual disappearance of *Pascendi* from the quasi-official collection, the 'manual' of Denzinger. The edition of 1913 (the 12th, compiled by C. Bannwart), contains both the quotations mentioned (no. 2105 and 2109). The 20th edition, compiled in 1932 by J.B. Umberg, omits no. 2105 ('omnium haereseon collectum'), but the 25th, again compiled by Umberg, in 1948, includes it again. In the entirely new version by A. Schönmetzer (the 32nd edition of 1963), there are, of the thirty-four or so pages of the 1913 edition, only about seven left, and both of the quotations referred to above are left out. And this edition was prepared for publication before the Second Vatican Council.

⁴⁷See A.R. Vidler, *The Modernist Movement in the Roman Church, op. cit.*, 212 and 222.

⁴⁸See J. Rivière, *Le modernisme dans l'Église*, Paris 1929, 416 ff.

⁴⁹Veremundus (Karl Muth's pseudonym), *Steht die katholische Belletristik auf der Höhe der Zeit?* Mainz 1898.

⁵⁰'... Zähe, unauflässliche Fleiss'; see V. Berning, *Das Denken Herman Schells*, Essen 1964, 1.

⁵¹See W. Spael, *Das katholische Deutschland im 20. Jahrhundert*, Würzburg 1964, 163 ff.

⁵²See E. Przywara, 'Le mouvement théologique et religieux en Allemagne', *Nouvelle Revue Théologique* (56) 1929, 565 f.: 'Bewegung' and 'Wesen'.

⁵³'Die Rückkehr des deutschen Katholizismus aus dem Exil', *Kölnische Volkszeitung*, 21 and 22 May 1924; see also Spael, *Das katholische Deutschland im 20. Jahrhundert, op. cit.*, 260.

⁵⁴See C. Bilo, *Romano Guardini* (no. 13 in the series 'Denkers over God en Wereld'), Tielt and The Hague 1965, 21.

⁵⁵See F. Heiler, 'Zum Tode von Karl Adam', *Theologische Quartalschrift* (146) Tübingen 1966, 259.

⁵⁶See R. Aubert, *Le problème de la foi*, Louvain 1945, 532 ff.

⁵⁷F. Heiler, *Der Katholizismus, seine Idee und seine Erscheinung*, Munich 1923.

⁵⁸E. Przywara, 'Situation und Aufgabe im deutschen Gegenwartskatholizismus', *Stimmen der Zeit* (120) 1931, 166–167. This speech given on the Katholikentag of 1930 (4 September in Münster) has been republished in broad outline in E. Przywara, *Katholische Krise*, Düsseldorf 1967, in the essay entitled 'Der Ruf von heute', 89–105.

⁵⁹See H.J. Neuman, *Arthur Seyss-Inquart*, Utrecht 1967, 39–40, 240.

In Search of an Explanation in History 155

⁶⁰A summary of Archbishop Gröber's complaint can be found in H. Vorgrimler, *Karl Rahner: his Life, Thought and Work*, London 1963, 32 ff. A French summary is also provided in a review of the German liturgical movement in the French liturgical journal *La Maison-Dieu* (7) 1946. In addition to other documents, there is also Cardinal Innitzer's more optimistic and personal reply.

⁶¹See H. Vorgrimler, *Karl Rahner, op. cit.*, 34.

⁶²Y. Congar, *Dialogue between Christians* (no. 50 in the series 'Unam Sanctam') E. tr. P. Loretz, London and Dublin 1966, 32.

⁶³See *Informations catholiques internationales* (233) 1 Feb. 1965, 30.

⁶⁴*Une école de théologie*, Etiolles 1937. The main chapter of this book has been included in Chenu's *La foi dans l'intelligence*, Paris 1969, 243–68.

⁶⁵See *Informations catholiques internationales, op. cit.*, 29.

⁶⁶J.P. Jossua, *Le père Congar*, Paris 1967, 43–44.

⁶⁷'J'aime l'Angleterre, même si je m'y ennuie assez vite'; Y. Congar, *Chrétiens en dialogue* (E. tr. *Dialogue between Christians*, 16, 44).

⁶⁸See *Dialogue between Christians, op. cit.*, 19.

⁶⁹*Ibid.*, 21.

⁷⁰*Ibid.*, 45.

⁷¹J. P. Jossua, *Le père Congar, op. cit.*, 92–3.

⁷²'La nouvelle théologie où va-t-elle?', *Angelicum* (23) 1946, 126–45. In a later number of the journal, a dignified letter was published from the eighty-five-year-old Blondel, protesting against the distortion of his ideas and the suspicion of heterodoxy; see *Angelicum* (24) 1947, 210–11.

⁷³See H. Rahner, 'Wege zu einer "neuen" Theologie?', *Orientierung* (11) 1947, 214–15.

⁷⁴B. de Solages, 'Pour l'honneur de la théologie', *Bulletin de littérature ecclésiastique* (48) 1947, 65–84; see also J. Comblin, *Vers une théologie de l'action*, Brussels 1964, 49.

⁷⁵M. Labourdette, 'La théologie et ses sources', *Revue Thomiste* (46) 1946, 353–71.

⁷⁶H. de Lubac, *Histoire et Esprit. L'intelligence de l'Écriture d'après Origène* (no. 50 in the series 'Théologie'), Paris 1950, 13 ff.

⁷⁷'La théologie et ses sources. Réponse', *Recherches de science religieuse* (33) 1946, 390. In the later edition of the article published in *Dialogue théologique*, Saint-Maximin, Var, 1947, which also contains other essays by protagonists and antagonists, the quotation will be found on p. 81.

⁷⁸See J.M. Connolly, *The Voices of France*, New York 1961, 183.

⁷⁹See B. de Solages, *Bulletin de littérature ecclésiastique, op. cit.*, 135 and, as a criticism, M. Labourdette, *Revue Thomiste*, 1946, *op. cit.*, 371; *Dialogue théologique, op. cit.*, 62 f.

⁸⁰Garrigou-Lagrange, *Angelicum, op. cit.*, 126.

⁸¹See, for example, P. Teilhard de Chardin, *L'apparition de l'homme*, Oeuvres 2, Paris 1956, 362.

⁸²In a letter to G. Fessard dated 16 May 1936, he wrote of the work sent with the letter: 'Je m'y promène comme un éléphant dans les plates-bandes les mieux ratissées de la scholastique'; quoted in P. Grenet, *Teilhard de Chardin, un évolutionniste chrétien*, Paris 1961, 145.

[83]'désespérante sagesse'; quoted in C. Cuénot, *Pierre Teilhard de Chardin*, Paris 1958, 16.
[84]See P. Smulders, *The Design of Teilhard de Chardin*, New York and Westminster Md., n.d., 13.
[85]See the *Osservatore Romano* of 4 Dec. 1948 and 30 Jan. 1949. This incident was described by T. Deman in 'Tentatives françaises pour un renouvellement de la théologie; *Revue de l'Université d'Ottawa*, 1950, 138.
[86]See H. Engelmann and F. Ferrier, *Romano Guardini*, Paris 1966, 19.
[87]J. Matthes, *Die Emigration der Kirche aus der Gesellschaft*, Hamburg 1964.
[88]A. Kolping, *Katholische Theologie gestern und heute*, Bremen 1964, 220 and 228. The author is referring here to Guardini's *Das Ende der Neuzeit*, Würzburg 1950.
[89]'Geschichte und Geschichtserkenntnis im Geist der thomistischer Metaphysik'; see H. Rahner, 'Eucharisticon fratris', *Gott in Welt*, II (Festschrift Karl Rahner), Freiburg 1964, 897.
[90]T. Perez, *18 Propulsores del concilio*, Bilbao 1966, 16.
[91]C. Muller and H. Vorgrimler, *Karl Rahner*, Paris 1965, 13. Cf. also H. Vorgrimler, *Karl Rahner*, London 1963, 19.
[92]See the interview with Rahner in the *American Ecclesiastical Review* (153) 1965, 221.
[93]See *Geist in Welt*, Munich, 2nd ed. 1957, page 14 where the original introduction to the Innsbruck edition of 1939 has been reprinted: E. tr. *Spirit in the World*, London and Sydney 1968, lii.
[94]See *Zeitschrift für katholische Theologie* (63) 1939, 443-4.
[95]H. Vorgrimler, *Karl Rahner*, op. cit. 34 ff.
[96]See the *American Ecclesiastical Review*, op. cit., 219.
[97]See C. Muller and H. Vorgrimler, *Karl Rahner*, op. cit., 50.
[98]See J.B. Metz, *Tendenzen der Theologie im 20. Jahrhundert*, op. cit., 515.
[99]J.B. Metz, ibid., 517.
[100]See K. Rahner, *Zeitschrift für katholische Theologie* (75) 1953, 235.
[101]See J. Rivière, *Le modernisme dans l'Eglise*, op. cit., 70-71; see also L.J. Rogier and N. de Rooy, *In vrijheid herboren*, The Hague 1953, 519 f.
[102]*Christ the Sacrament of Encounter with God*, London and New York 1963.
[103]E. Schillebeeckx, *De sacramentele heilseconomie* I, Antwerp 1952, vi.
[104]E. Schillebeeckx, *Marriage: Secular Reality and Saving Mystery*, I: Marriage in the Old and New Testaments; II: Marriage in the History of the Church, London and Melbourne 1965.

FREEDOM FOR A NEW UNDERSTANDING OF THE GOSPEL

Only Via a Side-Road

In his very readable chapter on the 'pathology' of Catholicism ('Pathologie des katholischen Christentums') in his *Handbuch der Pastoraltheologie*, a book that is strongly marked by the ideas of Karl Rahner, A. Görres discusses, among other things, the gradual distortion of the Catholic principle of tradition. The content of the gospel as handed down in the Church has come to be too easily identified with the concrete forms which it has assumed in the Church in the course of history and these forms are regarded as guaranteed by the Church's 'infallibility'. As a result the normative power of what already exists in fact in the Church has become so firmly rooted in the Church's consciousness that anything new is regarded as a suspect who has to prove his innocence beyond all doubt. This became clear especially after the Reformation, with its accompanying polemics. The *via moderna* in thinking and 'modern devotion' were regarded as positive factors until the end of the Middle Ages, but the terms 'modernism' and 'new' theology were, in the recent past, only used by those who opposed them and were expressly avoided by their advocates.[1]

When viewed in this light, it is not really surprising, at least at first sight, that any quest for theological ideas about the right of a new understanding of the gospel to exist in the Catholic Church produces very meagre results. There is undoubtedly an element of truth in the witticism that the

Catholic theologian studies for many years to discover something new and then goes on studying for at least the same number of years to prove that what he has discovered is not new at all. Given the structure of the Church as it was until the very recent past, there could scarcely have been any other possibility. The modernists and, far more hesitantly, the supporters of the 'new' theology explicitly raised the question of pluriformity in theology, although at first they did so very cautiously and principally in order to defend themselves against official criticism from the Church. In both cases, an encyclical soon put an end to their hopes, expressing the view that the traditional system of thought, neo-scholasticism, had to be maintained, and offering very little latitude indeed within this rigid framework.

In spite of this, some Catholic theologians were compelled, by their experience of the world and the Church, to undertake a renewal of their field of study and we have, in the preceding sections of this book, briefly examined their aims and achievements within the context of various attempts to renew the Church. Although they were not able to obtain permission to put up entirely new edifices of the kind put up by Barth, Bultmann, Tillich and later Pannenberg on the other side of the confessional boundary, they were able to carry out a valuable service in planning and undertaking certain smaller structural alterations in the old house of scholastic theology, some of which were hardly noticeable from the outside. If they were called upon to answer for this, they tried to give as realistic a report as possible about the urgent need for such limited adaptation, usually calling what they had done 'restoration', which it often was to a great extent. Anyone wishing to trace the search made by Catholic theologians for freedom for a new interpretation of the gospel, which is all that we are really concerned with here, might analyse the way in which the alterations which were in fact made came about and compare, one with another, the various ways in which these were justified and the official point of view of the Church. I have tried in the preceding sections to focus on this process at least in its broad outline, but the very many themes involved in this process would make it almost impossible to narrow it down to the more retrospective summary that I aim to provide in the remaining part of this book.

For this purpose, it ought to be enough to limit our excavation to a sample trench with perhaps a single side channel—the most promising being the theme of the development of dogma. I choose this theme because this question seems to present us at once with such fundamental concepts as revelation, faith, Scripture, tradition, the Church and the Church's teaching authority and above all with the factor of history, a factor which has fascinated theologians since the beginning of the nineteenth century—many of them specialised in historical theology. These are the central aspects of the theme of the development of dogma. On closer inspection, all these basic elements that I have mentioned are in fact discussed in the context of the search for freedom of movement in theology and both problems often merge into each other almost imperceptibly—for example, in the case of modernism. Anyone who has once recognised the factor of historicity in the development of dogma would certainly be very naïve if he were to assume that this development suddenly ceased at a definite point of time in the past. It would therefore appear that Catholic theologians have also tended to regard the debate about the development of dogma as a kind of test case in which the chances that any 'new' theology might have of success could be tentatively measured by discussing analogous situations which raised less resistance, either because they were not 'new' or because they were more readily acceptable to the experience of the Church. An example of this latter category is the dogma of the Assumption of Mary. Development could, of course, also be traced via the constantly changing views about the whole structure of theology and this is especially noticeable in the increasing unity between historical and speculative theology. A fairly strong magnifying glass, however, is needed to observe this and it is probably advisable therefore simply to refer to this question from time to time in passing.

The problem of the development of dogma has, in any case, led to one of the most obvious trials of strength that have taken place between neo-scholasticism and a new theological approach. It was precisely in connection with the development of dogma that neo-scholasticism was confronted with almost insuperable difficulties, yet it was the neo-scholastic version of the draft constitution on revelation which was presented to the Fathers of the Second Vatican Council. The dramatic rejection of this draft during the first session of the Council marked a definite turning-point. After this, Catholic theologians used the material that had been accumulated in connection with the question of the development of dogma in their attempts to formulate explicit 'rules' for man's new, contemporary and developing understanding of the gospel which might assure their due parts both to man's contemporary experience and to the continuity of Christ's message within the community of the Church.

The Unchanging Truth

As a theological problem, the development of dogma is ultimately based on certain fundamental data shared by all the Christian Churches although the emphasis, of course, varies in each case—that our faith has a certain content of truths or judgements about reality which are expressed in human terms, that God's revelation took place within a clearly defined period of time and in a historical situation which is now past, that later Christian tradition has nonetheless accepted elements of truth which are, in comparison with the original revelation, clearly new or different and which consequently give rise to questions about their continuity with the gospel. In the narrower sense, however, the development of dogma is a typically Roman Catholic problem—the characteristic concepts of infallibility and of development of dogma make the question particularly urgent. As the Protestant theologian, H.M. Kuitert, has said, the Catholic Church has to re-interpret, but Reformed Christianity can go further and re-formulate, re-opening superseded or faulty doctrinal decisions.[2] The infallibility which the Catholic Church claims with such conviction and the emphasis given to this infallibility in clearly defined pronouncements by the Church's teaching office would seem to place that Church in a very vulnerable position, especially since she also believes that God's revelation came definitively to an end when the direct followers of Christ died and that the holy Spirit only calls to mind and elucidates what has already been proclaimed by Jesus, but what those who heard him directly 'could not bear'. The official interpretations of Christ's gospel which the Church has laid down in certain cases—a clear example of this is the very 'factual' pronouncements that the Church has made concerning Mary—must therefore be consistent with the gospel and with each other. If they are not, the Church would, so to speak, be able to catch the holy Spirit out in making mistakes.

This emerged most clearly when, during the post-Reformation period especially, the Catholic Church presented 'faith' more and more as a form of knowing, as an acceptance of a number of truths which were not open to human insight and for which God's authority, represented in the Church and confirmed by certain visible signs, was the guarantee. The polemics of the Reformation resulted in the attention of the Catholic Church being concentrated on 'points of doctrine' which were used as theses. What is more, because Christians of the Reformation tended to stress the subjective aspect of faith as a complete surrender in trust, Catholic theologians reacted by placing even more emphasis on the objective aspect of truth as something which man could know. When finally, after the time of Descartes, knowledge itself became more and more concerned with abstract and therefore clear concepts, the concepts of faith also began to assume the character of pure unchanging truth, the characteristic of God's own knowledge. It was not difficult to graft rationalistic thought—a purely mental activity which took place 'somewhere in a lofty chamber full of pure light where the turbulent movements of life itself never penetrated'[3]—on to formalised scholasticism and the reactions against this process were few. Thus, externally, the method of scholasticism was retained, while the living content of scholastic thought lost more and more of its basic ideas.

The Catholic Church was, then, convinced that this clearly defined content of faith and even the concrete institutions and practices of the Church went back directly to explicit pronouncements and decisions on the part of Christ and his apostles. With the aid of the holy Spirit promised to the Church, they had been handed down intact, almost literally from hand to hand. Different words were, of course, used from time to time, but only to prevent the possible occurrence of misunderstanding by defining even more clearly and precisely what had already been known for a long time. Just as an American looking for 'suspenders' in a shop in England learns quickly enough to ask for 'braces' if he is to be given what he wants, but certainly knows from the very beginning what he means,[4] so too has the Church never been in doubt as to what she means and has therefore always been able to recognise something new or different at once as something alien and as not an essential part of Christ's revelation—the source, in other words, of the distortion in Catholic understanding of tradition already referred to.

Bossuet made spectacular use of this idea as the central point of his apologetics against the Reformation—challenging his opponents to prove that the slightest change had ever occurred in dogma during the history of the Catholic Church and saying that, if they did succeed in demonstrating this, he would withdraw his argument. Understandably enough, the Protestant theologian P. Jurieu could not refrain from taking up the gauntlet and pointed out errors and gaps in the writings of the early Fathers of the Church. He brought the Jesuit Pétau as heavy artillery into the field,[5] but Bossuet, the celebrated representative of triumphant French Catholicism under the Sun King, had no need to take up a defensive position as quickly as this—in the case of the early Fathers, he maintained, it was simply a question of a difference in terms. The modern reader would hardly be prepared to believe in Bossuet's good faith in connection with this explanation, but it was accepted almost without question by the Church of Bossuet's own times. How could the divine truth, guaranteed by so many wonders, be imperfect—in other words, how could it change? Bossuet himself expressed this principle as 'the Catholic truth which has come from God has its perfection from the very beginning'.[6] In the zealous search for proof in the Church's past, whenever texts were brought to light which were contrary to everyone's expectations, the most fantastic theories were put forward to disprove such unwelcome evidence provided by historical research. Such awkward documents were, for example, called deliberate forgeries by heretics or else they were regarded as pieces of camouflage put up to conceal from those outside the Church her most profound mysteries, which were supposed to be preserved exclusively by oral tradition. Finally, if all else failed, it was always possible to withdraw to the last line of defence and argue that the unanimous teaching of the Church provided a more certain guarantee than historical research, which was, in this way, placed as a whole outside the law. Most theologians were moreover hardly concerned at all with historical discoveries and tended to resort, without knowing very much about the matter, to Bossuet's carefree affirmation that everything could be explained as a difference in terminology or, at the most, in what was made explicit and what remained implicit.[7] The unchanging character of the truth of faith—unchanging even in the forms in which it was expressed in the Church—remained, for the time being at least, axiomatic.

Bibliography

I have made grateful use of H. Hammans' very clear survey of the development of dogma, *Die neueren katholische t Erklärungen der Dogmenentwicklung* (Essen 1965), in my discussion of this problem in the foregoing sections. An American translation of this book has been announced. It is especially important as a study based on the bibliography of this subject from the nineteenth century onwards—and has a bibliography which is one of those discouraging but useful lists of books and articles which adorn all theses. The author's survey of the most recent 'theological' views will be found spread over different themes, which does not always help the reader's understanding of the subject. Hammans published a summary of his book in *Concilium* (3/1) 1967, and this number of the journal also contains other interesting studies of revelation, faith, theology, the Church and the Church's teaching authority. H. Rondet's book *Do Dogmas Change?* ('Faith and Fact' series, London 1961), which was written for a wider public in 1960, also provides a good insight into the problem. J.H. Walgrave's article 'Révélation foi et développement du dogme' in his *Parole de Dieu et existence* (Cahiers de l'actualité religieuse, 22), Tournai 1967, is a penetrating statement of the problem with a marked historical emphasis. The substance of this article is to be found in the *New Catholic Encyclopedia*, IV under the heading 'Dogma, Development of'. A major work by Walgrave entitled *Unfolding Revelation: the Nature of Doctrinal Development* is scheduled to appear in the course of 1970 in the series 'Theological Resources' (Washington, D.C.). A number of the articles on the development of dogma in the most readily available Catholic encyclopedias are characterised by the personal views of their authors. Examples of these are Rahner's article, 'Dogma' in *Sacramentum Mundi* II, Schillebeeckx' article, 'Dogmaontwikkeling', in the *Theologisch Woordenboek* I, 1952, which also appeared in his *Revelation and Theology*, London and Melbourne 1967, pp. 63ff., and

Geiselmann's articles 'Dogme' and 'Tradition' in the *Encyclopédie de la Foi*, I and IV, which deal especially with the attitude of the Tübingen school towards this problem. P.A. Liégé's contribution (entitled 'Dogme') in *Catholicisme hier, aujourd'hui, demain* III (Paris 1952) and E. Dublanchy's in some ways rather out of date, but nonetheless very detailed study of 'Dogme' in the *Dictionnaire de théologie catholique* IV, 1911, are more general in their orientation. Dublanchy's article contains many data about Bossuet, but the history of the whole problem will be found, very scientifically based on accurate historical research and equally well presented—a combination which the British seem above all to be able to bring off so successfully—in O. Chadwick's book, *From Bossuet to Newman, op. cit.* (see bibliography, p.44). For the narrowing down of the concept of faith since the Council of Trent, M. Seckler's article 'Glaube', in the *Encyclopédie de la foi* II, may be consulted.

Several Protestant studies on the development of dogma according to Catholic theology either by G.C. Berkouwer himself or in some way connected with him deserve special mention, especially because they often throw a completely new light on the problem for the Catholic reader. In English the only one of these works available is Berkouwer's reflections about the Second Vatican Council: *The Second Vatican Council and the New Catholicism* (Grand Rapids 1965: original ed. Kampen 1964) see especially chapter III.

The Tübingen School

Following Sailer, the Catholic members of the Tübingen school reacted creatively against such a narrow concentration on pure knowledge. Influenced by the theology of experience and the dialectic philosophy of their own times, they were able to reveal new depths in the scriptural and patristic views about tradition especially and thus to give a new, fuller and more dynamic content to revelation, faith and the Church also. Their theological achievement within the Catholic Church was that they did not allow any element of the Catholic tradition to slip through their fingers, even though it did, in the course of time, become apparent that their originally rather vague definitions needed to be more precisely formulated. They were convinced that man's personal experience of revelation had a decisive influence on his integration of that revelation, but they placed this personal faith from the very beginning within the framework of the community and placed it, what is more, within the community of the Church over the entire range of her history. Individual faith learns Christ's word as living tradition hands it down. Von Drey emphasised the dynamic power of the holy Spirit in the community of the Church and, on the basis of this, re-interpreted the current form of the doctrine and the organisation of the Church—unchangeable in their essence, these nonetheless adapt themselves in their outward form to the needs of succeeding generations; in this way the rich content of revelation is unfolded. This is also what Christ expected of his Church—that she would be a living organism in constant growth, dynamically and actively handing on his word and work and bringing it to fulfilment. The development in the life of the Church and consequently also in her dogmas, which have gained a more realistic place in this much more comprehensive whole, need not therefore arouse any surprise. This progress is inevitable and healthy and should not be explained away. The development of a living organism such as the Church is simply a sign of vitality. This progress has not, however, been in a straight line. The many different modes of human experience and the many ways in which this is determined by history mean that this growth is a dialectic process. The theologian in search of the gospel in the living tradition of the Church will therefore have to consider the whole life of the Church in his investigation within the whole of history, which is equally moved by the Spirit. The criterion for a lawful development is therefore the agreement of the whole Church, within which the Church's teaching authority has a supervisory function.

This is a surprisingly new vision within the sphere of Catholic theology, though certain of its aspects clearly need further elaboration. The place occupied by Scripture and the criterion for continuity with Christ's gospel are still not clear and the concrete course and scope of the development and the relationships between the various stages have so far been given scant attention. The later members of the Tübingen school defined many of these aspects more clearly, but their elaboration owed most to the work of the leader of the school. The fact that the theology of development of the Tübingen school was later attributed to Möhler is largely because his two major works were so popular, whereas von Drey's youthful work which was given up to this question was not published until 1940 in a book edited by the tireless advocate of the school of Tübingen, J. Geiselmann.

The idea of development in Möhler's work, *Unity in the Church*, which was published (in the original German edition) almost ten years after von Drey's manuscript, was a personal extension of von Drey's basic insights. In Möhler, the holy Spirit is presented even more consistently than in von Drey as the origin of the event of the Church. Individual Christians are formed by the Spirit in an invisible manner into a living unity by an inward power which is concealed from human experience and which goes on procreating itself through the centuries. This power is the tradition of the Church. The Spirit thus arouses, within the Church, a common, shared consciousness of faith that is comparable with the *Volksgeist*, the 'spirit of the people', which sustains God's revelation throughout history. On the basis of this inward principle of life, the Spirit also calls the body of the Church, the visible forms, into being—the outward institutions and offices, the outward tradition and the living word of proclamation, which is itself 'embodied' in Scripture, creeds and other writings. These outward, visible forms keep the inward tradition alive, in other words, they enable it to continue to grow. This process is directed by the Spirit, but it takes place, at the level of the outward forms, in a dialectical movement, in which not only all kinds of time factors in the life of the Church, but also explicit heresies act as antitheses. This confrontation also enables unconscious material of faith to penetrate to the explicit consciousness of the Church. The criterion for an authentic development is the agreement in faith of the whole of the Church, in which the Church of the past also plays an important part.

Möhler partly revised this rather vague and romantic conception later, taking the outward instead of the inward aspect as his point of departure. The origin of the tradition of the Church is now no longer the holy Spirit, but Christ—the Church's preaching, which emanates from him, evokes faith and builds up the community of the Church. In addition to the common, shared consciousness of faith, which Möhler now called subjective tradition, Möhler also postulated an objective tradition in his later writings, the Church's deposit of faith built up in the course of history. Tradition itself is also more clearly distinguished—the divine revelation which is handed down in this tradition is unchanging, but the human factors which play a part in this give rise to variation in the outward forms. An arbitrator, a visible, living authority which can distinguish the truth with certainty, is needed to judge in the conflict of interpretation brought about by this dialectical process and the development can only be a gradual unfolding of what has already been given in its fullness by Christ, an increasing consciousness of the unchanging Christian truth.

Like so many schools of theology in Europe, Tübingen became more and more right-wing after the first quarter of the nineteenth century, as Chadwick has commented, clearly rather regretfully.[8] In any case, it was a conscious change of direction which was not made under pressure from the *magisterium*. The reaction against pure knowledge had clearly overreached itself in the early stages of the movement. The basic ideas were, however, preserved, even by the later generations of the Tübingen school. Kuhn also saw in tradition not only a principle of identity, but also a principle of evolution. This striking combination of conservation and development, which, almost paradoxically, makes tradition a principle of progress, was one of the greatest achievements of the Catholic members of the school of Tübungen. Tradition, which had hitherto been regarded in the Catholic Church above all as an additional treasury for truths of revelation, was given back its ancient character of being the living representative of Christ's speaking and acting in the Church. This function was furthermore placed once again within its whole human and social context as an expression of the contemporary life of the Church, but was also referred back, in matters of faith, to the early Fathers. By virtue of its shared sense of faith which is inspired by the holy Spirit, the living community of the Church judges the authenticity of this interpretation of Christ's revelation and the teaching authority of the Church acts as the ultimate arbitrator within this community. Kuhn concentrated, in his speculative thought, above all on the implications of the dialectical process of development and completely abandoned the image of the organism. The unfolding of the content of revelation takes place, he maintained, at the level of the speculative spirit, which gains an increasingly wide knowledge of faith through the dynamism of the contrasting ideas and concepts which base the message of the gospel on the various New Testament authors while at the same time taking full account of the religious knowledge gained since their time. A retrograde step in Kuhn's otherwise very fruitful synthesis was, however, his identification of the living tradition of the Church with the activity of the Church's teaching authority.

Kuhn also did not define the relationships between the various stages in the development of faith very clearly. The Englishman Newman, who from the very beginning thought not in terms of an organism, but of human life, was able by his more concrete approach to throw more light on this question. It was, after all, his own, personal problem.

Bibliography

Most of the general surveys devote a fair amount of attention to the theology of the Tübingen school in so far as this was concerned with the development of dogma. The only special studies which need to be mentioned in this context are those of J.R. Geiselmann, which are far ahead of all others in this field. In addition to his general survey of the school of Tübingen, *Die katholische Tübinger Schule. Ihre theologische Eigenart* (Herder of Freiburg 1964), Geiselmann has also written two other studies that are well worth reading, one of Möhler in particular, *Lebendiger Glaube aus geheiligter Überlieferung* (Mainz 1942), and one of Kuhn in particular, *Die lebendige Überlieferung als Norm des christlichen Glaubens* (Freiburg 1959). Von Drey's youthful work is published in *Geist des Christentums und des Katholizismus* (Mainz 1940: this is part V of *Deutsche Klassiker der katholischen Theologie aus neuerer Zeit*). A concise summary will be found in Geiselmann's article 'Dogme' in the *Encyclopédie de la foi,* to which I have already referred. There is an American thesis on *Johann Adam Möhler's Theory of Doctrinal Development* (Washington D.C. 1959) but it does not appear to be easily available.

Newman's Way

There are astonishing parallels between Newman's ideas and those of the Catholic theologians of Tübingen although specialists in the field have, with some surprise, come to the conclusion that it is only in a very remote sense that any connection can be made between Newman, who began to look in very much the same direction as the Tübingen school at least twenty-five years after von Drey, and that school or even any German philosophical movement concerned with the idea of development. The fact that he was English and that he had an Anglican background gave a very distinctive colouring to his ideas, but he too found himself opposing those (in the concrete, many of his colleagues at Oxford) who

Freedom for a New Understanding of the Gospel 171

narrowed down the content of Christian faith to what could be clearly pointed out by rational and historical research. He could not believe in such a reduction on the basis of his own experience—human knowledge embraced much more than those explicitly conscious concepts which could be pointed out. Whereas the idea of the full content of the Christian revelation, as this had existed in the patristic period, had been for the whole of the Oxford Movement a reason for stressing certain 'Catholic' elements in the Church of England which had become blurred in the Anglican tradition, Newman himself found it increasingly difficult to believe that the later 'development' of these elements in the Roman Catholic Church would have been a misgrowth. He also recognised various factors in the thought and life of the whole Church which were the guarantee of healthy development in personal thought and life, and became gradually more and more convinced that there was a clear pattern to be discerned in the sequence of historical events. Newman's invaluable contribution to the theology of the development of dogma consisted above all of an extremely concrete and consequently all the more convincing description of the various factors which play a part in the historical development of the Church's consciousness of faith, a process which he had personally experienced in his own development. I can do no more here than simply summarise his ideas without attempting either to justify them or to distinguish between the various stages through which they passed in Newman's thinking.

Newman himself made an explicit distinction between the two problems inherent in this development—how the content of faith in fact grew and how the identity of this growth with the gospel was guaranteed. Newman, convinced of the value of a comparison between this process of growth and the development of the individual personal thought, did not have recourse to the image of the growing organism so favoured by the theologians of Tübingen, but insisted again and again that the whole man was involved in development, but that this progress of the whole man only became a really human progress when it was guided by conscious human thought, which was in turn always directly concerned with man's life in the concrete. Although he fully recognised the usefulness and even the necessity of abstract thought, especially in order to achieve clarity and to make indispensable communication possible, he insisted that not only the basis but also the aim of this abstract or 'notional' knowledge was always concrete, personal or 'real' knowledge. This polarity was, he claimed, also experienced in the development of thought. In the first place, thinking is an implicit, not yet non-reflexively conscious maturation in which the whole of man's personal life and especially his total orientation towards reality, his moral attitude, is involved. The (provisional) end of this development is a firm conviction which has not yet been analysed and which is strictly personal and uncommunicable. In the second place, it is possible to stand at a distance from this process of development, to reconstruct its stages and to reason in more personal, abstract terms about it, exercising supervision, so to speak, after the event, so as to make the result communicable to others, but without adding anything new or enabling the whole wealth of concrete experiential thought to be registered. This is why there is, in our attempt to justify our personal convictions, a place for a function which Newman called the 'illative sense' and which can, in the light of man's total orientation towards reality, estimate the true value of the bond which exists between man's different insights. It is especially by means of this illative sense that man's developing thought can keep in touch with concrete data. Human thinking thus develops from man's first, concrete and all-embracing experience of reality or 'idea'—and is, in this process, guided by 'first principles' which are at the same time closely connected with the whole person—via implicit and explicit stages forward to an explicitly new knowledge.

In the same way, man's thinking about faith also develops from a concrete experience of Christ's revelation—which comes to us through Scripture and preaching—via implicit and explicit movements forward—in other words, via faith and theology—and subject to the constant supervision of the illative sense of faith, which is itself nourished by a very real contact—'real' in the sense in which Newman used the word—with the reality of faith, under the impulse of the Spirit. In man's thinking about faith, however, the social aspects, which automatically condition all thinking, emerge particularly prominently. Like every community, the Church also has a collective 'idea' towards which she is, to a great extent non-reflexively, orientated and which provides the point of departure within the community for development. This is the whole of Christ's gospel, the sum total of all the 'impressions' of the apostles of the event of Christ—a real knowledge which covers the whole of Christ's revelation, which has, however, as yet hardly been worked out in detail. It is clear from the astonishing fertility of theology in the early Church that this collective experience of reality possessed a powerful dynamism which needed to be expressed. The collective idea of the Church is not, however, a pure datum of man's thinking, but is contained in everything that is 'handed down'—the community of the Church herself in her orientation towards Christ, her liturgical forms and normative structures and Christian life itself. This idea has brought about a Christian 'atmosphere' which is handed on from generation to generation and which expresses itself in collective 'first principles' of thinking and acting. In an argument which is clearly similar in many ways to that put forward by the Tübingen school about the function of the dialectical process, but which is different in its manner of thought, Newman also stressed the confrontation that takes place between the different forms in which Christians throughout the history of the Church have reacted and still react to concrete situations and how these different reactions are all inwardly directed by the Spirit and subject to the outward supervision of the Church's teaching office. It was through this confrontation, Newman maintained, that the

Christian idea, in the course of its development, became more and more explicit.

This, then is a concise description simply of the fact of development according to Newman. How does he show the faithfulness of this growth to the basic datum, the Christian idea? In the first place, he stresses the probability of God's coming forward to meet the doubts of the individual who accepted the revelation of Christ with a visible Church possessing a teaching authority which was, as far as certain crucial elements were concerned, infallible and he claims that this probability became certainty as soon as it was recognised that there was in fact a community which regarded itself as such. Newman also believed, however, that there were certain characteristics which indicated a development faithful to the Christian idea and pointed out seven of these, without aiming to provide an exhaustive list: the preservation of characteristic outward forms of the idea, the continuity of guiding principles, the ability to assimilate earlier stages and their continued existence in a more comprehensive whole, the presence in embryo of later stages in an earlier stage, logical inter-connection and finally the lasting life of the idea without its falling into sterile conservatism. Newman was convinced that these characteristics, all of which could be traced in history, provided support, especially when they occurred together, for the collective judgement of faith which was inwardly directed by the Spirit and which was, in Newman's opinion, decisive.

Walgrave has remarked that Catholic theology was not prepared for Newman's originality.[9] This was strikingly apparent when he sent a summary of his views in elegant Latin to the very open Italian theologian, G. Perrone, for his approval. Perrone's comments were unimportant and showed very little understanding of what Newman was saying. The Church was, of course, passing through the critical years of the mid-nineteenth century, and neo-scholasticism, on the defensive, could spare little attention for new ideas, especially for those concerned in one way or another with the changeable character of the truth of revelation. What is more, it was just about this time that Günther had filled the Church with a deep fear of everything new because of his much more challenging theories. The work of the Tübingen school and that of Newman was forgotten until the beginning of the twentieth century, when it was eventually rediscovered by the theologians of renewal and gratefully accorded a place in their own studies, including those of revelation, faith, the Church, tradition and theology in a wider context.

Bibliography

A great deal has been written about Newman's theology of development, both in general works and in special studies, but, as in the case of the theology of Tübingen, one of the interpreters is outstanding among the rest. J.H. Walgrave's synthesis, on which I have to a great extent relied in the preceding section, will be found in an English edition, *Newman the Theologian* (London 1960), which is ultimately based on the original Dutch publication of 1944. A summary will be found in Walgrave's studies already mentioned in the general bibliography on doctrinal development (see p. 164). The recently translated book by C. Biemer, *Newman on Tradition* (London and New York 1967) can also be recommended. What Chadwick has to say about Newman in the book that I have mentioned several times in different contexts, *From Bossuet to Newman* (see bibliography, p. 44), should not be read without consulting Walgrave's detailed criticism in the *Tijdschrift voor Philosophie* (20) 1958, p. 510 ff. There are paperback editions both of Newman's *Essay on the Development of Christian Doctrine* and of his *Grammar of Assent*. Newman's most concise summary will be found in the Latin abridgement of his ideas sent to G. Perrone. This was published in *Gregorianum* (16) 1935, p. 402 ff.

Neo-Scholasticism and the First Vatican Council

The most important change suggested by Perrone in

Newman's summary of his ideas was that 'new teaching' should be altered to 'new definitions',[10] which gives quite a clear indication of the horizon of neo-scholastic theology—that revelation is a collection of truths contained in propositions and preferably officially promulgated. This limited perspective certainly restricted the Church's vision, even when the Roman theologians were open to let new light shine on obscure questions, which was to some extent the case before the Church withdrew to a defensive position. Perrone had come across the problem in an early work by Newman and afterwards referred appreciatively to Möhler's *Symbolik*. Henceforward, he too saw tradition as an all-embracing datum in the Church, as a divine yet human event 'like the incarnation', but identified it in practice with the activity of the Church's teaching office, so that there was hardly any place in his view for criticism of the Church's teaching in the light of Scripture and tradition. Thus, in connection with the declaration of the dogma of the Immaculate Conception, he affirmed that a few unquestionable indications of this truth had at least to be found in Scripture and tradition, but that the really decisive factor was the conviction of the 'shepherds and faithful' as evidenced, for example, by the centuries-old liturgical celebration of the feast. The Church—and in this case the Church is in fact the teaching authority of the Church—has always been in conscious possession of all truths of faith. The development of dogma can therefore only be conceptual clarification. Traces can be found in other theologians of the neo-scholastic school, especially Passaglia and Schrader, of a concept of faith that was not purely intellectual, but this scarcely functioned in practice. Scheeben was representative of a more rewarding movement, with his concept of faith based on personal surrender and his view of theology as a science essentially characterised by its supernatural object which therefore does not lose touch with faith in thought, but aims to disclose the intelligibility of the data of revelation. The influence of these ideas is still noticeable even today, but they

Freedom for a New Understanding of the Gospel 177

were not directly concerned with the development of dogma —Scheeben's thinking about this was in accordance with the schematic views current in his scholastic environment.

Opposition to Günther made the neo-scholastic concept of faith with its emphasis on the intellect even more clearly the centre of attention. Because of his one-sided concentration on intellectual knowing, Günther's mode of thought could in fact be understood more easily by the neo-scholastic theologians of the time than that of the Tübingen school or Newman, both of whom kept close to the living experience of tradition and Scripture. On closer inspection, though, Günther's ideas are more comprehensive and more subtle than his opponents seem to have believed. They are also more apostolic. He had surprising insights into the problem of the development of dogma, but made practically no attempt at all to throw light on the question of historical revelation and living tradition with all its implications. Briefly summarised, his teaching amounts to this. Once the truths of revelation have been received in faith, this 'material' can be unfolded by Christian reflection, helped by the Spirit. It is, however, only with the help of philosophy that the believer can understand the 'why' of the truth of faith. In this way, his faith may become rational knowledge. In the whole of the Church and throughout her whole history, this has been a difficult way. The apostles did not attain the highest possible insight, nor did the Fathers of the Church. With the advance of knowledge, the earlier stages of insight would be constantly transcended The Church's task is to establish the highest insight gained at every period. In this, the Church is infallible, but her definitions do not comprise the whole truth and will therefore have to be corrected or supplemented in the course of time.

In 1857, Pius IX rejected Günther's ideas in a significant statement which was reminiscent of Bossuet. In this pronouncement, Pius IX said that Günther assigned the function of the Church's teaching authority to philosophy and in this way threw everything into confusion, especially 'the constantly unchangeable character of faith, which is always one and the same, whereas philosophy . . . is never consistent with itself and is always subject to a wide variety of errors'.[11] The First Vatican Council returned to the problems raised by Günther and discussed them in detail in the Constitution on Faith. This was the first time that the teaching office of the Church spoke clearly about the question of the development of dogma and related problems. The finally approved document—in which the views of the two leading neo-scholastic theologians who collaborated in the final version can be clearly recognised—namely Franzelin and Kleutgen—does leave latitude for a more comprehensive concept of faith, but clearly takes as its point of departure the view of faith based on intellectual knowledge: 'helped by the grace of God, we believe that what is revealed by him is *true*'.[12] Faith is a manner of knowing which is different from 'natural' knowledge 'not only in principle, but also in its object', although reason, 'illuminated by faith', can attain 'some understanding of the mysteries of God'. But the 'doctrine of faith revealed by God has not been offered to human minds as a philosophical invention to be perfected, but as a divine pledge entrusted to the bride of Christ to be guarded faithfully and declared infallibly. That is why that meaning of the sacred dogmas which . . . the Church has once and for all time declared must always be retained and no deviation must ever be made from this meaning either in the name of or under the pretext of a deeper understanding'.[13] That there is a development in our understanding of faith is confirmed by the well-known quotation of Vincent of Lérins which it is so difficult to interpret, but then only 'in its own lineage, in the same teaching, in the same sense and with the same meaning'. For Vincent's norm of faith was 'what is believed everywhere, always and by everyone'.[14]

It was even more apparent in the theological discussions both before and after the First Vatican Council that the sphere within which neo-scholasticism operated was extremely limited. The argument was in fact confined to an investigation into the logical relationships between truths of faith defined by the Church. Kleutgen, for example, tried to limit the extent of the development as far as possible by showing the clearest possible logical bonds between the various 'truths'. To do this, an old argument was set up once more—the notorious question of the status of a theological conclusion drawn from a revealed and a non-revealed premise. Could not, perhaps, a truth concluded in this way be connected so closely with Christ's revelation that real development could be denied?

In all this controversy, Newman and the Catholic theologians of Tübingen were completely lost from sight. Their answer to Günther's 'ideal reconstruction of Christianity'[15] would no doubt have been that the development of dogma was not primarily a question of philosophical thought, but something which took place in the whole multi-coloured life of the Church. This attitude was quite outside the experience of neo-scholasticism, which was as much a victim of pure 'thought' as Günther was. Furthermore, the ideal of a truth that was unchangeable even in its human forms so preoccupied neo-scholastic theologians that every attempt was made to limit the development of dogma to what was absolutely inescapable. Papal infallibility, which was dogmatically defined at the First Vatican Council, can also be interpreted as a new guarantee for the permanently unchangeable quality of truth. Infallibility has the function of 'guarding the deposit of faith intact and interpreting it faithfully'.[16]

The polemics with Günther did, however, give prominence to a new aspect. Neither the Tübingen theologians nor Newman had a change in the prevailing formulations of dogma in mind. All that they wanted to do was to justify the historical development of dogma and to enrich the faith of the Church by assimilating traditional data that had become blurred into theology. Henceforward, the possibility of development or re-interpretation of the Church's dogmas would be an issue in theology. This question was to be discussed with some acerbity in modernism.

Bibliography

Information about nineteenth-century neo-scholastic theology will only be found in general works. There is, however, one exception, W. Kasper's remarkable monograph on the Roman school, *Die Lehre von der Tradition in der Römischen Schule* (Freiburg 1962). There has recently been a revival of interest in Günther's theology, but very little is to be found about his theory of development. There is also very little to be found dealing with the paragraphs on development in the Constitution on Faith of the First Vatican Council other than L. Orbán's *Theologia Güntheriana et Concilium Vaticanum*, 2 volumes (Rome 1942 and 1949). There was in fact little debate about it and the original draft remained almost unchanged. For the First Vatican Council in general, R. Aubert's book *Le pontificat de Pie IX 1846–1878* (see bibliography, p. 43) should be consulted, or his later book, *Vatican I* (Paris 1964), which also contains a French translation of the Constitution on Faith, the Latin text of which will be found in H. Denzinger's *Enchiridion*.

History and Dogma in Modernism

Baron von Hügel happened, almost by chance, to get hold of Möhler's *Symbolik* and was so impressed by it that he advised Loisy to read it. Loisy never did in fact read Möhler's book, but he did make the Baron share in his enthusiasm for Newman, the 'most open theologian since Origen' who had, he believed, only lacked followers.[17] When Loisy became familiar with Newman's ideas, his own fundamental ideas had already taken shape. Very broadly speaking, one may say that these ideas developed from his historical exegetical studies and were his own justification of the assumptions that he had made in confrontation with the points of departure of his colleagues outside the Catholic Church. As a typical representative of the 'historians' who, in the second half of the nineteenth century, were so inclined to research that was 'free of metaphysical preoccupations' and were therefore all the more absorbed in the reconstruction of factual evolutions, Loisy was almost diametrically opposed to the official theology of his own times, with its obsession with the unchangeable character of faith. These official theologians regarded the historical theologians as the inhabitants of an unknown territory who had to be approached with great suspicion. This made Loisy's surprise that Newman should postulate that the development of dogma was something characteristically Catholic all the greater. Seen in this light, it is also understandable that Loisy should take over from Newman what he believed provided an answer to his own questions, in other words, principally the more external, social and historical elements in Newman's works, all of which he certainly did not know, for that matter. In any case, he undoubtedly underestimated the ultimately intellectual character of Newman's theory of development. He himself had a vital, almost blind evolution in mind, not what Newman envisaged—a process, guided by thought and constantly supervised, of development in the Church of intelligible ideas which were entrusted to the Church, however much they were linked to the whole richly varied life of the Church.

Loisy himself was very well aware of what was at stake. Shortly before his final break with the Church, he presented his work 'firstly as a historical outline and explanation of the development of Christianity and secondly as a general philosophy of religion and an attempt to interpret the formulations of dogma, the official creeds and the conciliar definitions, with the aim of reconciling them, by sacrificing the letter in favour of the spirit, with the data of history and with the attitude of mind of our own contemporaries'.[18] He based his hermeneutics, in this attempt to re-interpret Christianity, principally on the conviction that, in comparison with the original, supernatural intuition and religious experience of the gospel, the dogmatic formulations which attempt to express this religious intuition suffer from two weaknesses—a metaphysical relativity, because they are not capable of reproducing their object adequately, and a historical relativity, because they have to be continuously adapted to changing thought. The living rule of faith of the Church's teaching authority is our guarantee that these socially conditioned expressions do really point to the inexpressible original religious experience. This authority, established by God, indicates the forms in which Christian experience can be expressed in the most adequate way within a given historical situation. The gospel is thus progressively realised in history, in changing historical forms. The gospel did not, as Harnack insisted, continue to live in this inward experience *despite* the Church—it *had* to go on living *in* the Church. But this inward experience, towards which the expressions of the Church point in their faltering way, is itself not a clearly defined content of consciousness and therefore eludes knowledge.

This assured Loisy of the necessary latitude for historical research. The price that he paid for this, however, meant a far-reaching inflation of the concepts of faith towards which his research was, after all, ultimately directed. The reality of the formulations of faith, however, was almost entirely outside his sphere of interest—he was so completely preoccupied by historical research and the historical method that he expected these to supply the answer to every question. On the other hand, as Duméry has observed, he shared the illusion which haunted so many of his contemporaries in the same field of study and which we have now to a very great extent seen through—that it should be possible to demolish the theological superstructure and practise pure history, investigate pure facts without reference to their significance.[19] Blondel's intervention made the consequences of this position strikingly apparent.

It was quite clear that Blondel had high hopes of Loisy when he sent him a complimentary copy of his *Lettre* about contemporary apologetics in 1897. Loisy's *L'Évangile et l'Église*, however, made him enthusiastic at first, but later raised certain questions in his mind. These questions, which he eventually put to Loisy, were all concerned in one way or another with the wall that Loisy appeared to have erected around the historical facts—if these facts were thus isolated, how could they ever be brought into contact with faith and was not an isolation of this kind as unreal as the division made by neo-scholasticism between the different sciences or the different approaches to reality? Historical facts were, Blondel insisted, themselves part of reality, and consequently the essential problem was not whether or not historical development took place, but whether this historical development was authentic or not. This problem could not be resolved without recourse to Christ's consciousness of his mission. Could this question be answered by pure historical research? The general tone of Loisy's answers, which become progressively less and less patient, is revealing—he had never thought that metaphysics would be irrelevant to history, but he had to protect his autonomy as a critic by defending the territory which was still immune from the tyrannical supervision of the prevailing theology. As a historian, he could do no more than simply describe Christ and his mission by reconstructing these from the testimonies of the time.[20] Blondel was, however, unable to convince himself that Loisy based his position entirely on practical grounds. In fact, he felt compelled to make a public stand.

He published, in the journal *La Quinzaine,* several articles on 'history and dogma' in which he not only dissociated himself, without mentioning any names, from what he had recognised as Loisy's 'historicism', which suggested that dogma was the exclusive product of history, but also from the 'extrinsicism' of the prevailing theology, which suggested that history was totally dependent on an unchanging and amply clear dogmatic ideology, without any influence being exerted on it by the indisputable data of the critical sciences. The most valuable contribution to the discussion was, however, Blondel's own view of the bond between dogma and history, in which he provided a new interpretation, clearly inspired by his philosophy of action, of the tradition of the Church. This can be outlined briefly as follows. The gospel is more than simply a message recorded in written documents or contained in the preaching of the Church—it is a living reality which has been given form in the whole life and experience of the community of the Church. This reality is above all handed down in the Church's tradition, an action in which God's grace goes together in the concrete with man's activity. (This is one of Blondel's fundamental insights.) From the very beginning, then, there has always been a living unity between (divine) dogma and (human) history in the Church, a collective consciousness which is more than simply intellectual. This includes the whole content of revelation—both, for example, in its written documents and in its outward institutions—and preserves it, but it must also, in its explicit implications and consequences, take possession of this content again and again by Christian action. This tradition, 'which includes within itself the data of history, the efforts of reason and the experiences of faithful action',[21] is in the concrete the bond between the gospel and man's contemporary convictions of faith.

Blondel did not, however, succeed in convincing Loisy, who was unable to recognise his own intention in Blondel's ideas. It cannot be denied, on the other hand, that, even for Blondel, the demands of modern historical research continued to be alien—and it was modern historical research that Loisy most wanted to do within the Church and still hoped to be able to do without hindrance. He aimed above all to enclose his historical reserve within the fence of his 'philosophical' arguments and it was tragic that there was, at that time, no one within the Catholic Church who had sufficient insight and sufficient influence to guarantee that his investigations would gain a real place in theology, with the result that the expressions of faith at the time might be criticised in the light, for example, of a return to the sources of Scripture and tradition. Blondel, however, certainly put his finger on one very weak spot in historicism—it was almost as fanatically concerned with pure facts as neo-scholasticism was preoccupied with pure truths. This is perhaps the reason why the confrontation between these two points of view continued for so long to be a pure antithesis. The wider context which Blondel indicated might have been a better basis for more realistic discussion.

Tyrrell's views were very similar to those of Loisy, but he expressed them with prophetic eloquence and was more open and radical and consequently clearer. By nature he lacked the patience and caution of the scholar. He was more directly concerned with Christian life itself and with Christian mystical experience and believed that these could no longer be nourished by the dried up formulae of the prevailing theology. It is interesting to observe how he interpreted Newman's 'idea' as a 'spiritual power or impulse'[22] which took from the surrounding cultural environment expressions which as symbols pointed to the religious experience that is given with the gospel. Tyrrell freely admitted that he had, in accepting this view, departed from the Roman Catholic belief in a treasury of faith 'deposited' with the apostolic Church and in the infallibility of the Church. His attitude contrasts sharply with that of the devout philosopher E. le Roy, who tried explicitly to achieve harmony between strict orthodoxy and modern scientific thought by defining the concepts of faith as an orientation towards community with God and Christian action. He was, however, insufficiently adept in the use of the traditional vocabulary of the Church to be able to avoid the suspicion that—as became clear later on—he had no intention of denying that the Church's formulations referred to reality.

As Vidler has observed, it was almost inevitable that, in their attempts to bring the gospel into harmony with the results of historical research and to restore its relevance for men of their own times, the modernists went astray in this virtually uncharted territory and became the victims of the one-sided pragmatism and anti-intellectual evolutionism of their age.[23] Spiritual experience is certainly one aspect of faith and the Church has never thought that it was possible for the concepts of faith to reproduce the reality of revelation adequately. But the modernists gave an exaggerated emphasis to the immanence of God and to the empirical aspects of the data of revelation. This overemphasis was, however, a reaction to the one-sided concentration on the transcendence of God and on rational thought in the theology of the period. No solution to the real problem was provided by the powerful confirmation of this in the papal condemnations of modernism.

Among the affirmations condemned in *Lamentabili* are Loisy's famous aphorism, that dogmas are 'not truths which have come down to us from heaven',[24] the statement that 'the dogmas of faith have only to be retained in accordance with their practical meaning . . . and not as the norm of faith'[25] and the assertion that 'truth is no more unchangeable than man himself'.[26] The encyclical *Pascendi* did not really discuss the problems raised in a direct and positive manner. All that it in fact did was to cut off a new road, insisting that the old road was still quite good enough and had been—so it would seem by implication—mapped out often enough. About two thirds of this quite lengthy document was devoted to a logical exposition of modernism—an achievement which, in view of the very divergent material, certainly commands respect. The result, however, is very reminiscent of an impressionistic composition by a romantic pupil after it has been corrected by his classical teacher. As Tyrrell himself said, in his famous reaction in *The Times:* 'When the Encyclical tries to show the modernist that he is no Catholic, it mostly succeeds only in showing that he is no Scholastic—which he knew'.[27] The teaching of the Church, for the most part, only emerges indirectly in the ironical descriptions of the modernist 'system', sometimes supplemented by earlier pronouncements made by the Church. Thus, the development of dogma is rejected in *Pascendi* with quotations from Vatican I, especially the condemnation of Günther already referred to, and with the words of Pius IX on 'those enemies of divine revelation' who 'wish to introduce . . . with great audacity . . . human progress . . . into the Catholic religion, as though that religion were not the work of God, but that of men or some philosophical invention which was capable of being perfected by human means'.[28] In a later section, the 'first and most important cause' of the errors of the modernists was explicitly called their 'ignorance'.[29] It was only because they did not know scholastic philosophy— Tyrrell, who had once been a convinced Thomist, must have sighed when he read this—that they embraced modern thinking with its 'deceits and trickery'.[30] One of the recommended cures for modernism, therefore, was the promotion of neo-scholastic thought, but an insertion was also made recommending positive theology, on condition that 'no harm was done to scholasticism', because 'more importance must clearly be attached to positive theology than in the past'.[31]

The task that had to be fulfilled by this theology is not mentioned in *Pascendi*, but it was clearly not to be a 'deliberate mutilation of history', of which the modernists were accused in their research under the inspiration of a false philosophy. It is also hardly possible that it would include a reconstruction of the development of dogma, in view of what had been said before this mention of positive theology. Many Catholic historians must have agreed in their hearts with what Dom Cuthbert Butler wrote to Baron von Hügel: 'The only freedom in Biblical things and the rest [Butler was here referring to the development of dogma] is that of a tram, to go ahead as fast as you like on rails, but if you try to arrive at any station not on the line, you are derailed'.[32]

Bibliography

Not only general works, but also several special studies of modernism, especially those by Rivière, Vidler, Poulat and Duméry (see bibliography, pp. 70–72), provide a good survey of the ideas of the modernists on the development of dogma. L. da Veiga Coutinho's Roman dissertation,

Tradition et histoire dans la controverse moderniste 1898–1910 (Gregorian University, Rome 1954) gives a useful picture of the different points of view and is explicitly written in the spirit of J. Rivière. There is also H. Gouhier's more sympathetic contribution to *Herméneutique et tradition*, an account of one of the colloquies organised in Rome by E. Castelli and published in Rome and Paris in 1963.

As for the authors discussed in the preceding section, Blondel's 'Histoire et dogme' has been republished in *Les premiers écrits de Maurice Blondel* (Paris 1956), in the series 'Bibliothèque de philosophie contemporaine', and is therefore fairly easily obtainable. The English translation is *The Letter on Apologetics and History and Dogma*, London 1964. Apart from Tyrrell's *Christianity at the Crossroads*, which was reprinted in London in 1963, the works of the modernists are no longer very easy to find. Loisy's most representative writing on the question of the development of dogma is his chapter on the origin and authority of dogmas, 'Sur l'origine et l'autorité des dogmes', in his *Autour d'un petit livre*, Paris, 1903, and Tyrrell's is not his reprinted book, but his *Through Scylla and Charybdis*, London, 1907, a collection of essays, some of them already previously published, in which the author, in his own words, 'throws down his cards on the table'.[33] The book by E. le Roy, to whom I have referred in the preceding section, is called *Dogme et critique* and was published in Paris in 1907. The article to which I have already referred by Walgrave in his *Parole de Dieu et existence*, defines the limits between Newman's ideas, the modernist view and the most recent interpretations.

Re-orientation within Neo-Scholasticism

Modernism was certainly the most daring venture in the search for freedom for a new understanding of the gospel in the recent history of the Catholic Church. The answer to the modernist challenge to scholasticism was, however, not entirely negative—new impulses within the theological tradition of neo-scholastic thought itself gave rise to an interior tension between those who continued to follow the course that had been set since the change in direction brought about by the polemics against the Reformation and post-Cartesian rationalistic thinking, and those who, confronted by the modern problem, went back to the medieval vision. This scholastic return to the original sources was, in turn, evident in two different directions and traces of the differences between the two directions that this new movement within neo-scholasticism took can still be discerned in the quite distinctive approaches of the later representatives of the two schools—the Dominican school which began with Gardeil and later included, among others, Chenu, Congar and Schillebeeckx, and the Jesuit school which goes back above all to Rousselot and continued with de Lubac, Bouillard, Rahner, Schoonenberg and others. Compared with the older, 'authentic' neo-scholasticism, however, there is also a very striking similarity between these two schools in their approach and in the results that they achieved, even though Rousselot, for example, experienced rather more opposition from the prevailing neo-scholastic theologians than did Gardeil.

Faith is at the same time both a human reality and a reality that is sustained by God's grace. This was the central point from which all the questions about faith radiated. To what extent can human experience lead to faith? Is faith itself a religious experience? How is this religious experience related to man's explicit knowledge of the truths of faith (which has consequences for the development of dogma)? How is faith as an experience related to theology and especially to positive or historical theology? In the technical neo-scholastic formulae, then, the fundamental questions raised by modernism were realistically discussed.

Gardeil's basic rediscovery would seem to have been the function of the light of faith, the inward illumination by the Spirit who brings to light the truths of revelation as religious values and thus makes faith into an inward experience—although this term was, Chenu remarked later, too suspect when Gardeil was writing for him to use it explicitly.[34] Faith is therefore not a purely neutral acceptance of the truths of revelation, guaranteed by God's authority and imposed by the will. It is an inward recognition of truth, truth that concerns one's own salvation. Theology tries to let this inward light penetrate as deeply as possible with the help of scientific means, not only into the content of faith which comes to us through the Church, but also into the human, philosophical context of this. Theology, therefore, is not a neutral science which can simply be practised without faith. The only way in which the science of faith, theology, can be practised is by keeping in touch with and being totally committed to the data of revelation. This means that theology must be historical, but this research directed by the light of faith is a quest not for 'pure facts', but for the religious meaning of history. The theologian is therefore able to envisage the development of dogma quite calmly. All the concepts of faith suffer from 'metaphysical relativity'—Loisy was not wrong when he claimed that neo-scholasticism also accepted this—and they are only an analogous grasp of the divine reality. This is the basis that makes historical specifications of the concepts of faith possible. The model in which Gardeil saw this possibility made concrete was still that of premises leading to a new theological conclusion. His pupil Marin-Sola was to apply these principles and all their consequences to the development of dogma.[35] In this way he was also to put his finger unintentionally on the weakness of the still too formal point of departure. It was only when Chenu and Congar and later Schillebeeckx also turned explicitly to consider the living reality from which the formal procedure had been abstracted that Gardeil's vision reached its real aim.

Rousselot also emphasised the light of faith—I should mention here that Gardeil was greatly indebted, as far as his ultimate position, which I have outlined briefly above, was concerned, to Rousselot's criticism of his earlier formulations—but he concentrated his attention especially on the elements which played a part in man's way towards faith. Impressed by Blondel's philosophy of action, he rediscovered Thomas' dynamic concept of faith and consistently stressed that God's grace was already at work in the concrete attitude with which man was open to revelation as preached and as confirmed by outward signs. Because he had at the same time come to the conclusion that, for Thomas, knowledge was characterised not by discursive reason, but by a much more deeply rooted 'sense for the real',[36] he too was able to see more in faith than simply a neutral acceptance of the truths of revelation and more in the development of dogma than simply a process of logical steps. The only document by Rousselot on the latter question that is still preserved, apart from a note of no more than a few pages, is a youthful work which has been recently published. This contains several very striking ideas and a number of significant references to Möhler, Newman and Blondel's 'Histoire et dogme'. Rousselot's great achievement was that he made a place within the scholastic tradition for the genuinely scholastic data of spontaneous judgement inspired by the whole of man's attitude to life and for love as the basis of all real knowledge.

The German theologians of the period between the two world wars did not reveal any new points of view in connection with the problem of the development of dogma, at least not directly. The subject was no more than incidentally discussed in the theology of renewal in the German-speaking countries. Schell made the general affirmation that, on the basis of the 'dialogical structure' of the event of revelation, the association of God's revelation of himself and man's trusting surrender of himself, a development of dogma was not simply possible, but even required. Revelation was in principle closed with Christ and deposited, as far as its content was concerned, in Scripture and tradition, but this content of revelation in fact required a further unfolding which was not a strictly logical deduction. Schell's dynamic and existential thought, in which theology functioned as the extension of the concrete, personal surrender in faith, includes many important points of departure for a new approach to the theme of the development of dogma, but these ideas have found very little response until quite recently and can consequently be given no place in this very general survey.

Guardini, Adam and the kerygmatic theologians centred in Innsbruck found the freedom to reflect about faith in contemporary terms mainly outside the framework of the prevalent theology. They too did not concern themselves directly with the debate that was taking place elsewhere about the development of dogma. Not even Karl Adam, who had gone deeply into the history of dogma when he was at Munich and had explicitly followed the tradition of his predecessors at Tübingen, dealt directly with this subject. Nonetheless, both Guardini and Adam, together with their contemporaries G. Söhngen, E. Przywara and K. Eschweiler, did make important, though indirect contributions to the discussion about the development of dogma. What they did above all was to reconsider the distinctive character of the knowledge of faith and therefore of theology as a science, taking especially Scheeben's approach to the problem as their point of departure.

It was natural, of course, that greater personal depth was given to faith within the dynamic 'movements' with their intense social consciousness, their feeling for the Church, their interest in the liturgy and its symbolic language and their concentration on Christ. The narrow basis of 'accepting truths on the authority of the Church' was broadened in many different directions. The reaction against the neutral, purely rational knowledge of faith which had begun with Blondel, Rousselot and Gardeil was strengthened by the influence of the phenomenological ideas of Max Scheler, who described man's orientation towards the highest religious values and his experience of God which was sustained by this, and by the inspiration of the basically related ideas of Augustine and Newman. On the one hand, faith was more deeply rooted in the human personality with its many-sided, concrete dimensions and associations, while, on the other hand, it was also inwardly orientated towards the living God, who comes forward to meet us personally and makes faith a specifically religious knowledge. This specific knowledge of faith had, these theologians believed, to be given a more important place in theology. Theologians could not, they insisted, analyse the truths of faith, after these had been accepted, with purely rational means, but could only attempt to unfold the intelligible element inherent in the vision of faith itself. This ideal of a theology continuously sustained by the life of faith was to play a very important part in the ensuing discussions about the development of dogma.

Bibliography

Gardeil expressed his views about faith and theology in *Le donné révélé et la théologie*. This book was published in Paris in 1932 with an introduction by Chenu, which can also be found, together with a commemorative note of 1956, in Chenu's *La foi dans l'intelligence*, Paris 1964, pp. 269 ff. (see p. 190, footnote 34). R. Aubert's thesis, *Le problème de l'acte de foi*, Louvain, 3rd ed. 1958, a book which is still unrivalled in its field, can also be consulted in connection with both Gardeil and Rousselot, a detailed exposition of whose work is contained in Aubert's thesis. Many more articles have been published, mainly in theological journals, about Rousselot than about Gardeil, but it should be sufficient to refer here to H. Holstein's study, 'Le théologien de la foi' which appeared in the special number devoted to Rousselot of the Fourvière journal, *Recherches de science religieuse* (53), 1965, which also contains Rousselot's youthful work on the development of dogma, presented by de Lubac. Rousselot's later 'Note sur le développement du dogme' was also published in the same journal—vol. 37, 1950, p. 113 ff. The two best books on the German debate about faith and science are undoubtedly Karl Adam's *Glaube und Glaubenswissenschaft im Katholizismus* (2nd ed. Rottenburg 1923) and K.

Eschweiler, *Die zwei Wege der neueren Theologie, Georg Hermes-Matth. Jos. Scheeben* (Augsburg 1926). As a footnote to Eschweiler's book, it may be said that the conventional neo-scholastic theologians did not greatly appreciate the striking likeness drawn by the author between the neo-scholasticism officially approved by the Church and Hermes' semi-rationalism which was condemned by the Church.

The Development of Dogma in Le Saulchoir

Similar ideas were also expressed in France and even explicitly applied to the problems of the development of dogma and the position of theology, although in the less spectacular and more technical language of traditional neo-scholasticism. Chenu's theology, so concerned with life and so fundamentally linked to history, has already been briefly mentioned in the preceding section in connection with Gardeil's work—Gardeil's rather barren vision was ultimately transformed by Chenu's emphasis on the contemporary context, his realistic approach to history and his consistent elaboration of the full humanity of the scientific study of theology.

Chenu reacted, with the Germans, against a purely rational approach to the data of faith and fully accepted their emphasis, which originated with Scheeben, on an inward unfolding of the vision of faith itself. He, however, regarded this as already implied in Thomas' authentic view of faith and theology. Chenu's idea of faith and theology, based on this point of departure, can be outlined as follows. Faith is directed towards 'God as my salvation' and is therefore a knowledge in which a decisive part is played by the will by spurring thought on to a never completed, but also never ceasing, attempt to fathom the transcendent mystery. The impatience of a faith which has surrendered itself to a reality which is constantly eluding the grasp of human understanding impels the believer to a restless quest in thought, with the aim of deepening and throwing light on his own inward experience of God by means of the 'outward' revelation in history—in other words, in Scripture, in tradition and in man's contemporary experience of faith. In this way, our religious attitude is given backbone[37] in a process which is constantly supported by the inward light of faith, but which at the same time uses every possible means of human, technical thought.

The knowledge of faith is therefore entirely 'divine' and has its own consistency on the basis of the light of faith, but it is also entirely 'human' in its mode—a paradox which forms the basis of a God-centred or 'theologal' humanism. Theology can therefore never go outside the sphere of the experience of faith without running the risk of letting the 'object' of its study slip through its fingers. The use of the scientific method makes this risk very real—there will inevitably be a certain divergence between the theological 'conclusions' and the experience of faith as such, but that is precisely why theologians have to study the original experience of faith again and again, and especially this experience as recorded in history. They can try to gain an insight into the problem in two ways—by means of philosophy, which is concerned with what is universal, necessary and unchanging, and by means of history, which considers the incalculable datum of the concrete reality of faith. The theologian does try to gain as universal an insight as possible, but only in so far as the history of salvation in the concrete is not opposed to this. 'As soon as it is authentic, the smallest *fact* is normative':[38] if no place can be found for it in the theory, the theory must be discarded. This primacy of the facts also explains the tension between the experience of faith and theological formulation, a tension which results in there being no possibility of theology 'without new birth', a saying of the Tübingen theologian Kuhn which Chenu used as a motto to introduce one of his articles.[39]

Chenu only applied this incidentally to the development of dogma. But, when he did define his position in greater detail, he provided an elucidation, once again based on Thomas, which, in principle, overcame the impasse of scholasticism. Looking back, it seems almost incredible that Chenu should have been the first to point explicitly to this distinction which is now so obvious to us, or at least that he should have rediscovered it in the scholastic heritage, because he freely acknowledged that, in so doing, he was only incorporating Newman's description into the Thomist doctrine of knowledge. The weight of the absolutely unchangeable character of the truths of revelation pressed heavily down on Catholic thought and Chenu pointed out the only place where the revealed truth was in fact unchangeable—the reality of God himself who is the real end of all our judgements about faith which are built up of limited and therefore changing concepts. For, according to Thomas' pregnant phrase, 'the terminus of the act of faith is not the proposition, but the reality',[40] just as every judgement, by the connection or separation of different conceptual contents, comes into contact with the reality itself under constantly new aspects.

Of course, even before Chenu the scholastic theologians were aware of the analogy between the development of dogma and the progress of human knowledge, but only Chenu seems to have realised that this process of knowledge was not simply an analogy, but the very principle and psychological basis of the development of dogma. 'What is known is adapted in the knower to his mode of knowing':[41] God could only speak to us in a human manner, that is, in human words which, with the progress of human thought, become more and more numerous and more and more explicit. Although Thomas only applied this to the progress of revelation, it can just as well be applied to the development of the deposit of faith entrusted to the Church. With the help of the Spirit in the light of faith for every believer and therefore in the whole of the Church, our knowledge of faith is directed towards the unchanging reality of God, but this is only attained in accordance with the necessarily limited content of the concepts of faith, which consequently need to be inwardly supplemented and deepened.

Freedom for a New Understanding of the Gospel 197

This fundamental idea, which can be called humanistic, and which secularises man's knowledge of faith in principle, was not elaborated by Chenu in all its consequences. The theme was, however, taken up again by Congar, who encountered the problem in a much wider context—that of the question put by non-Catholic Christians to the Catholic Church. This almost automatically raised the problem of the relationships within the Catholic Church between Scripture, tradition and infallibility in particular and Congar, under the pressure of his ecumenical contacts, became more and more 'conformed to the gospel'.[42] The different steps in his development cannot, unfortunately, be considered here.

The basis of Congar's theology was very little different from that of Chenu. In working it out in the concrete, however, he brought out more and more clearly an element which not only set the problem of the development of dogma against a more realistic background, but also threw light on a neglected aspect of this subject—the fact that the life of the Church consists of both tradition and reformation and has an unchangeable pole, to which the word, the sacraments and the apostolic office belong, and a reformable pole, the life of the Church and her institutions. The development of dogma is only one aspect of this whole. These two poles evoke each other and complement each other—a fact which can be understood when they are seen as the concrete result of God's activity in the world, which is a history of God's invitation to salvation and man's response to this. God is faithful to his promise of salvation and the faithful realisation of this promise is reflected in the constant progress of tradition. Man's inconsistency and the freedom of God's initiative, however, give rise to breaks and re-orientations in this tradition and, since the full revelation of salvation in the event of Christ, these breaks and new orientations are brought about in the concrete by a return to this original source.

Christ's revelation 'once and for all time' continues to live in the Church as tradition, but this is not regarded, according to the distinctions which have become prevalent since the teaching of the Tübingen theologians and which Congar defined, simply as the activity of handing down itself, but also as the very content of that activity—what is, in fact, handed down. This includes everything that the Church passes on as Christ's heritage—Scripture, for example, and the Church's practices, forms of life, liturgy and Church order. In addition, the meaning of the 'unwritten' tradition that has been accentuated by polemics must also be borne in mind here. Tradition, then, is fundamentally God's invitation to salvation in Christ as handed down in concrete forms from generation to generation within the community of the 'people of God on the way'. Tradition is continuous with the gospel and this continuity is realised not in spite of, but precisely within, this progress through history. Tradition takes place in the midst of the challenging changes of history and, in confrontation with these, its unique invitation to salvation assumes new forms and expressions. In this process, too, the content of knowledge of the data of revelation is also developed, under the impulse of Christian life itself, which has its focal point in communal worship and personal prayer and its expression both in spontaneous reflection and in scientific elaboration. The light of faith of the community of the Church as a whole, which is sustained by the Spirit, guarantees that this progress will be homogeneous. This light forms the basis of an inner 'sense', which directs the faith of the whole people of God and the proclamation and the ultimate interpretation of that faith towards the authentic revelation of Christ.

By no means everything in the Church is guaranteed, however, by God's promise or by the help of the Spirit. Even in Old Testament times, it was clear that it was necessary for the unwilling people of God to be corrected again and again and, after the definitive offer of salvation in Christ, man's response continued to be fickle. Congar, therefore prefers not to call the Church the continuation of the incarnation. Within the Church, he has explicitly pointed to such a reformation, which has as its aim a return to the central truth of revelation, only in the life of the Church, including the decisions of the hierarchy, and not in the authoritative proclamation and interpretation of the data of revelation. Because of the wide context within which this is discussed, however, Congar's view at least implies the possibility that elements of the Church's faith can be given too much or too little emphasis within the whole of the Church's tradition and that their importance can be increased or diminished according to the function that they fulfil in the life of the Church. For example, under the influence of the polemics directed against the Protestant Reformation, the meaning of tradition itself became narrowed down. In the present ecumenical situation, however, tradition can take on a much wider significance in the light of the source of the living gospel itself. Congar has shown—and here he is consistent with the whole development of his thinking—a certain preference for the idea that the Church is 'indefectible' rather than 'infallible'. The term 'infallibility', which, with its emphasis on knowledge, became, as it were, 'established' only in the nineteenth century, obscures the Church's hesitations and the errors she may make in her speaking in bearing witness to the gospel. Certain *acts* of the Church are infallible, but the Church herself or the pope are not simply infallible.[43]

In building up on the basis of Thomism a synthesis of the ideas of Newman, the Tübingen school and Blondel, a work of integration which Chenu had already begun, Congar infused new life into scholasticism. The real value of his contribution can, however, only be seen fully against the background of his own efforts to renew the teaching of the Church, which even resulted in Möhler being involved in posthumous difficulties with the Church more than a hundred years after his death—there were official objections to his *Unity in the Church* being included in Congar's series 'Unam Sanctam'. Congar's theology itself is a prophetic search for freedom for a new form of theology, a reform of theology and the Church, which, in the nineteen-fifties, gave rise to considerable scandal.

Bibliography

Chenu gives quite a clear indication of his own ideas in his articles on Gardeil, but only in some of his other articles, collected in *La foi dans l'intelligence* (Paris 1964), did he outline systematically his plan of theology based on history and the modern world and the Church. Two of these articles are particularly worth reading—'Position de la théologie', *op. cit.*, p. 115 ff. and 'La théologie au Saulchoir', p. 243 ff. Only the first of these has been included in *Faith and Theology, op. cit.* The second was the central chapter of Chenu's private edition dealing with the direction of the theology of the Dominican house of studies (see footnote 64, p. 155). His contribution to the theme of the development of dogma will be found in the same collection between his articles on faith —'La raison psychologique du développement du dogme d'après saint Thomas', p. 51 ff.

Congar's ideas can be found in the two volumes of *La tradition et les traditions,* Paris 1960 and 1963 (see especially the first chapter of volume II): the English translation is *Tradition and Traditions,* London 1966; and in part 20 of his series 'Unam Sanctam', *Vraie et fausse réforme dans l'Église* (Paris 1950), a book which caused a great stir when it was published. It was republished in 1969 as part 72 of the same series with revisions and retrospective reflections by Congar. A shorter work by Congar on tradition is a part of the series *Je sais, je crois,* which led to the greater work, *La tradition et la vie de l'Église* (Paris 1963); the English translation is *Tradition and the Life of the Church,* No. 3 in the 'Faith and Fact' series (London 1969). The two poles of tradition and reform have been explicitly brought together in Jossua's study of Congar (see bibliography, p. 119). I am greatly indebted to Jossua in my outline of Congar's work in the preceding section.

The Heart of the Problem in the 'New' Theology

In the years preceding 1950, Catholic theologians began to get nearer to the real heart of the problem of the development of dogma which had been discussed since the nineteenth century—the status of the concepts of faith that were in fact used in the Church. After centuries of unquestioned acceptance, these concepts were quite suddenly placed in an awkward position. As a result of historical studies, questions were asked about the identity of these concepts with the authentic gospel of Christ and, thanks to an increasing awareness of the fact that man's thinking was closely interwoven with the progress of history and society, doubt was cast on their value as an interpretation of modern Christian experience.

After various attempts at a solution had, for the time being at least, failed or died out and the way followed by the modernists had been closed, the problem became rooted within the quasi-official theology of the Church. A creative group of neo-scholastic theologians accepted the contributions that had been made by the Tübingen school, Newman and Blondel especially, and tried to integrate their ideas into neo-scholastic thought by referring this back in certain points to its original source. They described knowledge as a view of reality which was borne up by man's whole attitude to life and especially by love and which transcended the purely discursive use of concepts. They also rediscovered the function of the light of faith as the basis of Christian experience and specified the function of the concepts of faith by showing that these concepts were not in themselves the reality of revelation, but only pointed to that reality, which was the real end of all knowledge about faith. The increasingly urgent question now was how this relationship between the concepts and the experience of faith, which would, for example, throw clear light on the model which was currently used, that of 'explicit' and 'implicit', was to be interpreted. The pressure of external circumstances, such as the debate about the theological method, the facts leading to the controversy around the 'new' theology and the expected definition of the dogma of the Assumption of Mary which was already casting its shadow on theology, also sharpened the reactions of the conventional neo-scholastic theologians.

The current neo-scholastic theories put forward by M. Tuyaerts, R. Schultes and F. Marin-Sola especially to explain the development of dogma were basically extensions of the logical interpretations of the nineteenth-century neo-scholastics and attempts to define the extent to which the theological conclusion could provide an explanation. Because of their conceptual view of revelation and faith, they took it for granted that this could only be found in reasoning. One dilemma, however, caused them sleepless nights. If, on the one hand, it was accepted that the conclusion of reasoned argument yielded a really new insight, how could such a result of human reason be revealed by God? On the other hand, the alternative was to cling to the older view that all that could be found for truths that had already been known for a long time were new words. But how could this be reconciled with the findings of historical research? There seemed to be no solution to this fundamental difficulty, despite the introduction of the most ingenious distinctions and an appeal for support to the spontaneous life of faith.

This impasse was underlined by L. Charlier, who pointed out, in a book which dealt directly with the 'scientific' character of theology, that Chenu had already looked for a solution to this problem outside the sphere of the theological conclusion by asserting that the end of all knowledge of faith was the reality of revelation.[44] In this context, Charlier himself had been one of the first to affirm explicitly that revelation was not primarily the communication of a number of truths, which might then become the principles of ordinary deductive science, but above all a reality: 'God, giving himself to us through Christ in the mystery of the incarnation, of which the mystery of the Church is only the extension'.[45] This reality of revelation evolves, as given to the Church, and this very growth is the source of our evolving knowledge. This progress, however, is determined by the divine logic of the reality of revelation itself, which is wrapped in mystery and which only becomes clear to human knowledge in so far as God himself plays a part in the processes of human thought. Ultimately, then, the development of dogma cannot be registered either by deductive thought or by strictly historical research, but only by the Church's consciousness of faith. In coming to this conclusion, however, Charlier accepted a simplification that is always present as a real danger in Catholic thinking—that the Church's consciousness of faith is in fact the same as the teaching authority, which is in turn equated with 'active tradition'. It is not surprising, then, that Charlier's book was sharply criticised. One exception to this was his professor at Louvain, R. Draguet, who in any case shared his opinion about the decisive role of the teaching authority in the Church. Nonetheless, Charlier's point of departure—that revelation was a reality—was worked out in greater detail and in various ways later.

Replying to an article by the Roman theologian, C. Boyer, de Lubac also joined in the fray after the war with a study in which he reacted against the purely logical explanation— the mystery of salvation, he insisted, shatters our human concepts. In this, he took, as the point of departure for the development of Christ's act of redemption, the 'totality of dogma'[46] which is contained in a very concrete, living knowledge that embraces the later formulations in a higher unity. (Although this idea of de Lubac's is very reminiscent of Newman, surprisingly enough it was apparently not derived directly from him.)

This more limited debate about the development of dogma was, however, quickly eclipsed by the fundamental discussion about the concepts of faith in which the whole of the 'new' theology was involved. The preference which the theologians who were associated with the Jesuit faculty at Fourvière showed for the categories of Scripture and patristic literature, which were closer to Christian experience and less conceptualised, and above all their adoption of the typological and allegorical interpretation of Scripture, were the principal reasons for this change in the centre of theological interest. Daniélou regarded this typology as the best possible means of expressing the development of thinking about faith, as indeed the Fathers of the Church had done. What is more, the new theology pointed out that, after heretical views had been condemned by the Church, it frequently happened that the Church's preaching overemphasised the opposite view, with the result that authentic elements in the Christian tradition were thrust into the background of the Church's consciousness of faith. A reaction on the part of the Church against error—the anti-modernist oath, for example—does not necessarily comprise the whole teaching of the Church. As de Lubac said, even before the war, and using the familiar terminology of the Church as a fortification, a part of the rampart is not the whole city.[47] Various statements made more or less in passing, for example, that there had been more than one theology throughout the centuries in the Church and that we do not attain one absolute truth, but only reach more or less perfect approximations of the truth, in the end culminated in the more fundamentally constructed argument which Bouillard set out in connection with his study of the medieval doctrine of grace.

The point of departure which Bouillard took for his theory was a distinction in the theological process of knowledge between the judgement that is pronounced and the idea or representation that is used to contain that about which a statement is made. The judgement of faith covers the absolute, unchanging reality, but the ideas that have to be used for that judgement are taken from changing social patterns and ways of thinking and are therefore determined by the prevailing time and situation—they are, in other words, relative. They do, however, form a connected whole. The statement about unchangeable truth which is meant to be absolute can therefore be retained because the ideas connected with it are at the same time constantly evolving, with the result that the relationships between the statement and the ideas remain the same. Bouillard's much debated slogan, that 'a theology which is not actual must be a false theology',[48] has also to be seen in this light—the evolution of the ideas of such a theology has ceased somewhere, with the result that the whole balance is upset. Several aspects of Bouillard's theory, however, are still obscure. Did he, for example, regard idea or representation and concept as the same? Did he intend to apply his distinction to dogmatic statements as well? Did he, in other words, equate theological concepts with concepts of faith? As far as the last question is concerned, he spoke in principle only about the theological process of knowledge, although the examples that he gave do seem to indicate a wider application.

The challenge was accepted in the *Revue Thomiste* first by M. Labourdette and later also by M. Nicolas. They insisted that the 'new' theology made all human formulations of the truth of revelation relative and that the cause of this was an inclination to regard everything in the light of history and from the point of view of the subject. In their passionate joint reply, the 'new' theologians pointed out that there was also a form of relativism in the exclusive choice of the theology of the thirteenth century, which they saw as a criterion that had to be used to measure everything. Even more important, however, was the fact that, in this debate, two different views of the Christian revelation emerged. The argument of the 'new' theologians, in which the hand of de Lubac is clearly discernible, was that revelation was not the communication of a system of ideas. Revelation, according to this interpretation, was 'first and foremost—and will always be—the manifestation of a Person, of the Truth in Person . . . This does not mean that revelation never has to express itself in concepts and that the passing of time does not make it necessary for this conceptual expression to be defined more precisely and to be amplified . . . But it does mean that the Catholic truth will always go beyond its conceptual expression and, *a fortiori*, its scientific formulation in an organised system'.[49] Labourdette and Nicolas replied to this by stating that this revelation in Christ is only communicated to us in human language and human concepts. The way in which these concepts of faith are related to the reality of salvation is something that is beyond man's knowledge, but the existence of this relationship is guaranteed by God's authority. It is this which gives these concepts their absolute validity—and this is where the antithesis between Labourdette and Nicolas, on the one hand, and de Lubac and those like him, on the other, is clearly revealed. The concepts of faith can thus be used as bricks to build up a scientific, theological system. The truth of that system is founded on the concepts of faith, by virtue of their unseen but guaranteed relationship with the reality of salvation. The aim of theology must therefore be to define as precisely as possible the limits of what is expressed in the concepts of faith and to purify its content. Theological formulation must leave less and less latitude for misconception and in that way come closer and closer to absolute validity and unchanging truth. The official dogmatic formulations of the Church have attained this ideal and may therefore be regarded as definitive and unchangeable.

In this last formulation, one is aware of the whole environment of the century to which these two theologians ultimately go back—the time when human thought dissociated itself as completely as possible from the bewilderingly concrete character of man's individual and social life and when every attempt was made to strip concepts as fully as possible of their compromising human associations, until a point was reached when what was left was a precisely defined element which could be manipulated like a thing and was extremely suitable for the logical operations of reason. In the conventional neo-scholastic view, the reality itself is always out of reach—the conceptual content of the divinely guaranteed concepts of faith is not only the beginning but also the end of all thinking about faith. Outside these concepts, we are given nothing that could add anything essential to our knowledge of faith. The new theological approach, on the other hand, following Gardeil and Rousselot, regarded these concepts simply as a means of access to the concrete reality with which everything began and as the inadequate and socially conditioned interpretation of something that, by means of these concepts, can to some extent be seized hold of and understood. The aspects of man's concrete experience which are so determined by time and situation not only act as a brake on our knowledge of the reality that transcends us—they also make it possible for that knowledge to be objective. These concepts are, after all, only one function within the much more comprehensive knowledge of experience.

The discussion about the 'new' theology was made very difficult by this basic difference between the two ways of approaching reality. It was made even more difficult by the fact that the justification offered by the theologians of Fourvière appeared to be the result of thinking afterwards about the implications of a theological project inspired by historical studies, so that it was not a completely balanced reply to the criticism which their attempts to renew theology had rather unexpectedly evoked. Once the word 'modernism' had been uttered, the 'new' theology seemed indeed to provide reason for suspecting that the concepts of faith did not grasp the content of revelation really and objectively. Their opponents, on the other hand, spoke the discouragingly certain language of the teacher explaining yet again to a slow-witted pupil what he knew had been firmly established for centuries—and the encyclical *Humani Generis* seemed to prove them right.

This papal document pointed out that the view of reality as subject to 'evolution, by which everything that is absolute, firmly established and unchangeable is repudiated' was one of the principal errors outside the Church. It also added to the pernicious 'idealism, immanentism and pragmatism', which had already been condemned in the earlier encyclical *Pascendi*, not only the latest secular philosophy, existentialism, 'which considers the unchangeable essences of things as of little account', but also a 'false historicism', which, while confining its observations to the events of human life, overthrows the foundations of every truth and of every absolute law'. Catholic philosophers and theologians had the 'grave task' of 'guarding divine and human truth', but there were among them men who, for reasons which were not valued very highly in the encyclical, were trying to achieve a false irenism and not only to perfect, but even totally to reform current theology. The most important part of the encyclical was devoted to dogmatic relativism. This, the document maintained, was not only a constant danger in the new tendencies in theology, with their movement away from scholastic categories, their return to scriptural and patristic ways of speaking and their use of terms derived from modern philosophy—it was in fact already present in those theological tendencies.

The positive exposition in the encyclical was a balanced synthesis of traditional neo-scholastic principles—that towards which faith is directed is always described as 'truths', the concepts of which 'have, in a work lasting many centuries . . ., been formulated and worked out with the most subtle shades of meaning, with the purpose of expressing the truths of faith even more accurately'. These terms could be 'perfected and worked out even more subtly', but they could not be pushed on one side without making dogma 'like a reed shaken by the wind'. 'Whatever the human mind, in an authentic search, may be able to find in the way of truth cannot be in conflict with the truth that has already been acquired.' The Church's teaching office had been given the task of 'preserving, guarding and interpreting the deposit of faith' by Christ, 'in order to throw light on and explain in detail those things which are contained in an obscure form and so to speak implicitly in the deposit of faith'. 'The task of the theologian is to show how what is taught by the living teaching office of the Church is contained, "either explicitly or implicitly" in the sources of holy Scripture and divine tradition'—a definition of the theologian's task which was significantly adorned with a quotation from Pope Pius IX, and to which was added that Catholic exegetes should not replace the literal meaning by a 'symbolic' or a 'spiritual' meaning and should not explain clear statements by obscure data. The last comment was probably one more allusion to the return of the theologians of renewal to scriptural and patristic ways of speaking. In a later section of the encyclical, scholastic philosophy was defended in some detail against the criticisms of rationalism and once again prescribed for instruction in theology.

Schillebeeckx regarded the affirmation of the objective value of the concepts of faith and therefore of the theology that is built up on these concepts as the most important point in the encyclical. This objectivity had to be more precisely defined, especially with regard to the relationship between concept and experience, but the encyclical aimed to limit itself to indicating the boundaries within which a more precise definition might be looked for.[50] Schillebeeckx and Rahner, among others, did in fact take up this problem.

A few months after the publication of *Humani Generis*, Pius XII defined another boundary for theology by declaring the dogma of Mary's Assumption. In this way, he gave emphasis—to quote the words of *Humani Generis*—to one of the things 'which are contained in an obscure form . . . in the deposit of faith' and did not rely on strictly historical or rational arguments. It is said in Louvain that Draguet put out the flag to mark this confirmation of his theory about the development of dogma.

Bibliography

The classical neo-scholastic syntheses of Schultes, Tuyaerts and Marin-Sola, which are together known as the 'logical' or 'dialectical' theories, can be found, in essence, in the general scholastic works on the development of dogma. J.H. Walgrave has described very clearly the difficulties which confronted these logical theories in the article in his *Parole de Dieu et existence* that I have already quoted several times.

The discussion about the concepts of faith is not usually dealt with in the context of the development of dogma, but supplementary information will be found in the general works on the 'new' theology (see bibliography, p. 120-21). Two additional studies which may be consulted in this connection are the fundamental studies collected in E. Schillebeeckx' *Concept of Truth and Theological Renewal* (London and Sydney 1968) and T. Deman's well documented account, 'Tentatives françaises pour un renouvellement de la theologie', *Revue de l'Université d'Ottawa* 1950, 129-67. Deman was not a protagonist of the 'new' theology, but his study is objective.

Progress between 1950 and 1958

The extremely cautious and subtle wording of the dogmatic pronouncement in 1950 would seem to indicate that Draguet's conclusion that Pius XII had proved him right was itself not entirely founded on facts. Be this as it may, the theologians who continued to concern themselves with the central problem of the development of dogma after 1950 did not follow Draguet's narrow path. The theological tradition which had begun with the Catholic school of Tübingen and continued with Newman, Blondel and the theologians who had re-vitalised neo-scholasticism by going back to its sources, asserted itself more and more. In this, it was particularly influenced at this time by a renewed study of historical theology and by the use to which it had been put by the speculative theologians. Helped by the encouragement given to it shortly after the war by two of Pius XII's documents, patristic, liturgical and above all biblical theology flourished anew during this period and played a decisive part in the almost unanimous abandonment by the more advanced theologians of the idea that revelation, and consequently also tradition, did no more than simply provide a set of clear truths. Research into the Bible showed only too distinctly that the biblical 'stories', which seemed, at first sight, to be so translucent, and even more particularly the various expositions and testimonies contained in the Bible, were connected in many different and often barely tangible ways with other, similar texts and concealed allusions, combinations, extensions and sometimes even compelled changes in the traditional ideas. All this was recognised as a form of witness to God's speaking which consequently could no longer be seen in isolation from the total context, which included not only the historical context of the Old and New Testaments—in which lines of development were perceived with increasing clarity—but also the constantly changing context of the life and proclamation of the Church up to the present. The insight into the fact that God's word was also directed towards the post-apostolic Church led to the idea, inspired by the Church Fathers and the liturgy, of the 'fuller' sense of Scripture—a dynamism transcending the historically conditioned meaning of Scripture, in the same direction, on the basis of God's speaking which was also addressed to later historical situations. This led in turn to a renewed reflection about faith and the knowledge of faith, about speaking and listening and about the various psychological and 'logical' ways in which the content of knowledge could be contained in the whole of revelation, even according to the 'intention' of the divine speaker.

The most remarkable part of this debate took place, from about 1950 onwards, in the German and the Dutch-speaking countries. There was a great deal of sympathy in the Netherlands for the discussions among the French-speaking theologians about the theological method and I have already mentioned the highly personal way in which Schoonenberg decided in favour of the course followed by the theology of renewal. For him, theology is 'tracing back the mysteries of faith and uniting them'. It is more a question of rendering and interpreting than of justifying. 'At the end of a treatise, there is as much mystery as there was at the beginning.'[51] Since theological reflection can never take place outside faith, the concepts of theology contain more than those used by philosophy. Their content is also different, although they may well sound similar. A theological argument which employs both kinds of concept indifferently is consequently a syllogism with four terms. It is therefore necessary to refer the concepts of faith back to the source of revelation again and again. Speculative thought in the theological field must therefore always be subject to the criticism of historical theology. On the other hand, however, historical theology can never dispense with the light of faith, which is scientifically extended, as it were, in theology, because it is looking for God's word in history. According to *Humani Generis*, this tentative sounding out of tradition does not have to be restricted simply to laying bare the roots of the Church's already established teaching. It should also be extended to the hidden riches of revelation. In this way, theology is not primarily a question of going back to the New Testament and then, through the New Testament, to the Old Testament. 'Before being a dialogue with natural thought'—something which involves a renewal of scholasticism based on modern philosophy—'theology must be a dialogue with both testaments.'[52]

Schoonenberg, however, only applied these ideas in practice to the problem of the development of dogma in a short commentary on the definition of 1950. Rahner and Schillebeeckx, on the other hand, discussed this question in some detail. To illustrate the way in which the ideas of these two theologians converged in the period immediately preceding the Second Vatican Council, I shall conclude this general survey with a brief summary of their contributions. There are striking parallels between the ways in which both approached the subject. Both, for example, based their arguments on a palpable familiarity with the phenomenon of development and consequently confronted the concrete factors objectively, including those of the so-called 'logical' theories. Both theologians not only sought their inspiration in positive theology and even more especially in biblical

Freedom for a New Understanding of the Gospel 213

theology, but also tried to find a place for the various themes of those who had approached the problem before them by giving considerable attention to the psychological and sociological aspects and above all to the philosophy of man's knowledge and development. On the other hand, however, they clearly came from different theological schools, a fact which emerges with even more clarity because their contributions were made quite independently. Schillebeeckx' publication, in 1952, preceded Rahner's by six years, but it was written in the language which Rahner later said was 'only accessible with great difficulty to us poor non-Dutchmen'.[53] Although both Schillebeeckx' and Rahner's studies do no more than, in Schillebeeckx' words, offer 'perspectives for a synthesis',[54] scant justice can be done to their many-sided treatment of the problem in a summary and the final result can hardly be satisfactory.

In this rather difficult task, the most realistic course seems to be to give an outline of the last article which Rahner wrote on the subject of the development of dogma before the Council, in which he expressed his basic conviction that revelation was a revelation of God himself directed explicitly towards man—a communication of the very reality of God, in other words, and not simply a revelation of a number of truths. This reality, however, is made manifest as something intellectually knowable, in words. In this way, Rahner's views are very much in accordance with those of the increasingly numerous defenders of the idea of revelation as a reality, yet at the same time he does not underestimate the importance of the part played by human knowledge. The implications of this view are apparent in almost every aspect of his argument. What is remarkable in the first place is that, in accordance with modern exegesis, he also points in this article to the development of dogma within the Bible itself, including the New Testament, which does not detract in any way from the Bible's revelatory character, since the whole of the document, which came about by a process of theological growth, is revelation precisely as a whole. It would indeed have been surprising if there had been no history of the unfolding of revelation, since both the development and revelation itself take place through human forms in which God speaks to man, in other words, through history. This development is therefore unique and as unforeseeable as all history and cannot be embraced in adequate laws.

The difference between the two phases—revelation and the development of dogma—is based on what has been called the 'closing' of revelation at the end of the apostolic period—'closing' because God's communication of himself through incarnation and through grace as glorification already initiated, of its nature absolute and unsurpassable with regard to man, is eschatological. This calls for a definitive saving community, a Church which is the object of God's revelation of himself and which is also definitive in its response in faith as a community. If there were no 'hearers', there would be no reason for God's eschatological revelation of himself to exist. Because it is of necessity contained in human words and forms, this definitive revelation of reality is bound to have a part in the history of those who believe and, in the development that is given with this participation in history, various elements, such as the Church's teaching office, the inward grace of faith and the progress of human knowledge, also play a part. These elements are the inward consequence of the one whole of revelation and for this reason all of them always appear, though not always with the same degree of prominence. It is, however, useful to consider them separately.

The part played by the Spirit of God, who manifests himself humanly in the grace of the light of faith, is fundamental. Without this personal presence, revelation would not be God's revelation of himself and would not enable us to share in his reality. On the basis of this presence, we have not only a witness to God in his word, but also a contact in experience, although this only takes place in man's knowledge of the word. The part played by the Spirit in the development of dogma is therefore not purely negative, a help to prevent the Church from erring, but, on the contrary, a positive orientation which is present in an intangible form as the basis of various human factors in the Church.

The first of these factors which comes to mind is the teaching office of the Church. God's word comes to us in the proclamation of this witness to which full powers have been given and development thus takes place in constant dialogue with the teaching office. Nonetheless, progress does not, in the first place, rest with the teaching office of the Church, the fundamental task of which is to preserve and to distinguish what the charismatic dynamism of the life of the Church and theological thinking about faith propose as the development of revelation. This can indeed only be a proposal, because the only adequate bearer of the content of revelation is the Church's collective consciousness of faith. On the other hand, the Church's teaching authority must also receive the 'material' for its decisions from this collective consciousness of faith.

Another factor, which is a consequence of this, is that the development which takes place is determined by the human concepts and words within which God's revelation of himself has been given form. In this sense, the development of dogma is always a theological development and there must always be an inner connection between the ancient deposit of faith and any newly established dogma. It would, however, be unrealistic to expect this to take place simply on the grounds of syllogistic logic. Ordinary human experience provides grounds for certain knowledge which are not those of reason and Rahner's rather disconcerting example of this is the certainty that he has that his mother would not deliberately poison him. It is precisely because reason is not the only source of certainty that the theologian offers his justification to the whole Church and it is only if it is accepted by the Church that this justification can become valid.

This in turn opens up a view of the handing on of the content of revelation, of (active) tradition as a developing factor. The most essential aspect of this handing on of the content of revelation—a process marked by time and space and therefore with a perceptible historical course—is the activity of the Spirit of God and the part played by the light of faith. In the human process, after all, a speaking from person to person always takes place—the content of revelation is inwardly addressed to us. For an interpretation of the twofold movement which can be discerned in the development of dogma, Rahner points to his dynamic philosophy of knowledge, inspired by Maréchal. Just as being is the *a priori* sphere against which the spirit, in its transcendence, grasps individual objects and makes them intelligible, so too is the light of faith, borne up by the Spirit and ultimately identical with him, the *a priori* sphere within which the separate objects of revelation are grasped. On the one hand, the infinite breadth and intensity of this supernatural *a priori* of necessity urges a more and more articulated unfolding of the content of revelation contained within its sphere. On the other hand, every separate object is only grasped as an aspect of God's communication of himself, to be understood as an increasingly clear vision of the one mystery that the spirit is trying to grasp. By drawing attention to this dynamic progress towards an increasingly intense, yet simplified and concentrated knowledge and by applying it especially to the field of theological thought, Rahner has given an important, but frequently unnoticed element in the development of dogma its rightful place.

Finally, there is also another element to which Rahner has given special emphasis—the question of how the Church ultimately recognises a new element as a datum of revelation. This transition, which constitutes the central problem of the development of dogma, is traced back by Rahner surprisingly to the analogous question of how and where, on the way to faith, the transition of the preliminary human stages to consent to faith, inspired by God's light, takes place. This question has played some part, at least in the background, in all discussions about faith and in all apologetics. Rahner's

Freedom for a New Understanding of the Gospel 217

approach to this problem was made, in the spirit of Rousselot, from the vantage-point of the inner light of faith. In the development of dogma, there is also a decision in freedom, which cannot be traced back simply to insight, but which leads to a 'coming of the light'[55] in which the spirit recognises itself—a new confirmation of the basic idea that God's revelation of himself adapts itself to the 'hearers' to whom he addresses himself.

The article which Schillebeeckx first published in 1952 was a summary of a part of his course on faith and the part played by tradition in the Church. This article on the development of dogma, then, simply deals with one phase of his thought about tradition, with the result that his treatment of the subject is rather different from that of Rahner. Faith itself is, moreover, seen in Schillebeeckx' article as man's response, borne up by the inner revelation of the Spirit, to the 'outward' revelation and Schillebeeckx had already explicitly characterised this, in an earlier stage of the treatise, as sacramental saving history, in which the revelation in reality and the revelation in word formed an inseparable unity. Seen against this total background, then, there is a striking similarity between the views of the two theologians. I shall therefore draw special attention to the distinctive elements in Schillebeeckx' view in the following oversimplified outline wherever necessary.

On the basis of a broadly constructed, historical theological investigation, always one of the pillars of Schillebeeckx' studies, the limits of his synthesis are defined in advance. In the first place, he prefers to call his subject the development of tradition rather than the development of dogma, so as to relate the dynamic handing on of revelation to the entire reality. He also affirms that only the element of intelligibility in it—this is no more than an element, because knowledge must proceed from the terrestrial visibility of the transcendent reality—brings this development within our reach. Secondly, in order to gain as wide a perspective as possible, we have to ask, not about the bond between the

Church as she is now and the apostolic Church, with her Scripture and normative tradition, but about the principles which govern the close connection between the unchangeable and the developing elements within the whole history of the Church. If one speaks in this context, with the documents of the Church, about explicit and implicit, then one has to make this pair of concepts more concrete. What has to be made especially clear is how a later development, which, it is assumed, does not occur in its explicit form in Scripture or in the earliest tradition, does really form a part of God's speaking that is 'closed' in this deposit of faith.

Schillebeeckx considers this question, which Rahner also touched on in passing, in some detail in the light of studies by E. Dhanis and the linguistic philosopher K. Bühler, according to whom three aspects can be distinguished in speaking—a description of the subject of the discussion, a call to reaction (which may take the concrete form of an invitation to faith in the speaker's testimony) and finally a self-unveiling. Seen in this light, it is clear once more that revelation is essentially God's communication of himself and that the invitation to surrender in faith (the inward speaking which manifests itself in the light of faith) forms an essential part of this communication from the very beginning. This opens a way of making it clear that, if the Church should, at a later stage in history, discover some new depth in the original formulations of the apostolic deposit of faith, this can nonetheless form part of the historical revelation. After all, in this historical 'subject of conversation' God wanted to give form to his later revelation of himself and his invitation to faith. This idea of the 'double context' of the historical revelation, which is closely related to the idea of the 'fuller sense' of Scripture, has many points of contact in everyday life. Even such a trivial statement as 'Paul has written a novel' may, according to the intention of the speaker, have the meaning of 'Read the manuscript and publish it' in a specific context, namely, if the other person in the conversation is a publisher. An external factor may therefore be necessary to bring explicitly to light the meaning of a datum of revelation which is nonetheless (also) really intended. It is in this wider context that the essence of the truth which is present in the traditional concept of the 'theological conclusion' is rediscovered.

Once this point of departure has been clarified, the factual developments can be considered in a much more realistic light. Here Schillebeeckx avails himself of Newman's convincing description of the psychological and social factors in the process of development. On this basis, he is able, as a critic of the 'logical' theories, to state that the advocates of the logical view confused the progress in a straight line of logic with the richly varied psychological process of development. Even more important in this instance—and here Schillebeeckx deepens Newman's analysis—is the fact that the development of dogma is a progress of faith and consequently requires a principle which, indeed, does not bypass human knowledge, but nevertheless transcends it. The whole of Schillebeeckx' argument is thus based on the light of faith as the principle which gives direction to the development of tradition and which guarantees continuity in that progress.

Schillebeeckx thus follows a line of reasoning which goes back to Chenu's and Gardeil's interpretation of Thomas. He is moreover clearly inspired by Newman's 'illative sense' in his analysis of the concrete manner in which the light of faith functions in human knowledge and also at the same time bases his analysis on de Petter's philosophy of knowledge. The development of human knowledge takes place through the continuous conceptual explication of the intuition, related to the whole of reality, which is implied in every explicit item of knowledge, as the horizon one is implicitly aware of. Similarly, the development of our knowledge of faith also takes place through the continuous unfolding in concepts of faith of the intuition of the reality of revelation, the contact with reality which is, by virtue of the light of faith, implied in all explicit knowledge of faith.

The central point of this view is that contact with reality is based on the content of faith, the object, thus preventing any division between concept and experience. On the other hand, this interpretation also leaves latitude for all kinds of concrete factors of development, such as pre-reflexive and explicitly conscious 'reasoning' and psychological and social influences. In the complex totality of this development, both in the individual Christian and in the community, the light of faith is actively at work, that 'inner sense, "lost" as it were in the consciousness, that tells us what we should believe and what we should not', thus bringing about, within the community of the Church, 'a constant process of friction and purification, in which all members of the Church community play a part' and in which 'all the various voices eventually converge'. Finally, then, the new insight is seen to be 'like a fortunate word suggested to us for the purpose of formulating one of our most intimate ... convictions, but a word that so far we were simply unable to find'.[56] The Church's teaching office, finally, is able to declare whether a collective reaction on the part of the Church community has really come about by virtue of the light of faith.

One more striking aspect of Schillebeeckx' ideas on this subject is worth considering—the idea of what he rather paradoxically calls 'development through demolition'. This idea did not emerge explicitly in Schillebeeckx' thought until just before the Council.[57] It would seem to be closely related to Congar's pair of concepts to which I have already referred—tradition and reform—or to Rahner's idea of the 'Church of sinners', but Schillebeeckx explicitly applies it to the sphere of the knowledge of faith and formulates it positively. It is in fact an idea which most theologians have used in one form or another, but its explicit application to the problem of the development of dogma is something that I have not encountered in any theology except Schillebeeckx', although there are indications that there were attempts to use it in connection with this problem in the 'new' theology. The central element of this progress is that the dogmatic formulations contain representational elements which were determined by a particular historical period and situation and which must be relinquished later if the essential aspect of these formulations is to be preserved. Thus, the ascension of Christ was later stripped of its Ptolemaic mode of expression. Before a 'demolition' of this kind can take place, the Church does not have to be conscious of the distinction between the essence of what is said and the way in which it is said and this is, in fact, not usually the case. It is hardly necessary to say that man's thinking about faith is normally expressed in images and ideas taken from his contemporary view of the world. On the other hand, however, it is important to understand that, when man becomes conscious of the fact that it is possible to separate the essential underlying thought from the way in which it is expressed, this does not imply a retrogression from or a rejection of truths that were made explicit at an earlier stage in history under the pressure of modern ideas, but, on the contrary, it implies progress in man's thinking about faith.

This becomes especially relevant in the very practical context of, for example, marriage and Schillebeeckx has drawn attention to a very important fact in his study of the natural law and the Catholic view of marriage, the article in which he first made explicit use of this idea of 'development through demolition'. Our present, clearer insight into the distinctive character of *human* corporeality, he insisted, called for a renewed study of the earlier pronouncements made by the Church about the regulation of birth, which could not have passed an explicit judgement about a reality which did not at the time live explicitly in the Church's thinking about faith.

Bibliography

The most fully elaborated résumé of Schoonenberg's ideas about theology as the interpretation of faith will be found in his article 'Theologie in zelfbezinning' in *Annalen van het*

Thijmgenootschap (44) 1956, p. 225 ff. Rahner's most important studies of the development of dogma are his article 'The Development of Dogma' (1954) in *Theological Investigations* I and his two essays, 'Considerations on the Development of Dogma' (1958) and 'Virginitas in partu' (1962), both published in *Theological Investigations* IV. His article, 'Theology in the New Testament' (1962), in volume V of his collected essays and the questions that he asks in the light of fundamental theology about the components of theology in *Theological Investigations* VI also contribute to his study of the development of dogma. Schillebeeckx' article on the development of dogma will be found in the first volume of his translated articles, *Revelation and Theology*, London and Melbourne, 1967, where it is called 'The Development of the Apostolic Faith into the Dogma of the Church', p. 63 ff. Related studies will also be found in this first volume and in the second volume of his *Theological Soundings*: 'Revelation, Scripture, Tradition, and Teaching Authority' (1963), 'Revelation-in-reality and Revelation-in-word' (1960), 'What is Theology?' (1958), 'The Bible and Theology' (1963)—all the foregoing will be found in the first volume, *Revelation and Theology*, whereas the following will be found in the second volume, entitled in English *The Concept of Truth and Theological Renewal*: 'The Concept of "Truth"' (1962) and 'The Non-Conceptual Intellectual Element Dimension in our Knowledge of God according to Aquinas' (1952).

The Result

Even after the publication of *Humani Generis*, then, Catholic theologians did not cease looking for a more realistic understanding of the development of dogma in the Church. Among the various elements that were rediscovered were the light of faith as the basis of the Christian attitude which was embodied in the believer's whole experience, revelation as God's real communication of himself, the Church as the community in which this self-revelation of God is actually realised through human gestures and words, tradition as the historical progress of this handing on of the reality and interpretation of revelation to succeeding generations, and Scripture as the normative point of departure and the dynamic source of continuous insight into faith. If some of these rediscoveries already seem a little out of date now, this can only be taken as evidence of the very rapid development that has taken place in recent years. Compared with the official point of view of the Church, these theologians did seem, despite their care in integrating the traditional interpretations, like new modernists ten years ago. Their Protestant colleagues regarded them rather as commanders of distant outposts who had lost contact with the main force and who had perhaps even to act as spies, camouflaging the unchanged position of Rome.

On the other hand, it has become clear, especially since we have considered Rahner's and Schillebeeckx' contributions to the debate, that an increasingly urgent demand for freedom for a renewed practice of theology was expressed in the interpretation of the development of dogma. Thus, the very problem which had preoccupied Catholic theologians of renewal since the beginning of the nineteenth century had itself passed through a process of development. The difficult point was to find a way to the consciousness of faith of the whole Church. Looking back, it is possible to say that it was not only because the theologians were inhibited by the scholarly nature of their own achievements, which made it difficult for them to come into contact with everyday life, that their attempts were not entirely successful. The fact was that they hardly ever had the time and the opportunity to discuss their interpretations publicly in the Church. Every attempt that they made was followed extremely quickly by reactions on the part of the *magisterium,* which, because it was so closely bound to neo-scholastic thought with its absolute clarity and its firm emphasis on the unchangeable truths of Christian teaching standing outside the influence of history, could hardly be expected to need very much time for reflection before passing judgement. Because of the concentrated attention to the defence of the fortress, the work of the Tübingen school and of Newman was almost forgotten. But Loisy and Tyrrell, Chenu and Charlier, Congar, de Lubac, Teilhard de Chardin and those who supported them and finally, though less publicly, even Rahner and Schillebeeckx found out how difficult it was for their real intentions to be given a fair hearing.

Protestant observers have pointed out that this kind of impasse has occurred more than once in the history of the Catholic Church and has often given rise to a typically Roman phenomenon—looking forward to a reforming pope. This was certainly the case with Tyrrell and Reform Catholicism.[58] To a lesser extent, it also occurred in the underground reactions to the choice of Cardinal Roncalli as the successor to Pius XII—a seventy-seven year old man who appeared to lack the obvious interest in intellectual questions that his predecessor had possessed. After only a few days, however, disappointment changed to hope. This old man, a historian, was indeed going to grant the freedom that the theologians had been looking for to submit their ideas to a group, a group, what is more, which not only represented the experience of faith of the Church, but was also able to judge its 'development' authentically. The authoritative pronouncement of this group of men was to rehabilitate the theology of renewal and decisively improve its position in the Church.

NOTES

¹See A. Görres, *Handbuch der Pastoraltheologie* II/1, Freiburg i. Br. 1966, 304–7.
²H.M. Kuitert, *De realiteit van het geloof*, Kampen 1966, 187.
³J.H. Walgrave, 'Révélation, foi et développement du dogme', *Parole de Dieu et existence* (Cahiers de l'actualité religieuse, 22), Tournai 1967, 178.
⁴This telling example is taken from O. Chadwick, *From Bossuet to Newman*, op. cit., 19–20.
⁵See O. Chadwick, *From Bossuet to Newman*, op. cit., 74. This incident is also referred to in E. Dublanchy's article 'Dogma' in the *Dictionnaire de théologie catholique* IV, col. 1628 ff.
⁶'La vérité catholique venue de Dieu a d'abord sa perfection': quoted by Y. Congar in his article 'Théologie' in the *Dictionnaire de théologie catholique* XV, col. 439; E. tr. Congar, *A History of Theology*, New York 1968, 189— though Bossuet's phrase has been curiously misinterpreted by the translator.
⁷See O. Chadwick, *From Bossuet to Newman*, op. cit., 17–20.
⁸O. Chadwick, *From Bossuet to Newman*, op. cit., 110.
⁹See J.H. Walgrave, *Parole de Dieu et existence*, op. cit., 150.
¹⁰See J.H. Walgrave, *Newman the Theologian*, op. cit., 52. Perrone expressed this suggestion most clearly as follows: 'non oritur dogma novum sed vetus veritas nova definitione explicite credenda proponitur'; see *Gregorianum* (16) 1935, 417.
¹¹'De perenni fidei immutabilitate, quae semper una atque eadem est, dum philosophia . . . neque semper sibi consta(n)t neque (sunt) est a multiplici errorum varietate immun(i)s'; see Denz. 2829 (1656).
¹²'. . . Dei aspirante et adiuvante gratia, ab eo revelata vera esse credimus . . .'; see Denz. 3008 (1789).
¹³'. . . Non solum principio, sed obiecto distinctum'; '. . . ratio fide illustrata . . . aliquam Deo dante mysteriorum intelligentiam . . . assequitur'; 'Neque enim fidei doctrina, quam Deus revelavit, velut philosophicum inventum proposita est humanis ingeniis perficienda, sed tamquam divinum depositum Christi Sponsae tradita, fideliter custodienda et infallibiliter declaranda. Hinc sacrorum quoque dogmatum is sensus perpetuo est retinendus, quem semel declaravit . . . Ecclesia, nec umquam ab eo sensu alterioris intelligentiae specie et nomine recendendum'; see Denz. 3015–16 (1795–96).
¹⁴'. . . In suo genere, in eodem dogmate, eodem sensu eademque sententia'; 'Quod ubique, quod semper, quod ab omnibus creditum est'; see Denz. 3019–20 (1799–1800).
¹⁵To make an 'ideelle Rekonstruktion des Christentums' was Günther's aim in his book, *Vorschule zur Spekulativen Theologie des positiven Christentums*, Vienna 1828–29, 86; see Wenzel, *Das wissenschaftliche Anliegen des Güntherianismus*, op. cit. 13.
¹⁶'Ut . . . fidei depositum sancte custodirent et fideliter exponerent'; see Denz. 3070 (1836).
¹⁷See A.R. Vidler, *The Modernist Movement in the Roman Church*, op. cit., p. 37, and footnote 1, pp. 93 and 94.
¹⁸A. Loisy, 'Chronique biblique', *Revue d'histoire et de littérature religieuses* (11) 1906, 570.
¹⁹H. Duméry, 'Le modernisme', *Les grands courants*, op. cit., 132–4.

²⁰See Loisy's first letter to Blondel, 11 February 1903, in *Au coeur de la crise moderniste, op. cit.*, 80–85.

²¹M. Blondel, 'Histoire et dogme', *Les premiers écrits de Maurice Blondel* II, Paris 1951, 206–207: E. tr. *The Letter on Apologetics and History and Dogma*, London 1964, 269.

²²J. H. Walgrave, *Newman the Theologian, op. cit.*, 295.

²³See A.R. Vidler, *The Modernist Movement in the Roman Church, op. cit.*, 254.

²⁴'Dogmata . . . non sunt veritates e caelo delapsae'; see Denzinger 3422 (2022); see also above, p. 61 and its footnote 36.

²⁵'Dogmata fidei retinenda sunt tantummodo iuxta sensum practicum . . . non vero tamquam norma credendi'; see Denz. 3426 (2026).

²⁶'Veritas non est immutabilis plus quam ipse homo'; see Denz. 3458 (2058).

²⁷This quotation appeared in *The Times* of 30 September 1907; see J.J. Stam, *George Tyrrell, op. cit.*, 172, and Tyrrell's *Autobiography and Life, op. cit.*, II, 337.

²⁸'Isti divinae revelationis inimci . . . humanum progressum . . . in catholicam religionem temerario . . . inducere vellent, perinde ac si ipsa religio non Dei, sed hominum opus esset aut philosophicum aliquod inventum, quod humanis modis perfici queat'; see Pius IX's first encyclical, *Qui pluribus*, of 9 November 1846; see Denz. 2777 (1636). This quotation shows that, even before his 'conversion', Pius IX was, from the doctrinal point of view, far from 'liberal'.

²⁹'Prima ac potissima causa . . . ignorantia'; *Pascendi*, art. 28.

³⁰'. . . fuco et fallaciis'; *Pascendi*, art. 41.

³¹'Ut nihil scholasticum detrimenti capiat . . . maior profecto quam antehac positivae theologiae ratio est habenda'; *Pascendi*, art. 44.

³²See A.R. Vidler, *Twentieth Century Defenders of the Faith, op. cit.*, 37.

³³G. Tyrrell, *Through Scylla and Charybdis, op. cit.*, ix.

³⁴Chenu makes this comment in his preface to Gardeil's book in 1932; included in M.D. Chenu, *La foi dans l'intelligence*, Paris 1964, 278.

³⁵Marin-Sola did this in his book *La evolución homogénea del dogma católico*, Valencia 1923, a work which caused quite a sensation at the time in neo-scholastic circles.

³⁶'sens du réel'; on p. v of his *L'intellectualisme de Saint Thomas*, 2nd ed. Paris 1924, Rousselot called this concept programmatic for his book. The English translator used the expression 'faculty of the real', which seems rather too strong: see *The Intellectualism of St Thomas*, London 1935, 2.

³⁷'C'est le "donné" qui . . . s'invertèbre par l'intérieur et sous sa propre pression'; see 'La théologie au Saulchoir', 1937, included in M.D. Chenu, *La foi dans l'intelligence, op. cit.*, 246.

³⁸'Le plus petit *fait*, du moment qu'il est authentique, est régulateur'; Chenu, *La foi dans l'intelligence, op. cit.*, 127; E. tr. *Faith and Theology, op. cit.*, 26.

³⁹*Ibid.*, 116, at the head of the article 'Position de la théologie' (1935); E. tr. p. 15.

⁴⁰'Actus credentis non terminatur ad enuntiabile, sed ad rem'; *Summa Theol.* II–II, q. 1, a. 2 ad 2; see Chenu, *La foi dans l'intelligence, op. cit.*, 54.

⁴¹'Cognita sunt in cognoscente secundum modum cognoscentis'; *Summa Theol.* II–II, q. 1, a 2; see Chenu, *La foi dans l'intelligence, op. cit.*, 57.

⁴²'converti à l'Evangile'; see Congar, *Dialogue between Christians, op. cit.*, 19.

⁴³See Y. Congar, *Tradition and Traditions: An Historical Essay and a Theological Essay*, E. tr. Woodrow, London 1966, 308–14, especially p. 313.
⁴⁴L. Charlier, *Essai sur le problème théologique*, Thuilles 1938, p. 34, footnote 36.
⁴⁵*Ibid.*, 69.
⁴⁶'le tout du dogme'; see H. de Lubac, 'Le problème du développement du dogme', *Recherches de science religieuse* (35) 1948, 156.
⁴⁷See H. de Lubac, *Catholicism*, E. tr. Sheppard, London 1950 (no. 3 in the series 'Unam Sanctam'), 165.
⁴⁸'une théologie qui ne serait pas actuelle serait une théologie fausse'; see H. Bouillard, *Conversion et grâce chez S. Thomas d'Aquin*, Paris 1944, 219.
⁴⁹H. de Lubac, 'La théologie et ses sources. Réponse', *Recherches de science religieuse, op. cit.*, 396 f.
⁵⁰See E. Schillebeeckx, 'Humani Generis', *Theologisch Woordenboek* II, 1957, col. 2300–2302.
⁵¹P. Schoonenberg, 'Theologie in zelfbezinning', *Annalen van het Thijmgenootschap* (44) 1956, 228.
⁵²*Ibid.*, 236.
⁵³E. Schillebeeckx, 'Dogma-ontwikkeling', *Theologisch Woordenboek* I, Roermond and Maaseik 1952, col. 1087–1106; the same article was later published in the first volume of Schillebeeckx' collected articles under the title 'The Development of the Apostolic Faith into the Dogma of the Church', *Revelation and Theology*, London and Melbourne 1967, 63 f. For Rahner's comment, see p. 131, footnote 100.
⁵⁴See Schillebeeckx, *Revelation and Theology, op. cit.*, 81; cf. K. Rahner, *Theological Investigations* IV, Baltimore and London 1966, 5. Rahner's article was first published in 1958.
⁵⁵'Aufgehen des Lichts'; see Rahner, *Schriften zur Theologie* IV, *op. cit.*, 45; E. tr. *Theological Investigations* IV, *op. cit.*, 31.
⁵⁶For these quotations, see E. Schillebeeckx, *Revelation and Theology, op. cit.*, 84, 88–89.
⁵⁷E. Schillebeeckx, 'De natuurwet in verband met de katholieke huwelijksopvatting', Jaarboek 1961, *Werkgenootschap van katholieke theologen in Nederland*, Hilversum 1963, especially p. 26 ff.
⁵⁸See, for example, A.R. Vidler, *The Modernist Movement in the Roman Church, op. cit.*, 194 and G. Maron, 'Reformkatholizismus', *Die Religion in Geschichte und Gegenwart* V, *op. cit.*, col. 902–903.

THE APPEAL TO THE WORLD'S BISHOPS

Freedom for a Realistic Dialogue

Pope John's plan to hold a Council caused a considerable stir. This became only too obvious when he became the personal target of quite virulent criticism, despite the fact that he was inviolable as pope and at the same time irresistibly magnanimous as a man. The extremely right-wing Italian newspaper, *Corriere della Sera,* for example, printed the information that the Pope had, since his youth, been a modernist and had summoned the Council in order to renounce his infallibility.[1] This suspicion was, oddly enough, not entirely without foundation. At the beginning of the century, when he was secretary to the Bishop of Bergamo, John had in fact once been caught by the Holy Office writing a card to the modernist Buonaiuti, a fellow-student of his. He seems later to have made use of this incident as an excuse to Cardinal Ottaviani not to have to sign a special decree of the Index.[2] Moreover the word which he used as a motto for the idea of bringing the Church 'up to date'—*aggiornamento*—has a rather piquant flavour when one pauses to think how similar it is in meaning to the tabu word 'modernism'. As for the other accusation—his alleged desire to relinquish infallibility—during the visit of a number of prominent Protestants, he is reputed to have said, half deliberately, with his customary candour, that he was not infallible because he did not intend to use the chair of Peter officially to make a dogmatic pronouncement. Be this as it may, it was certainly his intention to set the papacy once more firmly within the whole Church, in an attempt, as Chenu has observed, to correct the overdeveloped vertical structures of the Church by concentrating on the horizontal relationships.[3]

Commentators have found it rather difficult to grasp hold of the exuberant personality of Pope John and they also seem to have been fascinated by the question of whether he foresaw the astonishing success of the Council. The 'progressives' certainly realised that his explicit theology was not theirs and that most of the world's bishops did not share their views. Generally speaking, the difficulty has been fairly well explained by saying that he had a strong affinity with the new approach which was not based on reasoning, but rather on intuition—an explanation which is reminiscent of Newman. What is in any case quite certain is firstly that he retained, from his education as a historian, a distinct feeling for relativity, secondly that he had known Cardinal Suhard when he was papal nuncio in France and had personally experienced there the hopes of the years immediately following the war and finally that he had always kept in touch with the Eastern Churches, in close and open contact. What emerges from his first statements as pope is a frank commitment to Christian unity and to the renewal of the Church. These were the two aims which he set the Council—both of them and their interconnection very reminiscent of Congar —and these two so to speak 'domestic' Church aims were in turn seen as a contribution to the peace and welfare of the whole world. After thinking about his programme as pope for three months, he deliberately decided, 'certainly trembling a little with emotion, but nonetheless with humble resolution',[4] on a very ancient form of consultation and decision in the Church—the word 'Council' suddenly came to him, as Schillebeeckx has suggested, 'from the old conjurer's box of theological tricks',[5] as the only proper expression of what had already been in his mind for a long time. Once his plan was fixed, he was not ashamed to say quite openly that his pontificate was 'on the point of occupying a more or less important place in history'.⁶

John XXIII's importance in the field of theology—which is the only aspect of the Second Vatican Council, so frequently described in all its dimensions, that I shall discuss here—is ultimately to be found in his pastoral and hierarchical activity. This was, surprisingly enough, exactly the same in the case of Pius IX, who was similar to and at the same time different from John in many other ways in character and in his conduct of affairs in the Church. According to the *Time* reporter, Kaiser, John made his intentions clear above all in his actions. He called the bishops of the world together and turned European theology and the practical sense of the Americans loose on them. He invited non-Catholics, including Russians, to the Council and let Cardinal Bea hold prayer services with them. He did not interfere with the Italian Catholics' political 'breakthrough to the left' and even invited Khrushchov's son-in-law to Rome.⁷ Above all, he wanted to create an atmosphere of freedom for a realistic dialogue, no more than this, but also no less. Before the opening of the Council, he conducted numerous discussions, led the central commission himself and dropped in unexpectedly on other meetings of conciliar commissions. Generally speaking, however, he kept in the background, fully expecting that his fellow-bishops would themselves discover their collegiality—an expectation which was not disappointed. It was only in one or two cases that he showed very clearly that he would not tolerate any attempt to restrict the openness of the Council. He must have been aware of the lack of sympathy for his adventure on the part of the hierarchical bodies in the Vatican, but he was at the same time realistic enough to appreciate that their presence during the preparatory stages of the Council was indispensable. In fact, the pre-conciliar commissions consisted for the most part of Vatican theologians, although de Lubac and Congar were members of the theological commission, Jungmann was on the liturgical commission and Karl Adam, who could unfortunately not take part in the work because of his old age, was on the commission for study. Rahner seems to have been added afterwards to the list of advisers to the commission on the sacraments. The fact that these theologians, who were not permitted to speak of their own accord, were not consulted, proved very difficult to change.

Their contribution would in any case have been of little use at that stage. In the doctrinal commissions, the 'Roman' theologians—the word 'Roman' is used in this context as a simplification to indicate the conventional neo-scholastic theology—were in an almost absolute majority and were busy composing the drafts in accordance with their own views and including in them all kinds of unfavourable references to the theology of 'renewal'. Their underlying inspiration seems to have been that, if at all costs there had to be a Council, then this dangerous relativisation of the Church's doctrine and of her age-old theology would have to be banned definitively. The bishops would recognise the theology that they had been taught in the Roman schemas and would hardly be able to vote against it. Other commissions, however, were more promising, especially, for example, the liturgical commission, many of the members of which were active in the liturgical movement, and the secretariat for Christian unity (not, it should be noted, for 'reunion'!), which, in order to keep the Curia out of it, had apparently deliberately not been set up as a commission. The president of this secretariat, the German Old Testament scholar, Cardinal Bea, chose his collaborators with great care from countries with a 'mixed' Christian population and, old as he was even then, set about the task of making contacts and sounding opinions and desires with very youthful energy. There was also enough frank speaking in the central commission, most of the members of which were bishops in residence in many different parts of the world and through which all the draft constitutions had to pass to be checked. It must have been in this commission that John began to realise for the first time that his plan was beginning to work.

When they had returned home and had received the first printed drafts, however, the members of this central commission noticed that their criticisms had only been taken minimally into account. This meant that the first four schemas, on the fundamental questions of dogmatic and moral theology, basically reproduced, in a polemically sharpened form, treatises from the current theological manuals. The representatives of the newer theology began to prepare those around them to be glad if any freedom were to remain for the theological counter-current. They saw through the situation clearly enough. If the first four draft schemas were accepted—and it looked very much as though they would be, in view of the theological training of most of the bishops—then the others would be adapted to the same pattern as their logical conclusions. 'Do not expect too much', 'hopeful but concerned', even 'possibility of failure'—these were recurring themes in the letters written by the travellers to Rome before they left in October 1962.

Pope John was conscious of the threat to that free and open dialogue on which he had from the beginning insisted. The rules of procedure for the Council contained clear guarantees for freedom of speech, but he did not want to take any risks. At the end of the baroque opening ceremony of the Council, he read, with an intensity which, even on the television, made it only too clear to everyone who heard it how affected he was by the ultimate fulfilment of his 'inspiration', a carefully considered speech, which was not the obligatory word of welcome that most of those present had expected and many had hoped for, but a programme which, stripped of the customary wordiness of such addresses, testified to his own directness. Against the prophets of gloom, he spoke about the great opportunity for the Church in the modern age and about the world's longing for peace and unity. He spoke too about the duty to preserve the gospel intact and to confess and proclaim it in full. Then followed these words which aroused such hope: 'Bravely and without

The Appeal to the World's Bishops   233

fear, we must set about the work that our present age requires us to do, continuing along the path which the Church has followed for almost twenty centuries. The first aim of our work is not . . . to repeat in greater detail the teaching handed down by the Fathers of the Church and by early and more recent theologians. We believe that this teaching is not unknown to you, but is rightly fixed in your minds. There was no need to convoke an ecumenical council to hold discussions of that kind . . . What has to be done is . . . to investigate and explain this certain and unchangeable doctrine . . . in such a way that it is adapted to our own times. For the substance of the deposit of faith or body of truths which are contained in our revered doctrine is not identical with the manner in which these truths are expressed, though the same sense and the same meaning must be preserved. If necessary, a great deal of time must be devoted to this manner of expression, and patience to elaborating it. Certainly, as for the methods by which this teaching is to be explained, those methods must be used which are most in accordance with the *magisterium,* the character of which is principally pastoral.'[8]

John's programme was received, to put it mildly, differently by different people. The protagonists of renewal were astonished by the Pope's unmistakable references to a distinction between content and mode of expression—something which they thought had been banished by *Humani Generis* from the Church's vocabulary. They also detected a barely disguised criticism of the dogmatic schemes of the theological manuals and an encouraging emphasis on the pastoral character of the Church's preaching. *Le Monde* proclaimed in a headline that John XXIII was insisting on the 'methods of investigation of modern thought'. The *Osservatore Romano,* on the other hand, regarded the 'First aim of the Council—Defence and Spreading of Doctrine'[9] as the essence of John's address, while several prominent Churchmen who were deeply concerned were happy to express their own views about the Pope's programme, from which they wished to dissociate themselves, to the Italian press.[10] After an intensive study of the texts, one progressive commentator even went so far as to say that he could prove that the distinction between content and mode of expression, which was most clearly formulated in the Italian text, which the Pope himself apparently wrote, had seemed too risky to the Latin translator, with the result that he felt obliged to touch up the text in translation.[11]

This incident gives a good indication of the edgy situation which had existed since before the opening of the Council, reached a climax halfway through the first session and in fact lasted until its conclusion. Those who had come to Rome hoping for a renewal felt extremely vulnerable in view of the course that the attempt to renew the Church's theology had followed in the recent past. They were conscious of many indications, not without a basis of truth, that those who reacted against a renewal were using most of the familiar means of neutralising the counter-current. These were playing a diplomatic game, employing all the juridical means available, and the progressives hardly regarded themselves as skilled at this. On the other hand, however, the established circles did not feel at all easy about the Pope's adventure. There were signs that the renewal might succeed this time. They had a presentiment that there would be a theological test of strength and they had not been trained to deal with this. Yet, so far, only the most superficial aspects of this opposition have been indicated. The contrast was much deeper than this and the atmosphere was so explosive because what was at stake for both 'parties' was their most profound inner conviction about the relevance of Christ's gospel. The ultimate basis of their opposition was in fact a completely different understanding of the relationship between content and mode of expression in revelation, Scripture and tradition, faith and theology.

It was therefore not a coincidence that the tension was released during the debate about the draft of the Constitution on Revelation. As the authors of these schemas had foreseen, the rest of the Council was really the conclusion of this debate, although the direction taken by this conclusion was the opposite of what they had expected. At the end of the Council, the Constitution on Revelation seemed to have developed together with the whole process of bringing the life and thinking of the Church up to date, which had itself gone much farther than anyone had imagined it would at the opening of the Council. Compared with some other conciliar documents of a more striking nature, such as the declaration of religious freedom, *Dignitatis humanae,* or the Pastoral Constitution on the Church and the World, the 'progressive' final version of the Dogmatic Constitution on Revelation, *Dei verbum,* has been called an impractical, irrelevant document by and for theologians. The same theologians, however, would be ready enough to admit that its direct utility is not the most obvious aspect of *Dei verbum.* But most people would similarly not get very excited about the foundations of the church of Notre Dame in Paris though there would not be much to see if these were unsound. If, at the close of the Council, many new themes had become firmly established in theology, this is because the theology of renewal as a whole had been accepted by an unexpectedly clear majority among the Fathers of the Council, which manifested itself for the first time in the rejection of the first schema of the Constitution on Revelation. One may safely say, then, that the whole status of Catholic theology underwent a deep and lasting change because of the freedom created during the first session of the Council. We have therefore to extend our excavation a little farther along the sample trench of the development of dogma.

The Fate of the 'Two Sources' Schema

A far less important place was given officially to the theologians at the Second Vatican Council than, for example, at Trent or at Vatican I. Several hundred 'experts' were nominated, but they were not supposed to speak of their own accord at the official meetings, even during the meetings of the various commissions. Their status was very similar to that of the non-Catholic observers, who had in fact more faculties. Nonetheless, both groups had a great influence— the observers in the first place by being present at all the official meetings. Congar says, in his account of the Council, that when he first met these official representatives of the other Churches there in Rome the tears came into his eyes[12] —it was exactly twenty-five years since his *Chrétiens désunis*. These non-Catholic observers were able to exert a decisive influence on the discussions by their written remarks and above all by their personal contacts. The European theologians of renewal especially established or re-established valuable contacts with them.

In addition to this, however, the Catholic theological 'experts' themselves formed mutual contacts which led to a regular collaboration and exchange of ideas for years, which in turn had a lasting influence on the development of the new Catholic theology. Among the theologians discussed in this book, Congar, de Lubac, Daniélou and Rahner were official experts, Chenu and Schillebeeckx were never able to achieve this status and Küng did not achieve it until the second session. The most important work done by these theologians, however, took place outside the official meetings. They advised the bishops when they were preparing their speeches, for instance, maintained contact between the various episcopal conferences and gave lectures, on invitation, to impressive numbers of Fathers of the Council. This latter fact in particular made some of them wonder, half seriously, who really made up the Church's 'teaching office'. Küng and Schillebeeckx, who had thought that their unofficial position would give them more time, received more invitations to lecture than they could possibly accept.

In the case of Küng, the reason for this was undoubtedly his striking publications on the Council and the structures of the Church. The bishops' attention was drawn to Schillebeeckx on account of some curious facts. In the first place, he was the only theologian whom the Dutch bishops thanked by name at the end of their pastoral letter about the Council in 1960 for his 'services' in its composition. The Italian translation of this letter, which in fact clearly reflected the most recent ideas about revelation, faith and the Church—ideas which were later to find their way into the conciliar documents—was withdrawn from circulation by the 'authorities', although this did not mean that it did not continue to be widely circulated unofficially and read. In addition to this, Schillebeeckx was also regarded as the author of an unofficial, but similarly widely circulated commentary on the first drafts of various conciliar documents, in which a number of weak points were critically examined and certain counter-suggestions were made. Apart from the chapter on evolution, this paper had indeed been written by Schillebeeckx. At the request of Mgr Bekkers, the Bishop of Den Bosch, who wanted to discuss the documents of the Council in advance, Schillebeeckx had put this paper together in a few days. The bishop became so enthusiastic that he had translations made and, after a later discussion, in which another seventeen colleagues, from Germany, among other places, took part, had these translations collected together and distributed in their hundreds among the Fathers of the Council.

Schillebeeckx' paper certainly achieved one positive result. His first suggestion was that the debates in the Council should begin with the last three draft constitutions and decrees to be sent in—those on the liturgy, means of communication and Christian unity—so as to gain time 'to study and to think about the following commentary' on the very one-sided fundamental schemas. The final sequence of the debates had not yet been decided and a number of petitions made to the ten presidents, who were mostly sympathetic, resulted in this important change. Encouraged by the Pope's opening speech and by their 'successes' in the election of new commissions, the more progressive Fathers set hopefully about the task of discussing the draft Constitution on the Liturgy, which was the most pastoral and the most adapted to modern needs. This gave the theologians time to try to get a favourable hearing among the bishops for the new theology. On the other hand, the bishops were already sufficiently interested in the commentary to send out invitations themselves, not only, of course. to the mysterious author of the commentary.

It is a rather strange experience to re-read this commentary in the new, post-conciliar situation—I was closely involved in the English translation at the time. But it is still a fascinating document. The extreme caution with regard to the prevailing theology, which was at that time the only theology that was universally accepted, seems a little unnecessary now. The originally private character of the comments is also occasionally revealed as the reason for this caution—that is to say not to provoke the opposition unnecessarily so that the positive elements that were already contained in the schemas would be removed. On the other hand, however, the careful attempt to point out the similarities between the older and the new approaches does not give the impression of being forced. In many respects, scholasticism which has been taken back to its sources is really no more than more open and more all-embracing than the theology represented in the original drafts, not in any fundamental way opposed to it. On the other hand, the commentary observes quite openly that the draft put forward the ideas of one particular theological school, went farther in this than Trent or Vatican I and, according to the footnotes, made no use of the sixteen thick volumes of suggestions which had been made in every part of the world. What is in any case still fascinating when one reads this paper again is the unerring anatomical analysis of the inconsistencies, the structural faults and the partly or completely wrong quotations and interpretations which were made especially when the new theology was under fire. Thomas, Trent, Vatican I and even *Humani Generis* were brought forward as witnesses for the defence of the new approach in Schillebeeckx' commentary.

The basic content of the schemas was, in broad outline, the well-known neo-scholastic view. Revelation was, in other words, regarded as the communication of a number of conceptual truths which could be found at two sources, Scripture and tradition. Faith was the acceptance of these revealed truths as proposed by the Church for man's faith on God's authority. Man's knowledge of the truth—a philosophical problem, which was dealt with in a separate chapter in the schema on the 'pure preservation of the deposit of faith'—was objective, grasped things *in se* in universal and abstract concepts and was able to attain necessary and unchangeable truths and pronounce judgements about them which were not subject to change. The concepts of faith were therefore not 'approximations always to be changed and corrected',[13] but a reflection of the unchangeable truth itself.

Schillebeeckx, on the other hand, in his commentary adhered to the fuller content of the biblical concept of revelation as God's revelation of himself interpreted in words. The rather simple proof put forward in the schema to show that revelation was only a communication in words could not really be upheld in the face of the biblical idea—despite, for example, the twenty texts, all quite literally interpreted, which were quoted as evidence in a footnote occupying two full pages, including one from the Twelve Articles of Faith: 'who *spoke* through the prophets'. All the same, in emphasising the 'manifestation of Christ', the idea of revelation in reality did find its way into the schema—and rightly, since Christ's humanity and life as a man was God's revelation of himself and any other view would have undermined Christology.

Scripture and tradition were, Schillebeeckx argued, testimonies closely connected to the one source which had been stressed by all the Councils ever held by the Church—Christ's gospel itself. And even Scripture and tradition did not bear witness primarily to a truth, but to a reality. Further, if God's inward speaking and the light of faith did not play a part, then faith was not 'divine' faith, in other words, it was not a virtue or attitude in which God himself was encountered. This was something which Thomas and all the traditional teachers of the Church had discussed in detail. Finally, the schema's theory of knowledge had failed to distinguish between the content itself and the manner in which we know—the concepts of faith do enable us to grasp hold of the unchangeable truth of God as an intelligible content, but the ideas which have to be used in this process are inadequate and are therefore subject to development and change. Compared with these basic principles of the schema, the short, carefully balanced chapter on the development of dogma, even though this was attributed to the living *teaching authority* of the Church, was clearly something quite different in kind.

The commentary also raised the question of whether or not the schema ought to be entirely rewritten and made many concrete suggestions for improvements. The bishops of the 'Rhine countries'—to use Wiltgen's handy phrase for Germany, France, Switzerland and the Low Countries—had, in fact, decided at an early stage to prepare such shadow schemas, and at the conclusion of the extensive debate on the liturgy, they put them forward as possible alternatives to the first schema on the 'sources of revelation' if this were rejected. Shortly before the opening of the debate on revelation, Cardinal Ottaviani called a meeting of the theological commission, in order to inform its members of the great value of the schema which had been compiled with such care. Most of the members of the new commission were protagonists of theological renewal. At this meeting, the cardinal's supporter, Mgr Parente, spent a whole hour attacking Rahner, whose work he rather surprisingly called 'romantic', and Schillebeeckx, whose commentary revealed an 'anti-conceptualistic neurosis and a modernistic view of revelation'. The atmosphere was unmistakably that of a law court. It was a harrowing time for the accused. Schillebeeckx alone had given twenty-three lectures and his views had in

The Appeal to the World's Bishops 241

this way been heard by more than fifteen hundred bishops. The theologians realised that the whole of theological renewal was at stake and that, if they lost, they could dispose of their theological books.

The verdict, which caused surprise at the time, is now common knowledge. The bishops had spent a month debating the draft Constitution on the Liturgy and had therefore been in close contact with the new theology that inspired it. In addition, they had personally met these new theologians themselves and had been impressed by their solid learning and their accurate knowledge of the whole tradition of the Church and especially of scholasticism. They had also met the non-Catholic observers, who were no less prominent in their own fields and who, in many respects, thought along similar lines. In this way, many of the bishops had been able to recognise, in the new theological ideas, a clear expression of their own pastoral experience. They had come together in an attempt to break through the impasse in their apostolic work. The older theology of the Church had shown itself to be incapable of helping them in this task, but the new approach, which many of them were now coming to know seriously and above all personally for the first time, did at least appear to provide positive perspectives. What also impressed them was that, unlike previous councils, one definite theology was forcibly put forward and that this was frequently done with clearly untheological means. This was particularly evident in the rather unedifying actions taken against the Jesuits' Pontifical Biblical Institute in Rome. As soon as they had arrived in Rome, all the Fathers of the Council had been warned against this college in a seditious brochure. In the autumn of 1962, two well-known professors, Lyonnet and Zerwick, were teaching, by order of Curia officials, only biblical linguistics and none of the other teachers at the college was an official expert at the Council.[14] The principles of Catholic biblical studies as expressed in the schemas on revelation were the theoretical reflection of this guerilla warfare. Entirely in accordance with the point of departure that the Bible was the depository for truths and historical 'facts' that could be easily manipulated, the modern methods, which were concerned with the relationships between the various traditions and literary forms in the Bible and which therefore placed the message of the Bible in a much wider context which was for this reason also less diaphonous, were severely criticised in the schema. In addition, the function of the 'living *magisterium*' of the Church with regard to the Bible (and tradition) was described as so all-embracing that it was not at all clear either what task was still left for biblical scholarship—the clarification and interpretation of obscure passages were regarded as the task of the Church's teaching office—or how the Bible and tradition could act as a norm for that office. In many respects, the schema meant a limitation of that freedom which biblical scholars in fact owed to the encyclical *Divino Afflante*, the document issued by Pius XII in 1943 at the insistence of and in collaboration with Cardinal Bea.[15]

Cardinal Ottaviani opened the official debate in St Peter's with a short statement that the schema was above all pastoral in character, because the 'most important duty of a pastor' was 'to teach the truth that is always the same everywhere'. The presentator, Mgr Garofalo, then added that the most important task of the Council was to defend Catholic doctrine and promulgate it in its most exact formulation.[16] A whole phalanx of prominent Fathers, however, including the Patriarch Maximos and Cardinals Frings, König, Bea, Liénart, Léger, Suenens, Alfrink and Ritter came forward and testified that they did not regard this intellectualistic approach as acceptable. To give only one example, Cardinal Alfrink compared the schema, in a very significant answer to Mgr Garofalo, with the programme that Pope John had outlined in his opening speech, quoting his remarks about the unnecessary repetition of the current theology, the pastoral character of the present Council and the distinction between content and mode of expression in the Church's

The Appeal to the World's Bishops 243

deposit of faith. The feeling on the third day was so obvious that one defender of the draft Constitution declared openly that he felt like Daniel in the lion's den.[17] In the following assembly, Cardinal Döpfner caused a stir by observing that similar objections to the ones that had been heard in the debate had been expressed not only in the theological commission, but also in the central preparatory commission, but they had simply been ignored.[18] On the next day, Mgr de Smedt of Bruges revealed that the Secretariat for Unity, in the name of which he was speaking, had, in accordance with its task, offered to collaborate with the theological commission, but that this offer had not been accepted 'for reasons which I am not entitled to judge'.[19]

The theologians calculated what their chances would be when it ultimately came to the vote—Schillebeeckx, with characteristic optimism and encouraged by his experience in his lectures, thought that sixty per cent of the votes would be cast against the schema. The majority would in fact have been even greater than this, but, because the question had, by a trick, been phrased differently—'must the debate about the schema be broken off?'—one-third of the votes cast were against the schema, which was not enough. The 'acquittal' did not in fact come until the Pope intervened, overriding the procedural rules. There are good reasons for thinking that the two pillars of the Holy Office, Cardinals Ottaviani and Browne, voted, in the confusion that prevailed because of the unexpected phrasing of the question, for the rejection of their own schema and thus, as the heads of the supreme doctrinal court in the Catholic Church, ironically condemned themselves as well.

Although John XXIII may or may not really have said, 'Now my Council is beginning',[20] he certainly had a clear understanding of what was going on. He was connected with St Peter's through a closed television circuit, so that he had no need to miss anything, but, as he said significantly to his secretary, he could always switch the set off. His solution to the crisis was a confirmation of his basic plan—to create the freedom for a real dialogue. He therefore entrusted the task of composing a new schema to a combination of the (new) theological commission and the Secretariat for Unity under the joint leadership of Ottaviani and Bea. By repeatedly stressing the function of the Secretariat for Unity, the Pope showed clearly enough that he believed that the deepest meaning of the Council, the meaning that he had had in mind since the idea of the Council had first come to him, was its ecumenical character. Another indication of this was the decree on ecumenism, in which theological pluriformity—the practical issue of the lawsuit with the Roman theology—was most obviously expressed.

After this climax, the theologians seemed to be, as it were, absent from the Council for a time. The schema on the means of communication did not, after all, give much opportunity for energetic action for or against and the last schema that was still available, that on Christian unity, was so clearly directed exclusively towards the Eastern Churches that it was soon decided to incorporate it into the more general projected schemas. It was not really until the debate on the hastily printed draft Constitution on the Church that interest revived. Although this document was better than the other products of the pre-conciliar theological commission, it was not essentially different from them in its general tendency. Its basic faults were, in the words of Mgr de Smedt that have since become classic, triumphalism, clericalism and legalism.[21] Even more influential, however, was the theme taken up by the hitherto rather reserved Cardinals Suenens and Montini in defining the function of the Church towards the world. Going back to the Pope's original aim and following the ideas that had already been expressed in the 'message to the world',[22] a half forgotten proclamation which had been inspired by the French 'secular' theology of Chenu and Congar and had been approved by the Fathers at the beginning of the Council, these two cardinals pleaded convincingly in favour of a breakthrough of the purely ecclesiastical problems and a concentration on such world problems as atheism, hunger, poverty and peace. This was in fact the origin of the Constitution on the Church and the World. The Council was, however, set on its course when, in response to a large number of suggestions, the Pope set up a small co-ordinating commission and gave it two main tasks. The first was to effect a drastic reduction in the overwhelming number of schemas. The second task was to supervise their compilation, in the spirit of the majority view that had emerged at the first session. As John himself said at the final meeting, 'This first session has been like a slow and solemn opening to the great work of the Council.' It had taken time for mutual contacts to be established, for pastoral experiences to be exchanged and for the Fathers to become acquainted with one another's ideas. If this had led to 'understandable but rather disturbing differences of opinion', it had nonetheless been beneficial in revealing 'the holy freedom of the children of God which flourishes in the Church'.[23] The Pope was beginning to witness the confirmation of his inspiration by the Spirit of God.

The Council could not fail now, even without John. At the end of September 1963, the participants went back to Rome, bereft because of the death of the Pope, but strengthened by his testament, *Pacem in terris,* in which he, so as to make quite sure, prophetically anticipated the debate on the Church and the world. Pope Paul VI, in an impressive speech which was both all-embracing and surprisingly animated, re-affirmed the fundamental ideas that his predecessor had already outlined and quoted the most striking statements from John's opening speech, The progressives, who still felt a little ill at ease in their recently acquired position as the majority, set to work with renewed vigour to deal with the reborn schemas. There were to be more than enough difficulties during the next three years, but by the end of the Council far more had been accomplished than had been expected before October 1962. Not only had the neo-scholastic theological terminology, which had been for so long accepted almost without question, been replaced by expressions taken from the Bible, the Church Fathers or modern thinking, but many of the themes of the theology of renewal had at last been officially accepted by the Catholic Church. The Constitution on the Liturgy, for example, contains echoes of Casel's theology of the paschal mystery and of the theology of the sacrament and the word which was inspired by him. In the Constitution on the Church, there is the central theme of the people of God, going through history and led by those holding office and collegially united, as the sign of mankind seeking unity. In the Decree on Ecumenism, there is an explicit affirmation that those Christian communities which are not united with Rome are nonetheless Churches and an ecumenical quest, emphasised by a relativisation of the expressions of faith, for the fullness of the one Church of Christ. Although the Decree on the Training of Priests is not entirely successful, it does not prescribe one uniform programme of studies, regards biblical theology as the basis and modern thought as an important ancillary means of priestly education and limits reference to scholasticism to a simple phrase, 'with Saint Thomas as teacher'.[24] In the Declaration of Religious Freedom, the inviolable value of personal conviction is openly recognised. The Decree on the Office and Life of Priests emphasises their prophetic task and their pastoral presence in the world of work, if necessary by themselves serving as workers. The Decree on the Missionary Activity of the Church makes use of the experience of the *Mission de France* by reformulating the concept of 'mission' as an essential mark of the Church. As a final example, the Pastoral Constitution on the Church and the Modern World opens the way for honest dialogue between the Church and the constantly evolving modern age and accepts in principle the autonomous 'laicity' of the world, for example, in the relationship between the Church and the state, in the structure of society, in marriage and in scientific research.

The whole process of development is, however, clearly

reflected in the progressive change that took place in the schema on Revelation—a striking example of the 'development of tradition' during the Council itself.

The Council's Final Judgement on Dogma and History

The dialogue between at least the 'Roman' members of the theological commission and the Secretariat for Christian Unity about a new draft Constitution on Revelation went off least smoothly of all when the question of the 'two sources' of revelation was discussed. Those who opposed this theory did so not only for ecumenical reasons, i.e. out of consideration for the emphasis placed on *sola scriptura* in Protestant teaching, but also because the limited vision of the Roman theology seemed to them to be impoverished in comparison with the fullness of the idea of revelation which had held from biblical times until the Middle Ages. To postulate tradition as an independent source of data which cannot be found in the Bible is to take too limited a view of the content of revelation—to regard it, in other words, as a number of clearly defined truths. What is more, a tradition which is regarded as independent of the Bible and which is 'deposited' in and interpreted by the Church, which means, in the concrete, by the teaching authority of the Church, is an element which is very liable to be dependent on the actual practice of the Church and which can therefore be easily used to neutralise Scriptural criticism of the life of the Church. For these reasons, the new theologians aimed to make the bond between the Bible and tradition as close as possible—the Bible is the essence of the apostolic tradition fixed in Scripture and tradition is the handing on of the realities of revelation and of the Church's developing understanding of Scripture. Historical studies had shown that these ideas were still assumed at Trent and that they had been rediscovered, as we have seen, from the time of the Tübingen school onwards. The Roman theologians, on the other hand, continued to uphold the views that had been developed in the polemics that followed the Council of Trent and were convinced that these constituted a point of faith that had been established in Trent and Vatican I. A special emphasis on control by the Church's teaching authority was almost automatically linked to this.

The combined commission, then, made hardly any progress in the discussion of a new schema until the decision was finally taken completely to avoid the controversial question of the 'addition' of tradition to Scripture. The second schema submitted to the bishops before the summer of 1963 contained many positive elements. The concept of revelation now also included God's actions, and the relationships between Scripture and tradition and between tradition and the Church's teaching office were defined in a more realistic manner. Nonetheless, according to their written reactions, the bishops had the ultimate impression that the new schema was not substantial enough, in comparison with the document on the liturgy and the new schema on the Church which had recently been submitted to the Fathers. Could they reach no more than a minimal agreement about such a fundamental point? In order to get round the difficulties, a suggestion that had already been made before was once again put forward, namely that it might be sufficient to incorporate a few fundamental ideas into the existing schema on the Church. Fortunately, however, this mood of discouragement was overcome and in March 1964 a subcommission of the theological commission, consisting of some seven bishops and twenty-one theologians, including Rahner and Congar, set to work on an entirely new schema. The Secretariat for Unity took no part in this preparatory work, preferring, after the experience of the good theological draft of the Constitution on the Church, to limit its collaboration to a final check of the document, which in fact did not result in any substantial alterations.

Deadlock was reached, however, once again when a plenary meeting of the theological commission discussed the schema on the 'two sources'. It was therefore decided to present both points of view to the whole Council and to leave the final decision to the Fathers. The decisive factor in this was that the majority report was entrusted to Archbishop Florit of Florence, who had been a faithful supporter of the older theology, but had become gradually convinced of the value of the newer approach. Many of the more hesitant Fathers of the Council were persuaded by his balanced argument, expressed as it was in the familiar terminology of the earlier theology. Because Florit's opponent, Mgr Franič, had in any case to admit that the new schema contained no error, but was merely incomplete, the way to an ultimately well balanced constitution was smoothed out,[25] even though the contrasts continued to be discernible even in the final amendments.

Anyone who compares the final version of the Constitution on Divine Revelation with the first, rejected schemas is bound, according to L. Bakker's suggestive image, to feel a bit dizzy now and then, as though he had performed a double jump.[26] Sometimes there is not very much difference between what is said in the final version and what was meant to be condemned in 1962. After a short introduction, in which it is significantly enough said that the Council *listens* to the word of God, the final document first describes revelation as God's sacramental communication of himself and as his invitation to men to fellowship with him, revealed and proclaimed in words. God speaks to man in his creation, but he has also, since the time of our ancestors, revealed *himself* in the history of the chosen people, as a constant preparation for the fullness of revelation in Christ's being and actions. To this revealing God, man must show 'the obedience of faith' (*Rom.* 16: 26) by which he 'entrusts his whole self freely to God' with 'full submission of intellect and will' made possible by 'the grace of God and the interior help of the Holy Spirit' which 'precedes and assists, moving the heart and turning it to God, opening the eyes of the mind'. The same holy Spirit also continues to 'bring about an ever deeper understanding of revelation'.[27] In comparison with this subtly worded exposition of the meaning of revelation, in which the themes of the theology of renewal are again and again discernible, the amendment proposed by 116 of the Fathers, but not accepted by the Council, to strike out the 'personalistic' definition of faith as free surrender[28] was no more than a rearguard action.

The second chapter of the Constitution on the 'handing on' of revelation, which is built up on this foundation, aroused more reaction. Only one bishop did not find it a good idea to relate the title of this chapter to the active handing on of revelation.[29] The advantages of this point of departure are obvious enough—it is only possible to throw any light on the relationship between Scripture, tradition and the Church from the general background as this is in fact described in the document. The first paragraph of the second chapter describes the task which Christ gave to his apostles 'to preach to all men that gospel which is the source of all saving truth and moral teaching', a task which they fulfilled faithfully by their oral proclamation of the word, by their personal example, by their institutions, and finally by committing the message of salvation to writing. Tradition and Scripture, handed on after the apostles by their successors, 'are like a mirror in which the pilgrim Church on earth looks at God'.[30] The first characteristic that strikes one in this exposition is the designation of the gospel as the one source of the truth of salvation—not of 'truths'—and the relativisation of this description by the addition of 'and moral teaching'. The second striking feature is the realistic description of the elements of tradition and the deliberately chosen word order, 'tradition and Scripture' which, unlike the opposite order, clearly characterises Scripture as the essence of the total tradition, but at the same time also as an element of tradition. It is remarkable that the section of the World Council of Churches known as 'Faith and Order' came to practically the same conclusion a year earlier at its world conference in Montreal.[31]

After a welcome reminder of the 'special way' in which

The Appeal to the World's Bishops 251

the preaching of the apostles is contained in the 'inspired books', the following section of the Constitution goes on to define more concretely how tradition 'includes everything which contributes to the holiness of life, and the increase of faith of the people of God; and so the Church, in her teaching, life, and worship perpetuates and hands on all that she herself is, all that she believes'.

The second paragraph of this section, which deals with the development of tradition—this broad term itself is almost a matter of course—merits full quotation here: 'This tradition which comes from the apostles, develops in the Church with the help of the Holy Spirit. For there is a growth in the understanding of the realities and the words which have been handed down. This happens through the contemplation and study made by believers, who treasure these things in their hearts . . ., through the intimate understanding of spiritual things they experience, and through the preaching of those who have received through episcopal succession the sure gift of truth. For, as the centuries succeed one another, the Church constantly moves forward towards the fullness of divine truth, until the words of God reach their complete fulfilment in her.'[32]

This paragraph, in which the fact that revelation is really determined by history was for the first time declared by a Council of the Church, caused considerable alarm and changes were suggested up to the very last moment. A group of 175 Fathers wanted to admit only a development in man's *understanding* of tradition and therefore to have both the beginning and the conclusion of this paragraph changed. A rather smaller number even wanted to have the words relating to man's growing 'understanding of the realities . . . handed down' removed, because, they argued, only truths were, in the proper sense of the word, capable of being understood by man. (The commission pointed out that these words in fact expressed the desire of the 175 Fathers.) In addition, the request was made that the text should also include a clear reference to the intact preservation of the deposit of faith and that the classical phrase of Vincent of Lérins, that is, that development took place 'in the same teaching, in the same sense and with the same meaning', should also be added to this paragraph.[33]

It will of course be clear that this fairly compact group of bishops formed the 'hard core' that was left of the 800 or so who had voted for the very first schema. The commission vindicated its latest draft by saying that most of the objections had been clearly met in the latter part of the text. There had been no intention to deny the 'closing' of revelation by suggesting that there was a growth in the content of tradition. On the other hand, however, it had seemed right, in addition to including a sentence which made development refer clearly to man's understanding, to speak of the development of tradition as a whole, in other words, of the whole life of the Church and not simply of the knowledge of a number of unchangeable 'truths'. In any case, the quotation from Vincent of Lérins was not included because its interpretation was, in the opinion of the members of the commission, uncertain[34]—a polite way of saying that the sentence excluded real development rather than recognising it.

The 175 bishops also asked that the function of the Church's teaching office should be added to the 'factors of development'—this function was entirely omitted from the penultimate version. They succeeded partly, but by no means entirely. The list of various factors in the development of tradition is in fact the most surprising detail in the whole paragraph. Originally, the development of man's understanding was attributed in the first place to the 'contemplation made by believers', but, to pay proper honour to the work of the theologians, the word 'study' was soon added. The second factor named in the schema was 'spiritual experience'—an almost too bold choice, considering the dubious connotation it had acquired in modernism. Cardinal Browne lost no time in pointing out this connection in protest,[35] but the only concession which the commission was prepared to make was to clarify the wording so that the final version read: 'the intimate understanding of spiritual things they experience'. The penultimate version thus still contained only these two factors—in striking contrast to, for example, the view expressed in *Humani Generis*, which attributed such a decisive role to the Church's teaching authority. The commission was clearly following the line which was most prominent in the theology of Rahner and Schillebeeckx, namely that the teaching authority formally had a judging function. Because in fact the preaching of the Church was a further factor of development, however, the commission decided to add it to the list, though not to mention the *magisterium* explicitly as this was not formally under discussion. The total perspective was therefore in no way changed—the preaching of the bishops of the Church was still placed third on the list of developing factors.

The third and final paragraph of this section (art. 8) deals with the concrete function of this living, growing tradition—how it penetrates the practice and life of the Church, how, through it, the Church comes to know Scripture, which is 'more profoundly understood and unceasingly made active in her'[36] by tradition. In this way, God's word, expressed in the gospel, continues to resound in the world through the holy Spirit, who leads believers to the full truth of Christ.

Two difficulties still remained—the relationship between tradition and Scripture, in itself, and the relationship between tradition and Scripture on the one hand and the whole Church and her teaching authority on the other. The first of these two problems is dealt with in article 9 of the Constitution, which still bears clear traces of the issue at stake—that of the 'addition' of tradition to Scripture—in the confrontation between the two opposing theologies of revelation. Nonetheless, a considerable measure of agreement was reached over quite a far-reaching basic formulation. Tradition and Scripture are closely connected and mutually interwoven, because they both come from the same source and are directed towards the same end. Both contain the word of God and in both cases it is the holy Spirit who guarantees that the word is preserved intact. Whereas revelation has been 'consigned to writing' in the Bible, it is preserved faithfully in tradition, explained and made widely known by preaching. That is why 'it is not from sacred Scripture alone that the Church draws her certainty about everything that has been revealed. Therefore both . . . are to be accepted and venerated with equal devotion and reverence'.[37]

The words 'with equal devotion' (in the original Latin document, the word *pari,* equal or like, is used here) in the second sentence of this quotation, which goes back to the Council of Trent, merit closer attention. Out of reverence for Scripture, there was a desire to avoid the word 'same' (*eadem*). The first quoted sentence is, however, clearly the central point of the dispute and marks the farthest limit to the agreement of both parties. In the penultimate version, the omission of this statement made 111 of the Fathers ask if the sentence 'Therefore not every Catholic truth can be (directly) proved from Scripture (alone)' might be added.[38] With good reason, the members of the commission refused to accept this emphatically neo-scholastic formulation, but finally decided in favour of one of the expressions suggested by the Pope. The result was clearly fortunate, affirming as it does tradition as the wider context of Scripture within the Church. The extent to which the Bible contains the whole truth of revelation, either explicitly or purely implicitly (a kind of Catholic *sola Scriptura*), is not discussed in this section of the Constitution, but tradition, as explanation and interpretation of Scripture, is affirmed as the basis of greater certainty about revelation.

The function of the Church's teaching office with regard to this one deposit of faith in Scripture and tradition is approached as it were from 'below', that is, from the point of view of the whole community of the Church, in the following section of the Constitution. The single-minded unity of bishops and people or the 'remarkable common effort on the part of the bishops and faithful' is based on the fact that the whole people of God remain steadfast 'in the teaching of the apostles, in the common life, in the breaking of the bread, and in prayers' and in 'holding to, practising, and professing the heritage of the faith', that is, tradition. It is only *after* stating this common responsibility on the part of the whole people of God that the 'task of authentically interpreting the word of God, whether written or handed on' and, what is more, of doing this 'in the name of Jesus Christ' is ascribed exclusively to the 'living teaching office of the Church'. This is in turn immediately followed by the affirmation: 'This teaching office is not above the word of God, but serves it, teaching only what has been handed on, listening to it devoutly, guarding it scrupulously, and explaining it faithfully by divine commission and with the help of the Holy Spirit'. This interconnection between tradition, Scripture and the Church's teaching office 'under the action of the one Holy Spirit' is then described as so close 'that one cannot stand without the others, and that . . . each in its own way . . . contribute effectively to the salvation of souls'.[39]

In Archbishop Florit's presentation, the collective consciousness of faith of the whole community of the Church was explicitly connected with the development of tradition: 'The authoritative intervention of the Church's *magisterium* has nothing of itself, unless it is precisely the charisma of infallible authority', through which it recognises and confirms, in teaching, the agreement with revelation, 'adding nothing to it and taking nothing away from it'.[40] In the proposed amendments to the draft Constitution there was practically no opposition any more to this statement, which rejected the idea that the Church's teaching office was the principal factor in the development of dogma. Finally, the suggestions made by some of the Fathers, who apparently identified the teaching office with the pope, gave the commission a good reason for referring to the Constitution on the Church and pointing once more explicitly to the collegial responsibility of the pope and the bishops.

In the remaining four chapters of the Constitution, these fundamental ideas are applied to Scripture, its divine and human origin and its interpretation and place in the Church. The broadminded principles of *Divino Afflante*, which were so disputed during the first session because of the action taken against the Papal Biblical Institute, are reaffirmed and extended in the rest of the Constitution. As God has spoken in a human manner in the Bible, the most important task is to find out what the sacred authors meant and, to do this, use must be made of all available exegetical means, especially in order to establish the 'literary forms' of the various parts of the Bible, since these are 'historical in varying modes'. In this work of interpretation, however, 'no less serious attention must be given to the content and unity of the whole of Scripture' and man's understanding of the Bible in the tradition of the whole Church 'must be taken into account'. This exegetical investigation is the 'preparatory study' through which the 'judgement of the Church may mature'. The exegetes' work is, however, 'subject finally'[41] to this judgement. What strikes one immediately in these final sentences is the very modest way of speaking about 'taking into account', the 'judgement of the Church' (not the judgement of the Church's teaching office) and 'finally'.

After stressing the importance of the Old Testament, the Constitution says, in very restrained language, that the four gospels are 'of apostolic origin',[42] and that the 'Church unhesitatingly asserts' their 'historical character', which above all means that they really bring us into contact with the historical saving events of Christ, for it is explicitly stated that, after the ascension of Christ, the apostles 'handed on to their hearers what he had said and done and did this with that clearer understanding which they enjoyed'. The section on the New Testament also says, moreover, that the authors of the gospels selected and interpreted their material 'in view of the situation of their churches'.[43]

In the concluding chapter (VI), the central place of

The Appeal to the World's Bishops

Scripture in the life of the Church is described in inspiring language. Scripture is, together with the apostolic tradition, the Church's 'supreme rule of faith', by which preaching and Christian thought must be 'nourished and ruled'.[44] So that the community of the Church may come to a 'deeper understanding' of the Bible, exegetes and theologians are actively encouraged to use, in sincere collaboration and subject to the guidance of the Church's teaching office, all available means to 'continue . . . with the work they have so well begun . . . with loyalty to the mind of the Church'.[45] The study of Scripture must, as it were, form the 'soul'[46] of theology.

It will therefore be abundantly clear that due honour is paid to the pioneering work of historical and especially biblical theologians—their 'return to the sources' made this Constitution on Revelation possible.

When the last proposed amendments were put to the vote, just under three years after the dramatic rejection of the 'Two Sources' Schema, only 27 of the Fathers of the Council were unable to agree with the general content of the Constitution and at the final count there were only six votes against. This may be compared with the final voting on the Schema of the Constitution on the Church and the Modern World, in which there were respectively 251 and 75 votes against. It may possibly cause surprise that, at the request of 175 alarmed Fathers, no more than about seven per cent of the total number, at the last moment changes in the text—some of them quite important—were in fact made. It was, however, a matter of vital importance to the Council and to the 'progressive' theologians in the commission to reach the greatest possible agreement about the basic document of the Christian faith. They were only too well aware of the fact that every light, even the light of faith of one single Father of the Council voting against, and even though it was concealed in a superseded theology, could be a welcome support for the understanding of the word of God. It was not a question of prescribing a practical rule of conduct, but of expressing man's understanding of an elusive mystery.

The theologians of renewal wondered afterwards, not without some surprise, how it had ever been possible to cover such an immeasurable distance in less than three years. Not only had a great deal of freedom been created for their interpretation—the essence of it had been recognised and gratefully accepted as an authentic development. Their argument, based on material evidence which they had been collecting for years, had always been that revelation and faith had never been enclosed, either in the biblical or even in the medieval tradition, in static, conceptual relationships and that an intellectualistic reduction of this kind contained no more than a fraction of the total wealth of human thought and experience. In the Council, this argument was listened to with increasing attentiveness and finally with consent. In this way then, two closely connected sets of data, which even in the Catholic Church had been forcing themselves on the attention—indeed, with increasing insistence since the beginning of the nineteenth century—were ultimately freely acknowledged as indisputable. These two sets of data were, on the one hand, the results of historical studies in the field of theology and, on the other, of the fact that human life and experience was something dynamic and conditioned by history.

Encouraged and rehabilitated by the decisions of the Council, Catholic theologians were able to set to work again afterwards with renewed energy and in greater freedom.

Bibliography

The lists of books and articles on the Second Vatican Council in theological bibliographies have in recent years become longer than those on mariology in the past. B. Ulianich has made a useful and reasonable selection in *Concilium* (2/7) 1966. Because of his personal involvement, Congar's account of the Council, *Vatican II, le concile au jour le jour*, 4 volumes, Paris 1963—is especially important. The first two volumes have been translated: *Report from Rome* (London 1963 and 1964). Apart from this work, the most reliable and informative accounts are those by A. Wenger, *Vatican II*, 4 volumes, Paris 1963, and R. Laurentin, *L'enjeu du concile*, 5 volumes, Paris 1962. One book which merits special mention because of its concise reporting and which was published since Ulianich compiled his list is *The Rhine Flows into the Tiber. The Unknown Council* (New York 1967), by R. Wiltgen, who was himself an untiring help during the Council to everyone who was disappointed by the official communiqués. R. Caporale's sociological study, *Vatican II. Last of the Councils* (Baltimore 1964), throws a surprising light on the expectations, backgrounds, contacts and influence of the different groups during the Council.

The theological background will be found in the above-mentioned work by Congar and in one of his separate studies, 'Le "théologiser" du concile', which is published in his collection, *Situation et tâches présentes de la théologie* (Paris 1967). There is also *The Theology of Vatican II* by Mgr C. Butler, who was himself a member of the theological commission, and Schillebeeckx' collected articles dating from 1959 and thus reflecting the development during the years of the Council. There is a complete French translation of these articles in two volumes: *L'Église du Christ et l'homme d'aujourd'hui selon Vatican II*, Le Puy 1965–66, and an English version of some of the same articles in *Vatican II, the Struggle of Minds* (Dublin 1963) and *Vatican II, the Real Achievement* (London 1967). The commentary of the non-Catholic observers is also extremely illuminating, especially that in *Dialogue on the Way* (Minneapolis 1965), a collection edited by G.A. Lindbeck, whose own contributions are the most substantial, and the reflections in G.C. Berkouwer's two studies, already referred to in the bibliography on page 165. Professor Berkouwer was the personal guest of the Secretariat for Unity at the Council. During the preparatory period especially, the books of H. Küng, and in particular his *Structures of the Church* (London 1965), had a very great influence within the Catholic Church.

Professor Lindbeck has himself recommended R. Kaiser's colourful account of the first session, *Inside the Council* (London 1963). The American edition, which was published in the same year in New York, is called *Pope, Council and World*. Interesting reflections about the contrasts that were revealed during the first session will be found in Schillebeeckx' *Vatican II: the Struggle of Minds, op. cit.* and in Chenu's article, 'Un concile "pastoral"', now included in *L'Evangile dans le temps* (Paris 1964), p. 655f., in which the author, following his own form of theology, shows that 'pastoral' theology is not a decoration or an application of theology, but the very essence of all theology, that it is, in other words, 'God's word in action'. John XXIII's statement about the *'magisterium,* the character of which is principally pastoral' (see p. 232–3) can readily be connected with this type of theological thinking. This is also expressed in many of the articles written on the death of the Pope. The most instructive of these are Chenu's 'In memoriam' in *Signes du temps* (7), July 1963, Schillebeeckx' article in the first volume of *L'Église du Christ, op. cit.,* and especially the very realistic portrait that Cardinal Suenens drew for the Fathers of the Council on 28 October 1963 to mark the fifth anniversary of John's coronation as Pope. This is included in English translation in M. Novak's book *The Open Church: Vatican II, Act II* (New York 1964) pp. 18–26. On John XXIII see also E.E.Y. Halis' *Pope John and his Revolution* (London 1965). The speeches which John XXIII and Paul VI made to the Council will be found in English in Xavier Rynne's *Letters from Vatican City, The Second Session, The Third Session, The Fourth Session* (London 1963–66).

The history of the development of the Constitution on Divine Revelation has been summarised by P.A. van Leeuwen in his article 'Genesis of the Constitution on Divine Revelation', *Concilium* (3/1) 1967, pp. 4–10. This same number also includes a study by L. Bakker on the background. Y. Congar has contributed an after-thought to the history of the constitution entitled 'La question de la révélation' in the collection edited by B. Lambert, *La nouvelle image de l'Eglise. Bilan du concile Vatican II*, Paris 1967. J. Ratzinger, who, like Congar, was also a member of the last sub-commission which dealt with the schema, has written a particularly important study in one of the supplementary volumes of the *Lexikon für Theologie und Kirche* on the documents of the Second Vatican Council, translated into English with the title *Commentary on the Documents of Vatican II*, London and New York 1968. Cf. also *The Dogmatic Constitution on Divine Revelation of Vatican II*, commentary and translation by George H. Tavard (London 1966). The English text is found in the standard translation *The Documents of Vatican II*, ed. Walter M. Abbott (London and Dublin 1966).

NOTES

[1]See *Dialogue on the Way*, Minneapolis 1965, 45, in a contribution by the editor, G.A. Lindbeck.

[2]See E. Buonaiuti, *Die exkommunizierte Kirche*, edited and with an introduction by E. Benz, Zürich 1966, 52.

[3]See M.D. Chenu, *Signes des Temps* (7) July 1963, 4, in which he wrote a tribute to the memory of John XXIII.

[4]'certo tremando un poco di commozione, ma insieme con umile risolutezza di proposito . . .'; See *Acta Apostolicae Sedis* (51) 1959, 68.

[5]See E. Schillebeeckx, *Het tweede vaticaans concilie* I, Tielt and The Hague 1964, 71 (E. tr. *Vatican II—The Real Achievement*, London 1967).

[6]'. . . un Pontificato, che sta prendendo il suo posto più o meno felicemente nella storia'; see *Acta Apostolicae Sedis, op. cit.*, 66.

[7]See R. Kaiser, *Inside the Council*, London 1963, 90.

[8]'. . . Alacres, sine timore, operi, quod nostra exigit aetas, nunc insistamus, iter pergentes, quod ecclesia a viginti fere saeculis fecit. Neque opus nostrum, quasi as finem primarium, eo spectat . . . fusius repetantur ea, quae Patres ac theologi veteres et recentiores tradiderunt, et quae a vobis non ignorari sed in mentibus vestris inhaerere merito putamus. Etenim ad huiusmodi tantum disputationes habendas non opus erat, ut concilium oecumenicum indiceretur . . . Oportet ut . . . haec doctrina certa et immutabilis . . . ea ratione pervestigetur et exponatur, quam tempora postulant nostra. Est enim aliud depositum fidei, seu veritates, quae veneranda doctrina nostra continentur, aliud modus quo eaedem enuntiantur, eodem tamen sensu eademque sententia. Huic quippe modo plurimum tribuendum erit et patienter, si opus fuerit, in eo elaborandum; scilicet eae inducendae erunt rationes res exponendi, quae cum magisterio, cuius indoles praesertim pastoralis est, magis congruant'; see *Acta Apostolicae Sedis* (54) 1962, 791f.

[9]See Y. Congar, *Vatican II, le concile au jour le jour*, 4 vols. Paris 1963, 25 f.

[10]For example, Cardinal Siri in a statement to the weekly newspaper *Orizzonti*; see R. Kaiser, *Inside the Council, op. cit.*, 85.

[11]See R. Laurentin, *Bilan du concile* I, Paris 1963, 15 and A. Wenger, *Vatican II*, Paris 1963, 47–50.

[12]Y. Congar, *Vatican II, le concile au jour le jour, op. cit.*, 36.

[13]'Non sunt approximationes semper mutabiles semperque denuo corrigendas'; see the 'Schema de deposito fidei pure custodiendo', c. IV, no. 22, in *Schemata Constitutionum et Decretum*, Series I, Vatican City 1962, 38. This phrase is an implicit quotation from *Humani Generis*; see Denz. 3882 (2310).

[14]See R. Laurentin, *Bilan du concile I, op. cit.*, 38.

[15]See G.A. Lindbeck, *Dialogue on the way, op. cit.*, 36.

[16]See R. Wiltgen, *The Rhine Flows into the Tiber*, New York 1967, 47; see also A. Wenger, *Vatican II, op. cit.*, 107.

[17]See R. Wiltgen, 48.

[18]*Ibid.*, 48.

[19]Laurentin has published this intervention in *Bilan du concile* I, *op. cit.*, 72–5; the quotation will be found on p. 74.

[20]See R. Kaiser, *Inside the Council, op. cit.*, 160.

The Appeal to the World's Bishops 263

[21]See, for example, A. Wenger, *Vatican II, op. cit.*, 153 and R. Wiltgen, *The Rhine Flows into the Tiber, op. cit.*, 57.

[22]See R. Laurentin, *Bilan du concile I, op. cit.*, p. 105, note 8 and J.P. Jossua, *Le père Congar, op. cit.*, 188.

[23]'Prima sessio, modo quodam lento et sollemni, quasi aditum aperuit ad magnum ipsum opus Concilii' . . . 'discrepantiae, minime quidem mirandae sed animos paulum sollicitantis . . . sancta libertas filiorum Dei, quae in ecclesia viget'; see *Acta Apostolicae Sedis* (55) 1963, 37. See also the sermon which the Pope gave on 25 November 1962 to a number of seminarists and in which he said that these weeks of the Council could be regarded as a kind of novitiate; cf. Wiltgen, *The Rhine Flows into the Tiber, op. cit.*, 51.

[24]See the Decree *Optatam totius* on the Training of Priests, art. 16: 'S. Thoma Magistro'.

[25]J. Ratzinger, 'The Dogmatic Constitution on Divine Revelation', *Commentary on the Documents of Vatican II*, III, London and New York 1968, 163.

[26]L. Bakker, 'Man's Place in Divine Revelation', *Concilium* (3/1) 1967, 14.

[27]The quotations in this paragraph are taken from article 5 of the Dogmatic Constitution, *Dei Verbum*, on Divine Revelation, *The Documents of Vatican II*, ed. Walter M. Abbott, London and Dublin, 1966. The third of these quotations, on the consent of the intellect and will, is itself a quotation from the Constitution on the Catholic Faith, *Dei Filius*, of the First Vatican Council, chapter III; see Denzinger 1789 (3008).

[28]See the draft Constitution on Revelation, *Schema Constitutionis de divina revelatione, Modi . . . a commissione doctrinali examinati*, Vatican City 1965, 9.

[29]*Ibid.*, 15.

[30]The two quotations in this paragraph from the Dogmatic Constitution, *Dei Verbum*, on Divine Revelation, *op. cit.*, will be found in article 7; for the first of these, see also the Decree *De canonicis Scripturis* of the Council of Trent; see Denzinger 783 (1501).

[31]See the report edited by P.C. Rodger and L. Vischer, *The Fourth World Conference on Faith and Order*, London 1964, 51.

[32]See the Dogmatic Constitution, *Dei Verbum*, on Divine Revelation, *op. cit.*, art. 8.

[33]See the *Schema constitutionis de divina revelatione, Modi . . . a commissione doctrinali examinati, op. cit.*, 20.

[34]*Ibid.*, 21.

[35]See E. Stakemeier, *Die Konzilskonstitution über die göttliche Offenbarung*, Paderborn 2nd ed. 1967, 307.

[36]See the Dogmatic Constitution, *Dei Verbum*, on Divine Revelation, *op. cit.*, art. 8.

[37]See the Dogmatic Constitution, *Dei Verbum*, on Divine Revelation, *op. cit.*, art. 9 with a correction of the current translation which is explained in the next paragraph. The second sentence in this quotation is taken from the Tridentine Decree *De canonicis Scripturis, op. cit.*; see Denzinger 783 (1501).

[38]'. . . quo fit ut non omnis doctrina catholica ex (sola) Scriptura (directe) probari queat'; see the *Schema constitutionis de divina revelatione, Modi . . . a commissione doctrinali examinati, op. cit.*, 24.

[39]See the Dogmatic Constitution, *Dei Verbum*, on Divine Revelation, *op. cit.*, art. 10 for this and the other quotations in this paragraph.

⁴⁰'Huiusmodi auctoritativa Magisterii interventio nihil continet sui, nisi ipsum infallibilis auctoritatis charisma . . . nihil eidem adiiciens, ab eadem nihil detrahans'; quoted by E. Stakemeier in *Die Konzilskonstitution über die göttliche Offenbarung, op. cit.*, 146.

⁴¹The quotations in this paragraph will be found in the Dogmatic Constitution, *Dei Verbum*, on Divine Revelation, *op. cit.*, art. 12.

⁴²*Ibid.*, art. 18.

⁴³For this and the two preceding quotations, see the Dogmatic Constitution, *Dei Verbum, op. cit.*, art. 19.

⁴⁴See the Dogmatic Constitution, *Dei Verbum*, on Divine Revelation, *op. cit.*, art. 21.

⁴⁵*Ibid.*, art. 23.

⁴⁶*Ibid.*, art. 24.

GETTING USED TO THE NEW FREEDOM

Shortly after the close of the Council, Congar wrote: 'The danger now is that we shall cease to search and simply go on drawing on the inexhaustible reserves of Vatican II . . . It would be a betrayal of the *aggiornamento* if this were regarded as permanently fixed in the texts of Vatican II.'[1]

Has this fear been realised? Anyone who thinks about it is at once confronted with the 'historical crisis' in the whole of the Christian world—the problem which was touched on in the introduction to this book, when the enigmatical place of theology in the Catholic Church was questioningly outlined. An initial surprise was caused by signs of 'breaking up' even in the unshakeable rock of Peter. It does, however, look as though the extent and the severity of the breaking up process has been, if anything, intensified by the Council, which was, after all, summoned to look for a Catholic answer to the challenge of the historical crisis. The openness in the Catholic Church that had to some extent been brought about by the Council meant, among other things, that the 'radical' theology which had originated outside Catholicism reached wide sections of the Catholic populations who had previously been protected and obedient, but who now found, to their surprise, that this Protestant theology accurately reflected their own experience. This caused an unexpected and apparently irresistible speeding up inside a Church that had hitherto been well ordered and well organised, so that the inevitable result was a sensation of dizziness. This vertigo soon affected the rest of the Christian world, where the certainty of Catholicism had at least always been envied.

The pressure of this unrest in the Church gave the theologians little opportunity to confine themselves simply to commenting on the conciliar documents. There has indeed been a flood of books on the Council, but very few of the books written by the representatives of the theology of renewal have been concerned with purely interpretative exegesis. These theologians still try to keep 'up to date', although they do seem to get out of breath from time to time because of the constant acceleration of the process of development in the Church. They avail themselves of the new freedom that has been gained by taking up a permanent position in the advance guard of Christian theology in general, where they are welcomed as strong support, especially in the present-day discussions within the World Council of Churches and in the ultimately even more important Christian dialogue with Marxism.

This dialogue, which is in many respects concerned with the implications of secularisation, the dominant concept in almost all debates nowadays, had been a focal point of interest in France as long ago as the immediately post-war years, when French theology had a distinctively secular context. The spectacular change of climate that has taken place in the Catholic Church in recent years is most apparent when this earlier theology of only twenty or so years ago is compared with the present contribution made by, for example, Karl Rahner and, even more, by the 'political' theologians around J.B. Metz, who, following E. Bloch's philosophy of hope and the Protestant theologies of hope outlined by, for example J. Moltmann and G. Sauter, do not aim simply at the re-interpretation of human existence, but at its reform. There are also important side-shoots of this dialogue in the Netherlands (they will be found, among others, in Schillebeeckx), especially since the challenge of the American 'death of God' theology, which at first asked for a more urgent response, seems to have lost much of its impetus.

This change in the Christian world looked very different, however, to those who had not left through the gates of the Catholic fortress when these were at last thrown open, but had watched others leaving with terror in their hearts. Cardinal Ottaviani, who for years was at the head of the present Congregation of Faith, still personifies this group. The heraldic motto which he chose as cardinal, *semper idem*, 'always the same', certainly deserves a prize for maximum application in life—it is the qualification used since the time of Bossuet for Catholic teaching about faith itself. The old, almost blind Cardinal has given this disarming portrait of himself in an interview: 'I am an old *carabiniere* who guards the gold reserve. If you tell an old *carabiniere* that the laws are being changed, he will think, "I am an old *carabiniere*", and he will do everything he can to prevent them from changing. But, if they are still changed, God will certainly give him the strength to guard a new treasure in which he believes. If the new laws have really become the treasure of the Church, supplementing her reserve of gold, then there is only one principle which counts—faithful service to the Church, . . . as a blind man—as the blind man who I am.'[2] It is not clear from this whether the 'laws' to which the cardinal refers in this interview are concerned with the changed norms for his department or with the whole renewal of the Church which was achieved, and certainly in spite of him, at the Second Vatican Council. In fact, the group that he represents was convinced that the process of bringing the Church up to date ended with the close of the Council and all that was necessary afterwards was to put it into practice. The fear expressed by Congar at the end of the Council, then, was in fact realised in the case of the Roman theologians.

It is also quite clear that the leading members of the Church's hierarchy who belonged to this group had some difficulty in getting used to the new situation. Their impression of unrest and disorder in the Church, even in Italy, strengthened their conviction that the whole Council had been a mistake. This prompted them to make a series of statements and to take measures to save what could be saved, if possible by going back inside the fortress. A year after the Council had ended, Cardinal Ottaviani sent a letter to all the bishops of the Church asking them to report to him whether and to what extent ten heresies, described in black terms, occurred among their subjects.[3] In so doing, the old policeman of the Vatican was indeed putting the new laws into practice by approaching the bishops, but his replacement of the name of his own department here and there by the 'Holy See' itself somehow betrayed his real intention. An extremely pessimistic report about 'dangerous modern views and atheism', which might well have been based on this enquiry, was made for the synod of bishops the following year and, in addition to this, there have also been other offensives, on a smaller scale and usually conducted underground, the best known being the campaign against the Dutch New Catechism for adults.[4] The most striking feature of the post-conciliar Roman documents is that even concepts and ideas which clearly bear the imprint of the minority opinion of the Council are used as though they were the only correct expression of the Church's teaching—almost absent-mindedly, references are sometimes made, for example, to rejected conciliar schemas. In this context, one can also observe the adverse effect of an ambiguity which the 'progressives' helped to establish at the Council: even the constitutions of the Council are considered to be 'purely' pastoral, with the result that the Roman theologians could continue to insist that the teaching about, for example, Scripture and tradition as laid down (in their opinion) at Trent and Vatican I is still the 'true' teaching of the Church. What is quite clear, anyway, in the published account of the official theological discussions about the Dutch New Catechism, for example, is how ill at ease the Roman theologians felt in the 'dialogue' which they explicitly wished to lead.[5]

Even the theologians who were in the majority at the Council have not, on the other hand, found it easy to adapt themselves to the new situation. Their most serious difficulty has not been that theology is a field which is rapidly becoming overrun by amateurs. On the contrary, most of them welcome this result of increased openness in the Church as the necessary breeding ground for their own research. At the very most, they are inclined perhaps to think that, as B. Willems has so tersely said, 'all theological statements have become and are still becoming more and more absolute as less is known about history'.[6] It is, however, much more of a change for the theologians of renewal that, since a great deal of external control has now ceased to exist—even their own reactions to the official warnings issued by the Church have changed remarkably since the Council—it has now become possible to practise theology in the manner of their non-Catholic colleagues, which involves facing new problems. If Catholic theologians are taking a special interest nowadays in the hermeneutical problem, this does not imply that they are simply following a similar tendency in the whole of Christian theology. The 'translation' of the gospel into contemporary language is in fact regarded as an urgent task for all Christians, Catholic as well as Protestant. Catholic theologians, however, are also clearly looking for a new direction in their own theological attitude. There has already been a remarkable change in the style of language used by theologians in the Catholic Church. Compared with the caution with which they expressed themselves and which was, if not irritating, then certainly enervating, and the scholastic jargon which they tended to use before the Council, theological writing has become and is still becoming much freer and fresher in tone. But theology properly so called involves more than a change of style. It has to develop its specific rules of procedure at a deeper level. The insights that have been gained into revelation, faith and the development of tradition, therefore, are now being applied—most clearly in the case of Schillebeeckx and Schoonenberg—to the new situation. Whereas previously the question as to whether progress was more than translation was always present in the background of the problem of the development of dogma, nowadays, following the line expressed in Schillebeeckx' 'development through demolition', more and more attention is given to translation for today which 'hermeneutics' ultimately is.

In this, Catholic theologians are criticised not only by the more conservative in their own Church, especially when they venture to apply hermeneutics also to the infallible pronouncements of the Church, but also by their Protestant colleagues, for whom the Catholic principle of tradition has long been a serious stumbling block, because it can deprive the Church's criticism of herself on the basis of Scripture of its compelling power. The Catholic Church is inclined to sanction what has developed historically on the basis of the principle of tradition without—and this is a further objection put forward by Protestant theologians—taking sufficiently into account the discontinuity between 'nature' and 'grace', in other words, without paying enough serious attention to the problem of human sinfulness in the Church.[7] It should be clear enough from what I have already said that there is good reason for this concern and the theologians of renewal, especially Congar and Rahner, have always stressed and continue to stress the need to reform the Church; and the Council took up their call. More particularly, though, Protestant criticism is applied to the latent possibility in the Catholic Church of 're-interpreting' the gospel untruthfully and too quickly. The tendency on the part of the Catholic theologians of renewal to trace all the Church's dogmas back to Scripture is, naturally, applauded by Protestant scholars, who, not quite without reason, were reminded, when the dogma of the Assumption of Mary was proclaimed, of what the modernists had advocated.[8] They are rather less enthusiastic, however, about the frequently rather circuitous or too perfunctory manner in which ideas such as the 'fuller sense' of Scripture are used in Catholic theology.[9] It rather looks as though a great deal more clarity will have to be reached in Catholic hermeneutics in this case. Now that the external control on the part of the official Church has become less, certainly in so far as its function within the community of the Church is concerned, the need for a 'built-in brake' in connection with the interpretation of the gospel has become greater.

Although there are certain one-sided emphases such as those outlined above, Catholic theology does have an important positive contribution to make to the universally Christian thought with which it wishes to establish closer and closer links. I have already suggested in the course of this book what this contribution consists of, but a brief summary of some of these elements, with the final emphasis on one in particular, would not be out of place here. In the first place, Catholic theology can offer a knowledge of the Christian tradition which is both wide and deep and which has been gained during the period when, for years, it had to be proved to the authorities that 'nothing new had been found'. Secondly, Catholic theology is fundamentally open to human thought in all its aspects—an openness based on the Catholic view that nature and grace form a single unity. Finally, and most important, though perhaps rather paradoxically as well, Catholic theologians are convinced, because of their history of difficulties with the Church's teaching office, that they can only *suggest* theological interpretations to the whole community of the Church and that they must wait until that whole community consents to those suggestions, which will then be ultimately sanctioned by the leaders of the community. Nowadays, theologians would prefer to underline heavily that word 'finally', which was first encountered explicitly in the Constitution on Revelation of Vatican II.[10] Especially now, in view of the change of climate in the Christian world, they hope that the Church's teaching office will not intervene too quickly in theological discussions. The Dutch bishops wrote in answer to Cardinal Ottaviani's alarmed letter: 'The theologians' exchange of polemics forms the best possible censorship of any exaggerations that may occur . . . If the Church's teaching authority trusted the theologians more, such exaggerations as may occur would disappear more quickly in free discussion than they would as the result of lists of errors ... A public pronouncement, after all, often results in a difference of opinion being over-emphasised and the harmony of believers being all too seriously disturbed.'[11] In the past many Catholic theologians have submitted inwardly to condemnations by the Church's teaching authority which were, in their opinion, made too promptly. Those who, like Loisy, were unable, in conscience, to do this have realised quickly enough that this meant the end of their attempts to renew theology in the Church. The link between this idea of the Church and the Catholic principle of tradition will be clear enough. Because the whole Church is the holder and protector of tradition, which includes not only Christ's word, but also his work, theology is also reflection about the community of the Church as the *reality* of salvation in the world interpreted by God's word.

This relationship with the Church and the Church's teaching office has already been suggested earlier on in this book as a possible reason why the theological peaks seem to be less high in the Catholic tradition than in the rest of the Christian world. The years ahead ought to prove the extent to which the stricter official control within the Catholic Church has been of direct influence. There are certainly indications that there are now very promising and comprehensive projects on the way, although I should like to be able to go as far as Macquarrie who, in acknowledging his debt to Rahner, has remarked: '. . . the leadership in theology, which even ten years ago lay with such Protestant giants as Barth, Brunner and Tillich, has now passed to Roman Catholic thinkers'.[12] In any case, the theologians themselves are more than ever convinced that they are still searching. In this connection, I should like to quote again from the Dutch bishops' reply to Cardinal Ottaviani, a section clearly written by a theologian, dealing with the fundamental question that has occupied us in this book: 'Theology itself has as yet no clear understanding of the relationship between man's experience of faith (on the basis of the infused light of faith) and the (dogmatic) concepts of faith. Theologians are still searching for this and it may happen that this or that theologian may place too much emphasis on this or that aspect. This is part of the groping search followed by theologians and, so long as one has confidence in this search, it cannot result in harm, because theologians correct each other in order to reach agreement.'[13] The same idea was expressed even more imaginatively by Blondel: 'The progress of religious truth resembles flowing water which is searching for a bed. It twists and turns, encounters a thousand obstacles, flows back, rises again, breaks through and flows on again unceasingly, even making use of the reserves of energy built up in meeting all these obstacles.'[14]

Congar may set his mind at rest. Even since the breakthrough of Pope John's *aggiornamento,* Catholic theologians, working in the new freedom that has been gained, will continue to search, 'scrutinising the signs of the times and . . . interpreting them in the light of the gospel',[15] for the unchanging truth and doing this as a service to what Pope Paul VI has called, in his encyclical *Populorum Progressio,* the 'full development of man and the progress of people'.

Bibliography

A few collections of articles which will give some idea of the direction followed by Catholic theology since the Second Vatican Council may be referred to: *From Anathema to Dialogue: the Challenge of Marxist-Christian Co-operation* (London 1967), in which Rahner and J.B. Metz discuss the relationship between Catholicism and Marxism today with R. Garaudy, the French Marxist; Rahner's most recent articles, collected in *Theological Investigations* VI and *Schriften zur Theologie* VIII; various issues of the international theological journal *Concilium,* in particular those on 'Dogma' edited by E. Schillebeeckx, and on 'Church and World' edited by J.B. Metz; Metz' own *Theology of the World* (London 1969), and his contribution on 'Political Theology' in *Sacramentum Mundi* V (London 1970); and, finally, a recent symposion of articles by two German, two Dutch and two French theologians—Rahner and Metz, Schoonenberg and Schillebeeckx, Congar and Daniélou—on various aspects of the problem of Christianity in a changing secularised world, published as *Crucial Questions* (New York 1969).

Several articles by Dutch theologians, so much in the news in these days, may be mentioned. These include the series in which Schillebeeckx discusses the problems raised by secularisation and radical theology, collected and translated into English in his *God, the Future of Man* (London and Sydney 1969). Schoonenberg has published various articles on hermeneutics, for example, in the *Tijdschrift voor Theologie* (8/1) 1968, and, together with various colleagues, in the third number of the same year, which was entirely devoted to this problem. This special issue has been translated into German: *Die Interpretation des Dogmas* (Düsseldorf 1968), while an abstract of Schoonenberg's earlier article has been published in *Theology Digest* (17/3) 1969, under the title 'Event and Happening: Hermeneutical Reflection on Some Contemporary Disputed Questions', pp. 196–202.

R. Rouquette has written an interesting survey of the first synod of bishops, *Une nouvelle chrétienté* (Paris 1968), and R. Laurentin has recently added two further volumes to his account of the Council: *L'enjeu du synode, suite du concile* (Paris 1967), and *Le premier synode, histoire et bilan* (Paris 1968), which also contain a useful account of the development of Catholic theology in the years immediately following the Council. The present state of theology in the Church is set forth in the report which Karl Rahner presented to the first meeting of the international commission of theologians in October 1969; this has been published in *IDOC International* (13), 1 Dec. 1969 (Ed. du Seuil, Paris), pp. 45–62.

NOTES

[1]See J.P. Jossua, *Le père Congar, op. cit.*, 209.

[2]Quoted from an interview published in the *Corriere della Sera*, in late October 1965, by M. von Galli and B. Moosbrugger in their book *Das Konzil und seine Folgen*, Lucerne and Frankfurt a.M. 1966, 187.

[3]This letter was published in *Acta Apostolicae Sedis* (58) 1966, 659–61.

[4]After several years of confused, official and unofficial activity, this campaign eventually resulted in a supplement to the Catechism composed by two Roman theologians, E. Dhanis and J. Visser, by order of a commission of cardinals who had already published their basic objections in *Acta Apostolicae Sedis* (60) 1968, pp. 685 ff. The authors of the Catechism rejected this supplement, which is at times certainly fussy or downright silly in its stylistic 'corrections'. The Dutch hierarchy let it be published without clearly endorsing it. In some editions it is sold separately, in other editions it is incorporated into the text—where it will be easily traced because of its radically different approach; in one language area it cannot be bought at all. A 'White Paper' with the details of the whole affair has appeared in Dutch and will soon be published in a French translation (Ed. du Centurion, Paris).

[5]See note 4.

[6]See *Tijdschrift voor Theologie* (8) 1968, 131.

[7]See, for example, G.A. Lindbeck, *Dialogue on the way, op. cit.*, 246 ff.; G.C. Berkouwer, *The Second Vatican Council and the New Catholicism, op. cit.*, Chapters II, IV and IX.

[8]See, for example, F. Heiler's bibliographical article, 'Assumptio', in *Theologische Literaturzeitung* (79) 1954, 1–47, especially p. 44.

[9]See, for example, G.C. Berkouwei, *The Second Vatican Council, op. cit.*, 226 ff.; G.A. Lindbeck, *Dialogue on the way, op. cit.*, 38 f.

[10]See the Dogmatic Constitution, *Dei Verbum*, on Divine Revelation, *op. cit.*, art. 12; see also above, p. 256.

[11]See *Katholiek Archief* (23) 1968, 127–8.

[12]J. Macquarrie, *Principles of Christian Theology*, London 1966, ix.

[13]See *Katholiek Archief, op. cit.*, 137.

[14]M. Blondel, *Attente du concile*, Paris 1964, 43.

[15]Pastoral Constitution, *Gaudium et Spes*, on the Church in the Modern World, art. 4, *The Documents of Vatican II*, ed. Walter M. Abbott, London and Dublin 1966.

EPILOGUE IN 2007

Before starting on this epilogue I re-read parts of my forty-year-old book. It was an eerie experience. *Aggiornamento*, to use its original title, was written during the years which followed Vatican II, a period of religious turbulence all over the world, but particularly in the Netherlands where the book was written. There Vatican II had provoked a strong current of hope for renewal of the Roman Catholic Church, which gradually merged with a growing mood of anxiety and doubt induced by the radical interpretation of Christianity in the bestseller of Anglican bishop J. A. T. Robinson, published at almost the same time. In the Netherlands the combination of these two currents resulted in a somewhat dizzying period during which the traditional Roman Catholic convictions and practices were questioned by ever more people, accompanied by various proposals to reform them. When the bishops returned from the Council they thought it best to give this process a chance to prove what it could contribute to church life in Holland. This lenient attitude led, in its turn, to commotion in traditional circles in the Dutch church and to conflicts with the central authorities in the Vatican, where the traditional forces meanwhile had started a counter-campaign against the conciliar renewal.

During this period the Catholic Church had become big news for the media. This interest dated from the years of the Council, where in a spectacular way more than two thousand bishops, stimulated by theologians who until then had been considered suspect by church authority, had managed to budge what was was supposed to be the most uncompromising institution in the world, the Roman Catholic Church. When after the Council the conflicting tendencies arose on an ever larger scale the media tried to follow the exciting developments as well as possible, but they found it difficult to disentangle what exactly was at stake in the conflicts or which position had the better prospects. The most baffling question for them was ultimately whether the traditional image of the Catholic Church had really changed since Vatican II. For this reason they felt a pressing need for information on the background of the confusing situation, especially on the part played by the theologians who now seemed to aim at widespread renewal. This question of the role of theology and theologians was to be the subject of my book, which it tried to approach from history—an intention more adequately expressed in the Irish (and Dutch) subtitle, "Beginnings of the *New* Catholic Theology," than in the far broader title of the American edition.

Forty years later the situation has changed considerably at many points. The Western world has known an incredible advance in technical prospects and in prosperity (though not for all people) and at the same time Christianity became widely secularized there. In Europe the public function of churches and theologians was marginalized more and more, while other world religions and new religious forces emerged ever more clearly in the Western world. This led to new forms of theology meant to address the new situation or special elements in it which required their attention: theology of liberation, feminist theology, and an open dialogue with other religions and world views. The Vatican tended to view these developments with great reserve, especially after the accession of the outspoken Polish Pope, John Paul II, and in reaction usually just repeated what it considered to be the unchangeable deposit of faith. The theologians who supported post-conciliar renewal reacted to the Vatican mistrust with growing disappointment, since according to them this posture was no more than a pre-conciliar view, itself (only another) a form of theology, and one hardly understandable for the modern Western world at that.

In spite of this heavily changed context it was suggested to me—e.g., by the publisher of a new Czech translation—that *Aggiornamento* even now can be of use as background information for the present situation. On a number of points it should be revised. In recent years there has been much new research on the theology of the nineteenth century which has resulted in an adjusted view of those developments of renewal, especially in German-speaking countries. In particular it has become much clearer that Neo-scholastic theology, expressly directed against modern tendencies, was strongly promoted—in ways which were often disgraceful—by measures inspired by church politics, from within and outside the Vatican center. It has also become much more evident that since the Middle Ages when theology became a university prerogative, fixed doctrine in Scholastic formulas had assumed a quasi-absolute authority in Catholic theology, often contrary to the genuine meaning of the gospel as it urges itself upon us in our days through newer hermeneutical interpretations.

In spite of these new data I think I could maintain that the main lines of my book have been confirmed rather than disconfirmed. Even in the concluding pages on "getting used to the new freedom," though still colored by the euphoria of the breakthrough of Vatican II, the later tensions already present themselves clearly. After 1968, when the book was finished, tensions and conflicts quite clearly accelerated, both in theological centers and in the central authority of the Church. In 1968 an almost revolutionary mood had emerged in the Western world as a whole, stirred up especially by students and—therefore—by their professors. For the Catholic Church, however, 1968 is first of all the year of the encyclical "Humanae vitae" of Pope Paul VI, who, against the advice of his own special committee—and of the hopes raised at Vatican II—substantially confirmed the traditional doctrine. This resulted in doubt and resistance even among bishops, not only about the sensitive matter of sexual ethics and birth control, but also about the function of papal primacy in the Church. Theologically this opposition focussed on the question which Hans Küng even made into the title of a challenging book, "Infallible?," which became the subject of a widespread and sometimes fierce discussion. At the same time this debate also stimulated innovators in their drive for the reform of the life and liturgy of the Church no longer to wait for central authority, which in their view just put on the brakes, but to take the responsibility for it themselves. The media in those years associated this process usually with developments in Holland, but this is due mainly to the fact that Dutch bishops were convinced they should themselves take part in the process of renewal, which therefore could run its course more openly.

In those years theologians had to work overtime, partly because at the same time Bishop Robinson's radical interpretation gained more and more ground, as was evidenced for instance in a movement in theology which started from the "death of God." All this made a theologian like Schillebeeckx state publicly that he was writing "with an almost feverish sense of urgency." Similar complaints were heard from his colleagues Karl Rahner, Hans Küng, Piet Schoonenberg and Yves Congar, and to some extent even from the ever-optimistic Marie-Dominique Chenu. Other prominent theologians who had supported the breakthrough of Vatican II—among them Jean Daniélou, Henri de Lubac, and Joseph Ratzinger—became convinced that the crisis in Christianity was dangerous enough to call for a countermovement. Two events illustrate this tension within theology: (1) at the end of 1968 more than 1300 theologians from all over the world put their signature to a declaration, initiated by theologians of the international journal *Concilium*, that "the freedom of theologians and of theology regained at Vatican II . . . should not be at risk once more"; and shortly afterwards (2) the initiative was taken to publish a theological antipode of Concilium, the "international catholic journal *Communio*," edited among others by Hans Urs von Balthasar and Joseph Ratzinger, to which also Daniélou and de Lubac were to contribute. At about the same time the Vatican started directly to intervene in the Dutch church, by a first investigation of Schillebeeckx's theology and by the appointment of more traditional bishops, clearly meant also as a warning to the rest of the Catholic Church.

Shortly after the Council the "Holy Office," since renamed "Congregation for the Doctrine of the Faith," increased its doctrinal surveillance, still taking for granted that Neo-scholasticism held the monopoly in theology, even though this position had officially been abandoned at the Council. In spite of some adaptations in the procedure for investigating the orthodoxy of theological writings—procedures often ignored or by-passed in practice—such investigations remained opaque for the Church and general public as a whole, except of course for their outcome and subsequent consequences for the theologians who had been investigated. From the documents of several investigations which have since been published, it is depressingly clear how little the consultants of the Congregation were able—or willing—to understand the newer approaches, much less to acknowledge them as expressions of the legitimate plurality in theology that the Council had recognized.

What was at stake in all these developments may become clearer from the elaboration in Catholic theology of a branch of fundamental theology known as hermeneutics. This "science of interpretation" was no longer applied only to biblical texts, but to all traditional statements of faith. An important element in the development of hermeneutics was the highly articulate reflection in Protestant theology elaborated in reaction to the ever more radical questions raised after Robinson's "Honest to God." In the course of this process, earlier ideas about the development of doctrine as they were sketched in the second part of this book (pp. 157–227) became incorporated into the new hermeneutics. In particular, reflections on the various forms and functions of language proved to be of great importance, notably for the understanding of traditional "fixed doctrine." And theologians started to realize the value of "ideology critique" as a means of exposing the background of fossilized conceptions and patterns of behavior and of the way they function within the Church's administration.

In the same vein new branches of theology developed, in dialogue with similar attempts in other Christian churches. On the one hand, such new approaches were meant to address expressly the many problems of present-day society (such as J. B. Metz's "new political theology"), repression in the Third World (several types of liberation theology), and the inferior position of women in a men's world (feminist theology). On the other hand, they were aimed at the ever growing plurality of religion and ideology in the Western world, as well as a broadening and extension of ecumenical approaches of which the development of Hans Küng's theology is a telling example. The new branches of theology can best be traced in the many thematic issues of the journal *Concilium*.

At the end of Vatican II most of the theologians described more explicitly in this book approached the end of their creative period: Chenu and de Lubac were about seventy, Congar, Daniélou, and Rahner about sixty years old by that time. With the exception of Daniélou, who died unexpectedly in 1974, they all lived to a respectable age (de Lubac, 96; Chenu, 95; and Congar, 90) and mostly continued in their final years to promote renewal. Chenu for example turned up at all sorts of exciting events in church and society, e.g., the revolutionary disturbances of 1968 in Paris. Rahner became one of the moving forces behind *Concilium* and various large series and encyclopaedias. He continued until his death to support colleagues (like Schillebeeckx) and projects (such as liberation and feminist theologies, and ecumenical rapprochement) that came under attack in the church. In the Netherlands Schoonenberg became deeply involved as a theologian in the controversial New Catechism. Schillebeeckx also emphatically related his theology to actual problems. As a result he was subjected to three Vatican investigations (none of which ended with negative sanctions). But now past the age of 93, he can no longer hope to complete a major new publication.

The younger generation of theologians has shown that in recent years Catholic theology could make use of the extended scope for research after Vatican II and could broaden its horizon considerably. Its historical and exegetical branches helped develop new approaches such as literary analysis and non-normative historical studies. The results of such new methods have been incorporated more extensively and intensively in dogmatic and moral theology, which also found inspiration in newer forms of philosophy (including process philosophy) and the human sciences. The latter were welcomed even more strongly in pastoral and practical theology, which also came to use psychological and sociological methods and data more directly. When this activity took place at universities and faculties in which ecclesiastical authority enjoyed a measure of control, various forms of "environmental protection" proved to be necessary, of which the "Cologne Declaration" of 1989—advocating an open, decentralized church—was the more important. Thus theology attempts to continue its time-honored charism and commitment, in more varied ways, with greater awareness of the concerns of other religions and world views, and more discretely looking for "traces of God" in everything present-day men and women meet on their path through life.

Errata

p. 22, just after the middle of the page: "Pope Paul VI . . . touchy Synof of Pistoria" should be "Pope *Pius* VI . . . *sympathetic* Synod of *Pistoia*."

p. 31, line 6 from bottom: "insistent mystique" should be "*near-idolization.*"

p. 90, line 10 from bottom: "as a practical reality": "*as*" should be deleted.

p. 94, line 15: "esprit of the Church": "*of the Church*" should be deleted (just *esprit* is emant).

p. 138, line 13 from bottom: "magnificent knowledge" should be "*extensive* knowledge."

p. 163, line 15: "has its perfection" should be "has *His* perfection" (meaning: God's).

www.ingramcontent.com/pod-product-compliance
Lightning Source LLC
Chambersburg PA
CBHW050339230426
43663CB00010B/1918